General Map of Kingsport Tennessee

Compiled in the Office of
John Nolen City Planner
Harvard Sq. Cambridge Mass.
1919

To Bristol

Golf Course (18 Holes)

Armstrong Village

The Oaks Reserved

Main Line

Federal Dyestuff & Chemical Co.

To Johnson City & Spartanburg

Scale

1000 500 0 1/8 1/4 3/8 1/2

Feet Miles

To Johnson City

KINGSPORT, TENNESSEE

KINGSPORT TENNESSEE

A PLANNED AMERICAN CITY

MARGARET RIPLEY WOLFE

THE UNIVERSITY PRESS OF KENTUCKY

Scholarly publisher for the Commonwealth,
serving Bellarmine College, Berea College, Centre
College of Kentucky, Eastern Kentucky University,
The Filson Club, Georgetown College, Kentucky
Historical Society, Kentucky State University,
Morehead State University, Murray State University,
Northern Kentucky University, Transylvania University,
University of Kentucky, University of Louisville,
and Western Kentucky University.

Editorial and Sales Offices: Lexington, Kentucky 40506-0024

Library of Congress Cataloging-in-Publication Data

Wolfe, Margaret Ripley, 1947-
Kingsport, Tennessee: a planned American city.

Bibliography: p.
Includes index.
1. Kingsport (Tenn.)—History. 2. City and town
life—Tennessee—History. 3. City planning—
Tennessee—History. I. Title.
F444.K5W65 1987 976.8'96 87-8299
ISBN 0-8131-1624-4

In loving memory of my father
CLARENCE E. RIPLEY
16 August 1919 – 16 December 1986

CONTENTS

MAPS

ACKNOWLEDGMENTS

When I began preliminary work on this study in 1977, I was blissfully unaware of some of the professional and personal challenges that lay ahead. Armed with a recently acquired doctoral specialty in American urban history, I was again living where I had grown up, on the outskirts of Kingsport, Tennessee, a planned twentieth-century city. This research project seemed to be made to order, and I soon found myself deeply involved with a subject that had both regional and national historical significance. Serious study of local topics rarely allows one the luxury of using only local sources. Research pertaining to Kingsport has taken me to such far-flung locations as Cornell University's archives at Ithaca, New York; a Wall Street law firm representing the Securities Company in New York City; the National Archives and Library of Congress, Washington, D.C.; and the Vero Beach, Florida, home of Earle Sumner Draper, who was involved in planning the town.

Although there is no dearth of material, my research has been affected by the absence of complete sets of manuscripts pertaining to the early history of modern Kingsport. Too many documents have been lost because the person responsible for their care neither knew nor understood their significance. The papers of the Kingsport Improvement Corporation, the agency that planned, financed, and established the city, came under the auspices of various New York City attorneys and accountants representing the Securities Company, the holding company for the ventures at Kingsport. That collection has been destroyed, although some fragmentary evidence still exists. The contract-labor records of the Carolina, Clinchfield and Ohio Railroad were disposed of in a similar fashion years ago; one can only surmise what they might have included pertinent to the planned city and the labor conditions of Southern Appalachia. A drawing for the proposed municipal center near Church Circle, which was once on file in the Tennessee Room of the Kingsport Public Library, was thrown away because no one who was there at the moment thought that it had any value. Such incidents point to the need for serious attempts to establish a photographic and documentary archives for the model city.

Kingsport has developed its own mythology, perhaps because of its Cinderella, or fairy-tale-like, origin, and it strains the historian sometimes to separate the myth from the reality. It does not take long, however, to discern the effects of incantation. After interviewing several of the town's pioneers, I discovered that I was hearing the same stories with slight individual improvisations. The same applies to the various Rotary Club and other civic publications pertaining to the town's history as well as to many newspaper stories. While these accounts, oral and written, should not be taken at face value, most of them contain useful information and have been helpful in reconstructing the town's past.

Bringing this research project to fruition has been further complicated by my close ties to this city, the region, and its people, and I have been careful to separate sentiment from statement of fact. Although not a resident of the incorporated town, I have spent most of my life on its periphery. From my study window, on a clear day, I have a beautiful view of Bays Mountain; at night, I can see the glow of the town's lights from my living-room windows. When the winds happen to be blowing from the wrong direction, from my front porch I can sometimes smell the pollution from the industries. I was born at Holston Valley Community Hospital, where, almost thirty years later, my daughter also came into the world. As a very small child, I rode the Clinchfield trains and the work buses from the Ross Camp Ground community into Kingsport; I can remember having meals with my father and mother at the old Phoenix Restaurant near Five Points. I have pleasant childhood memories of the American Legion Carnival and the Fourth of July parades. My parents bought my shoes at J. Fred Johnson's Department Store, and Dobyns-Taylor Hardware was a frequent stop; both are now defunct. "Going to town," for us, always meant going to Kingsport. I have been distressed to watch the decline of the town and the emergence of some of the problems that have plagued it in recent years. Although there is much to criticize, there is also much to commend, particularly the neighborhoods, the churches, the first-rate public-school system, the civic clubs, a fairly stable economic base provided by commerce and industry, and cultural events like those produced by the Fine Arts Center, the Kingsport Symphony, and the Community Concert Association. A renewed interest in the downtown has also materialized.

Along with being a resident of the area, I am a descendant of several generations of native-born Appalachians, those pure Anglo-Saxon Protestants who received so much fanfare in the early propaganda that was used to promote and boost Kingsport. These natives who have provided a relatively cheap labor supply are my people; I am one of them. My life as an Appalachian would probably have been remarkably different had it not been for the social and cultural influence of Kingsport. Not only was it a magnet that drew people of the hinterland for shopping, employment, and medical care; it was also a bastion of middle-class American values, serving as a yardstick for human hopes and aspirations in the surrounding rural setting. I have the good fortune to enjoy the blessings of urban life while residing on a "hillside farm" that has been in my family for over a century. Nonetheless, this study will disappoint enthusiasts of Appalachian Studies who venerate the folk as well as those who seek a denunciation of capitalism.

Numerous people around the Kingsport area and in various libraries and archives have aided me; when appropriate, they are recognized in the notes and text. All of them have received my personal expressions of appreciation. Perhaps there is some truth to the adage "You can't fight City Hall." Fortunately, for me, that has not been necessary. My special thanks go to the late Harry R. Egan, city recorder and finance director, and Bruce Sloop of the Planning Department. Several residents who rendered help and encouraged me have expired, among them Mrs. J. Fred (Elizabeth) Johnson, H.J. Shivell, Mrs. S. Phelps (Penelope) Platt, Howard Wilson, Karl Goerdel, J.T. Roller, and Edward J. Triebe. I am especially grateful to Dr. Merritt Shobe, who arranged a particularly timely and productive interview with three early Eastman employees.

The benefits of being a member of a university community become obvious in the course of writing a book. This one would never have been completed without the support of James Earl Wade, chairman of the Department of History at East Tennessee State University from 1979 through 1985, who arranged significant blocks of time in my work load so that I could do research and writing. Martha Egan, a history graduate student, became interested in my work and shared important bits of information that she discovered. Barbara Charlton, the faculty secretary at the Kingsport University center, typed portions of an earlier draft of this work and enthusiastically offered assistance and comfort. Edith Keys, a longtime reference librarian, now retired, at the Sherrod Library, spent countless hours arranging the acquisition of published materials through interlibrary loan during the early phase of work on this project. Her successor, Lisa Ridenour, followed suit. Eloise Haney and Julana Croy of the Kingsport University Center have also provided valuable service. Larry Smith, the university photographer, cheerfully met each request for the reproduction of old prints. My sister, Pamela Ripley, in Alumni and University Relations, and my friend and colleague Professor Al Tirman, in the Mathematics Department, read an earlier version of this manuscript, made corrections, and provided thoughtful, constructive criticism.

An unexpected joy of academic life is to be blessed with the friendships of generous and selfless individuals. One of my colleagues, James L. Odom, is such a person. I can never repay him for his many kindnesses; I can only offer him my heartfelt appreciation. Whatever its flaws, my work is far better than it might have been because of help so graciously offered by Thomas H. Appleton, Jr., managing editor of the Kentucky Historical Society. My dear friend and former classmate, he read every page of an earlier draft for style and content and offered invaluable suggestions.

The researching and writing of this study parallel my child's life, and neither would have come through as well without the many hours of baby-sitting provided by my relatives, especially my mother and father. The book is dedicated to my husband, David, and to my daughter, Stephanie, whose lives have been affected by this project and this city almost as much as has mine.

1

Introduction

Kingsport, Tennessee, is the first thoroughly diversified, professionally planned, and privately financed city in twentieth-century America. Located in the northeastern corner of the Volunteer State, just south of the Virginia border, bounded to the east by Interstate 81, and cut east to west by northbound I-181, the city sprawls for more than ten miles along highway 11W in Sullivan and Hawkins counties. Lying at 1,200 feet above sea level, the contemporary incorporation physically exceeds John Nolen's 1919 plan; but plumes of smoke and vapor that routinely rise from the floor of the Holston River valley testify to the presence of a modern industrial city anticipated some eighty years ago. Beyond the pale of urban development and relics of human progress, the intervening mountains, ridges, and hollows of the Appalachian chain offer some of the most spectacular scenery to be found anywhere in the United States. The coal towns of southwestern Virginia and the sedate old Tennessee communities and county seats of Blountville, Greeneville, Jonesborough, and Rogersville lie within a fifty-mile radius of Kingsport. The advent of the planned city, a glittering new industrial jewel in the green mountains, offered area residents an alternative to rural life and to staid village and small-town existence as the new century dawned. Neither an Appalachian hamlet nor a company town, it developed as an all-American city. From flaunting its patriotism with grandiose Fourth of July parades to being slightly defensive about its pollution, it has exhibited values almost stereotypically those of middle-class America. Produced by the marriage of New South philosophy and progressivism, born of a passing historical moment when capitalists turned their attentions to Southern Appalachia, and nurtured by the Protestant work ethic and an American credo, Kingsport reflects its heritage.

Being a planned city does not make Kingsport unique, for history is littered with examples. The United States alone offers dozens of cases. To cite but a few, Pullman, Illinois; Anniston, Alabama; Gary, Indiana; and Radburn, New Jersey, have all been the subjects of recent books.[1] Interest in urbanization over the past few decades likewise has produced a flurry of articles dealing with planning and landscape architecture, as well as several volumes worthy of note.[2] Private initiative at Kingsport and slightly later at Alcoa antedated such acclaimed federal undertakings in the mountains of Tennessee as those of the Tennessee Valley Authority at Norris and of the United States Army Corps of Engineers at Oak Ridge.[3] This capitalistic experiment in town planning spawned a prosperous industrial city in Southern Appalachia, a region that was considered to be in the backwash of major technological and urban growth, a retrograde environment. Kingsport owes its existence and its success to the coincidence of private development in Southern Appalachia with the onset of professional town planning in the United States.

Kingsport's founders rejected the haphazard growth of the boom town and the controlled, single-dimensional environment of the company town, while circumstances obviated the suburban-bedroom-community approach. Receptive to the efficiency-expertise strain that ran through the Progressive Era, they opted for professional assistance and enlisted the services of town planner John Nolen. Nolen's contribution, however, was marginal, although it has often been exaggerated; physical design was but one aspect of the overall plan for the city. Nonetheless, the decision to use a reputable planner and the timing of Kingsport's birth were auspicious. A plethora of urban problems during the late nineteenth century had fueled the rising interest in city planning, and the concomitant demand for technical assistance gave rise to a new profession. The first National Planning Conference was held in Washington, D.C., in 1909, bringing together an assortment of experts. That year was significant in Great Britain as well as in the United States, for Parliament passed an act that allowed local officials to undertake comprehensive land-use planning. A year later the Royal Institute of British Architects sponsored an international meeting in London. In 1917 the American City Planning Institute originated within the National Planning Conference. Specialized training had commenced at Harvard University, and city planning was well on its way to being recognized as a unique and specialized field.[4]

Kingsport's physical design reflects transitional patterns in American city planning. By the time of this town's inception, the City

Beautiful approach had run its course, and the City Practical, or City Functional, stratagem was gaining ground.[5] Nolen leaned heavily in that direction. Believing, however, that cities could be both beautiful and efficient, he did not reject the Garden City concept of Londoner Ebenezer Howard; indeed, English influence in architecture and landscaping remains apparent at Kingsport. The Tennessee town represents what one scholar calls "the first successful germination" of "American New Towns Policy" and what another, more recently, labels "Roads Not Taken." Commenting on two approaches to coping with urban congestion—namely, the American Garden City Movement and the building of company towns—the latter scholar maintains that neither of these became a part of American mainstream town building and city planning.[6] It must be stressed that Kingsport's founders eclectically drew on the expertise of a variety of professionals, of whom Nolen was but one. The founders, not the experts, discarded the company town and the mill village and charted the course for a multifaceted urban community of industry, commerce, and neighborhoods.

In recent Western culture, planned cities have often been the beachheads of capitalism. As investors have pursued cheap labor and exploited raw materials in undeveloped regions, the establishment of urban enclaves has signaled a commitment of sorts, albeit short-lived, and a claim or a control over the lives of workers and residents of the hinterland. This applies to the most primitive mining operations as well as to more sophisticated industrial environments—be they Pullman, Gary, and Kingsport in the United States; billionaire Daniel K. Ludwig's failed Jari in Brazil; or the Jubail project in Saudi Arabia, under the direction of the globe-girdling San Francisco-based Bechtel Group Incorporated.[7] During the late nineteenth and early twentieth centuries, Southern Appalachia had fired the imaginations of American as well as foreign investors.

The capitalists who masterminded developments in Southern Appalachia from the 1880s to the advent of the Great Depression introduced inhabitants to both the best and the worst aspects of an industrial urban society. Regular cash income, indoor plumbing, health care, electrification, recreational opportunities, a commitment to public education, and housing that was as good as or better than the norms of the area—all helped to elevate the standard of living for some. Meanwhile, capitalists exploited nonunion, unsophisticated laborers with comparatively low wages and often-dangerous working conditions, allowed company housing to fall into disrepair, and polluted the air and water while abusing the countryside. Rural Appalachians, for the most part, had industrialization imposed on them and their land; but some of them, in league with outside investors, actively promoted this transformation.[8]

Economic development that came to Appalachia during the late nineteenth century was hardly an aberration of capitalistic practice. It did, however, represent the superimposition of mature capitalism on a society that had not been sufficiently cushioned by the preceding economic stage, and therefore it affords an example of unrestrained capitalism allowed to run its course. Capitalists, by nature, seek to control raw materials, to manipulate the political system, and to dominate the labor force in the international arena, on the national front, and, indeed, on such regional levels as those of Appalachia and the American South.[9] Although Kingsport's beginnings owed a great deal to techniques and ideas from the Progressive Era, sometimes assumed to have been products of American liberalism, the city's conservative founders embraced them to further capitalism. The desire for success, however, is not exclusively a conservative or a liberal aspiration; and capitalism does not preclude conscience. The promoters and early industrialists in the planned city were men of conscience who fostered the development of community and who nurtured free enterprise.

The "model city" of Kingsport was a direct offshoot of the Carolina, Clinchfield and Ohio Railroad project, which brought Upper East Tennessee out of economic stagnation and helped to transform it into an industrial center. In 1909 a writer for the *Scientific American Supplement* likened this railroad to "a serpent" which "winds its way through chasms, gorges, ravines, between towering cliffs and mountains extending upward thousands of feet."[10] In a sense, the serpent had arrived in the garden; for this isolated, beautiful setting, for better or for worse, was irrevocably changed. Seven decades after incorporation, Kingsport's population stood in excess of 30,000, instead of the 50,000 mentioned in the early physical planning. Census figures indicated only a slight increase—from 31,938 to 32,027—between 1970 and 1980. In 1975, Kingsport became a part of the newly recognized Johnson City-Kingsport-Bristol Standard Metropolitan Statistical Area, which by 1977 had a population of more than 400,000 and rank of eighty-eighth among the SMSA's in the country. Figures for 1980 showed a count of 433,638.[11] The history of modern Kingsport falls naturally into two parts, that from 1916 to 1944—when its founders, John B. Dennis and J. Fred Johnson, directed its growth and development—and that since, when clear-cut leadership has not been apparent. The dynamism that typified the town early on gave way to complacency with the passing of the founding fathers. The second and third generations, while true to the primogenitors' pursuit of profits, have been essentially devoid of the vision that tempered the capitalistic practices of the originators.

The downtown, where remnants of the physical plan are still visible, has deteriorated. For the better part of two decades a prefabricated building blocked the view of the redbrick depot, the symbol of the city's ties to the Carolina, Clinchfield and Ohio Railroad. Around Thanksgiving, local merchants still bring Santa Claus to town on a Clinchfield train from Elkhorn City, Kentucky, to participate in the annual Christmas parade. The location of the Kingsport Inn—a gracious two-story hotel that once attracted tourists, accommodated visiting industrialists, and provided a graceful setting for social events—was long occupied by a large parking lot but is now the site of First American National Bank-Eastern. The store founded by J. Fred Johnson, "the father of Kingsport," has been sold to Millers of Knoxville, and even Millers has moved to the Fort Henry Mall, on the east side of town. Passing through the city by way of Stone Drive, the "Golden Mile" that now sprawls for several, one encounters Pizza Hut, McDonald's, K-Mart, Ramada Inn, and other links of the national chains—all of which give Kingsport the same monotonous appearance as hundreds of other towns. The industries pollute the air and the water, and emissions from their smokestacks often mar the view of the landscape. The zones of greenery have receded, and most of the disease-plagued elms that once lined the main streets of the downtown have been cut and never replaced. Suffice it to say, Kingsport in the 1980s is not "the magic city" envisaged before World War I.

The post–World War II situation is a common one in American urban history, marked by a deteriorating downtown, industrial pollution, the blighted strips of discount stores and fast-food establishments, the appearance of shopping malls, annexation battles, and the absence of outstanding public leadership. Serious social, physical, and political fragmentation has occurred, and residents of the outlying areas have resented the city's encroachment through annexation. Concerned citizens have expressed their views in various forms. Some have been flippant, as the lady who wrote: "That's not pollution you see in the air over Kingsport. It's just the dust from [Congressman] Jimmy Quillen's feet running around helping people." Others have been defensive, as the gentleman who commented on the opposition to annexation: "We cannot improve this city by adding 15,000 unwilling, uncooperative whiners who are dragged into the city like Faust being dragged to Hell by Mephistopheles.... If you don't really want to come into our city, we don't want you." Some have been facetious, like the man who remembered "when Kingsport [was] with a certain amount of pride referred to as the 'Model City.' Then someone became a little curious and consulted Webster's dictionary for the meaning of the word 'model' and discovered 'model' defined as 'a cheap imitation of the real thing.'" A few have been belligerent, as the citizen who observed: "We're not a 'Model City' or 'Gateway City' or any of those fine sounding things. We are a dirty, stinking, noisy milltown."[12]

Being a planned city and using the rubric "model city" gave Kingsport certain promotional assets, but it also carried liabilities. The history of the United States, for example, demonstrates that more is expected of a unit of government that purports to be an *ideal*, a *model*, or a *utopia* by those involved with the experiment as well as by observers. Whether a country or a municipality, it incurs a certain amount of jealousy from nonparticipants. Not infrequently, Kingsport's critics have used the town's label as a springboard, prefacing their assaults with "If Kingsport is a model city, why...?" The town's inception as a planned industrial community, which generated much of the initial momentum, also produced considerable self-satisfaction. By 1975 the core area was obviously experiencing difficulties, and the Chamber of Commerce had already established the Downtown Improvement Task Force; but John Stroud, then the chamber's executive vice-president, returned from a conference in New York City with an ill-timed publicized opinion that Kingsport was better off than other urban areas because it was "a planned city."[13] The tendency to rest on laurels has not been limited to Stroud and the Chamber of Commerce.

Closely related to this smugness has been the heavy reliance on experts. Johnson and Dennis had subscribed to the aspect of progressivism that glorified rationality, efficiency, and expertise; and they recruited an interesting array of experts to advise them. Johnson and Dennis, however, used the experts judiciously, while themselves retaining overall direction. Furthermore, they continued to maintain a vigilant supervision over city officials after Kingsport was chartered in 1917 under the arrangement of a city manager with the Board of Mayor and Aldermen. In later years, without the caliber of the earlier leadership, administration of the city fell to the specialists, among whom was an assistant city manager, fresh from a regional university, who confessed that not only his work schedule but his free time "was becoming intertwined with methods to expedite sewage plant construction and to solve routine city matters." Then there was a city manager who reportedly kept a Confederate flag and a Tennessee Eastman Company flag on his desk and sat picking his teeth during an appointment. "Professionalised knowledge" in the modern world creates "minds in a groove," wrote philosopher Alfred North Whitehead; and as a publisher of a local newspaper concluded, such people might "provide managerial skills... but someone else will have to provide the direction and leadership."[14]

Another major problem has been pollution, an enduring reminder of Kingsport's debt to industry. On his first visit in 1916, Earle S. Draper, later a nationally known landscape architect, recalled: "I got off the train, and the prevailing wind was blowing from the hill at the back of the station, and the cement dust was on everything.... I got up the next morning and cement dust was all over the bed.... I never went up on Cement Hill. I could not stand the odor. I only looked at it from a distance."[15] The belching smokestacks that once signified progress for an infant town came to represent pollution for a health-conscious society. In her best-selling novel *Kinflicks,* the Kingsport native Lisa Alther has Mr. Zed, the town father of Hullsport, propose kudzu as a final solution to the problems of industrialization. He would "plant it, under cover of night, at selected spots around the factory and the town. The vines would silently take hold and begin their stealthy spread. Before Hullsporters were even aware of their existence, the grasping tendrils would choke out all life in the Model City. The site would be returned to nature."[16] A 1978 article in *Southern Exposure* mentioned the reluctance of residents "to criticize the industries which put bread on their tables" and discussed the risks incident to pollution in Kingsport. An editorial in the *Kingsport Times-News,* acknowledging the problem, commented acidly: "One can argue with justification that Kingsport's best-known feature is not Bays Mountain, Church Circle or Netherland Inn—it is the air itself."[17]

Although the whims of politicians, the aspirations of businessmen and industrialists, the apathy of the citizens, and the myopia of municipal officials have undermined the founders' dream for a model city, the economic base has remained fairly strong. Internal factors have shaped much of the town's history, but Kingsport has not been immune to external forces. American cities have been called "Industrial Artifacts," and to some degree this description is applicable to Kingsport.[18] Because of Kingsport's comparatively small size, its relative youth, and its initial planning, the decentralization of the original industries has not been as pronounced as in northern and upper-midwestern cities. Nonetheless, Kingsport sprang from a phase of capitalistic development that is rapidly receding into the national past. Turn-of-the-century captains of industry from the North and the Midwest once foisted their attentions on Southern Appalachia because of its plentiful land, natural resources, and cheap nonunion labor. Now, American-based decision makers for multinational corporations, caught in fierce international competition, look hungrily to the inexpensive workers of Latin America, Southeast Asia, and other Third World locales. As the twentieth century draws to a close, Kingsport's economy is being buffeted by the winds of the high-tech revolution and of shifting world economies.

Closer to home, Kingsport's hinterland likewise has undergone alterations during the course of the twentieth century. For several decades, the town was an oasis of civilization, representing to many rural residents of the Virginia, Tennessee, Kentucky, and Carolina mountains a shining example of technological progress and culture. Gradually, and in part because of the town's contributions to the area, this section has changed. With significant strides in transportation and communication, improvements in education, continued economic development, and the impact of federal and state programs, a more enlightened citizenry is less awed by the model city than was the first generation of laborers who made the transition from farm to factory.[19]

Kingsport shares some of the general historical contours of American cities, but it remains a planned city and a Southern Appalachian phenomenon. It does not necessarily conform to scholarly models of urbanization or to those dealing with regional development. It may be that southern urbanization can best be understood within a regional context that features a rural life-style shaped by the predominance of staple agriculture, race, and a colonial economy.[20] All of these features have had some tangential influence on Kingsport, but colonialism looms most prominently because of the heavy dependence on northern capital and the magnetic attraction of Yankee investors to cheap southern labor.[21] The town and its region, Southern Appalachia, have been bastions of white Anglo-Saxon Protestants. The black population has generally ranged from around 4 to 6 percent in Kingsport, immigrants have been exceedingly rare, and race has never been a particularly significant factor. Residents, however, are not peculiarly southern. As one of the pioneers on this urban frontier has noted, Kingsport was "a very cosmopolitan town...neither southern nor northern."[22] While natives of Appalachia provided a reliable labor force, most of the managers and professionals have usually (but not always) hailed from elsewhere in the country.

Southern Appalachia is *in* but not necessarily *of* the South. It shares the ruralism and religiosity of points below the Mason-Dixon line, but long-standing political and economic ambiguities of the region have partially alienated it from the South of the "Lost Cause" and the "Confederate Dead." That is not to suggest that rebel heroes and folklore have been completely absent or that the population has been set apart totally from southern culture. Symphony belles, superstud athletes, souped-up automobiles, and other southern attributes have developed as the town has aged. Such artificialities are more the products of affectation than of decades of social fermentation.

Kingsport has possessed a curious cultural mix, with outside college-trained managers and technicians working alongside local laborers whose education rarely went beyond high school. The influx of outsiders and the newfound affluence of natives, however, have blurred any real or imagined Appalachian distinctiveness as the more ambitious of mountain families have moved into better homes and have seen the children through college.[23] From this population has emerged the usual spectrum: a few Rhodes Scholars, scores of Ph.D.'s, at least one Miss America finalist, successful politicians and businessmen, war heroes, skilled lawyers and physicians, and such notables as the National Broadcasting Company's correspondent and anchorman John Palmer and Congressman James H. ("Jimmy") Quillen, the ranking Republican on the House Rules Committee. Perhaps most important of all have been the general "garden variety" of Americans whose ambitions revolve around "one of those trim ranch houses, the good schools, the fine churches, a college education for the kids, and a new Chevy under the carport in Kingsport."[24]

Kingsport has been the subject of dozens of articles, numerous promotional tracts, and several Rotary Club publications. It has received passing mention in scholarly studies devoted to planning and landscape architecture. Given its evolution from lofty beginnings as a "model city" to a city suffering some rather ordinary urban problems, the time is auspicious for a comprehensive study. This book represents the first full-fledged treatment of this experiment by a trained historian. It is a biography of the city of Kingsport. By considering the special roles of capital, labor, industry, and government in the development of the town, it seeks to address "the city-building process in relation to technology and social organization," described several years ago by historian Roy Lubove. Such an approach, Lubove maintained, "can, potentially, help clarify the elusive relationship between personality, social organization, and environment."[25]

This account acknowledges the social and intellectual challenge of American urban history and examines the ideology that has shaped the town, as well as the altering perceptions that Kingsport citizens have had of themselves and their city. The organizational structure of the book reflects the complexity of the planned city's origins. Chapters 2 through 5 focus, respectively, on ideals, physical development, the economic base, and the population. Subsequent chapters detail the town's history since the late 1920s, at which time its continued existence seemed to be guaranteed.

2

Foundations of an American Dream

Kingsport's underpinnings were based on a potpourri of American ideology. The founders drew heavily on the ideals of a rural, agrarian society and sampled innovative thoughts of their own era that helped to shape the twentieth-century urban, industrial world. It has been suggested that the first utopia was "not a Hellenic speculative fantasy but a derivation from a historical event...the city itself."[1] Whatever the classical connection between utopias and cities, John B. Dennis, the financier for the Kingsport project, denied any effort to fantasize, claiming that the experiment had "simply been carried out on modern lines of business sense."[2] The right to dream, however, is a democratic privilege, and American dreams of the eighteenth century were converted into plans for an entire society. Indeed, those early national visions became an integral part of American history and life across three centuries.[3] Accepting Dennis's rejection of utopianism does not preclude labeling both him and J. Fred Johnson, his close associate, *dreamers,* whose idealism was tempered by practicality.

Whereas some of the social experiments of nineteenth-century America had been characterized by strange sexual behavior and peculiar notions about religion, Kingsport's code of conduct was embedded in Protestantism and middle-class values. The sober majority demonstrated as early as 1917, for instance, that they would not tolerate violation of the prohibition laws when they shut down the Days of 49 Dance Hall, with its "bevy of girls." A writer for the *Kingsport Times* self-righteously declared that Kingsport planned to be a model city of citizens as well as of streets.[4] Steeped in the sacredness of American economic theory, and devoid of socialism or communism, this "utopia" was anchored in capitalism.

Embracing such republican ideals as equality of opportunity, the desirability of land ownership, and the virtue of the people and endorsing a nineteenth-century credo of moral values, progress, and culture, Kingsport's founders attempted to build an industrial dream on a fractured foundation. A capitalistic utopia defies logic; it is a paradox. Republican ideals, too, are at variance with capitalism. Essentially, republicanism, with its reliance on civic virtue, is anticapitalistic and, in eighteenth-century America, represented an attempt to stave off an emerging individualistic society and to salvage a sense of community and social conscience that civilized people believed to be appropriate to human behavior.[5] By the time the Kingsport project was launched, yet another vital ingredient in the town's success, the Protestant work ethic, had been shaken by the realities of the Industrial Revolution in the United States. The work ethic originated as a middle-class affair and was likewise perpetuated by mill owners and managers who looked down from their comfortable hillside dwellings onto the factories and the humble abodes of the workers below. The retarded economic development of the area around the site of the new town favored the Kingsport experiment, for the work ethic was a distinctive feature of preindustrial capitalism, the ideology of an earlier, perhaps simpler, time and place.[6] Possessed of vision, intuition, energy, and commitment and personifying a type of leadership that antedated modern managerial approaches, capitalists at Kingsport conveyed their enthusiasm to residents of the surrounding countryside and mobilized them as staunch supporters of the project.

American dreams are not infrequently conceived close to nature.[7] On 5 February 1929, the Reverend Thomas P. Johnston presented the Kingsport Board of Mayor and Aldermen with a gavel. It was made from a limb of the "Big Elm" near Rotherwood, at the confluence of the north and south forks of the Holston River. He had salvaged it when a tree surgeon was at work trying to save the elm from disease. In the ceremony, the minister offered these words: "Now gentlemen, almost under the shade of this historic old tree our magic city of Kingsport has grown: a city that represents all that is best in the age in which we live."[8] As early as 1750, Dr. Thomas Walker had explored the land in the vicinity of the north and south forks of the Holston River for the Loyal Land Company of Virginia. Walker reported an elm tree whose trunk at a height of three feet from the ground measured twenty-five feet in circumference. It is probable that the tree he observed and the "Big Elm" were one and the same.[9]

This spectacular example of nature's handiwork was only one of many manifestations of natural beauty in the countryside near where the modern city of Kingsport was to be established. Walker also recorded that grass was "plenty in the low grounds," noted the presence of Indian inhabitants, and mentioned having "caught two young Buffaloes one of which was killed, and having cut and marked the other we turn'd him out." His party also observed "Perch, Mullets, and Carp in plenty, and caught one of the large Sort of Cat Fish."[10] The Southern Appalachian wilderness had provided such protective isolation for this garden that more than a century later the beauty and resources were still largely intact. The planner John Nolen, on his first visit to the site of modern Kingsport in 1916, "found a wasteland, temporary town laid out grid fashion in contrast to some of the most verdant countryside he had ever seen."[11] A newcomer from Michigan who took up residence in the infant town in 1919 recalled "the unspoiled natural beauty" of the area.[12]

The mountain barriers and the inadequate transportation systems help to explain the limited development in Upper East Tennessee, generally, and the Kingsport area, specifically, prior to the twentieth century. Although permanent settlements had been made in the vicinity of Long Island by the 1770s, no major town had risen along this section of the Holston River during the nineteenth century. The town of Boat Yard, on the north bank of the Holston just below the tip of Long Island, had originated toward the end of the eighteenth century. In 1822 it was incorporated as Kingsport.[13] The village of Old Kingsport—some controversy exists as to whether it was named for William King or for Colonel James King—would eventually be annexed into the modern city of Kingsport. The planned city of the twentieth century, however, had its beginnings on a nearby but different site. Old Kingsport was stymied by impediments to trade.

Boat Yard, during the early eighteenth century, had occupied a desirable location on the Holston River. It was also a station on the great post road that led from Philadelphia and Baltimore to frontier settlements in Kentucky and Tennessee. Technological and natural changes, however, had negated these advantages. Preindustrial manufacturing had withered, and the flourishing river trade had given way as the Holston became virtually unnavigable to Knoxville; and the railroad that was built through East Tennessee favored Jonesboro. As one local historian noted, "When the East Tennessee and Virginia Railroad joined the Virginia and Tennessee Railroad at Bristol in 1859

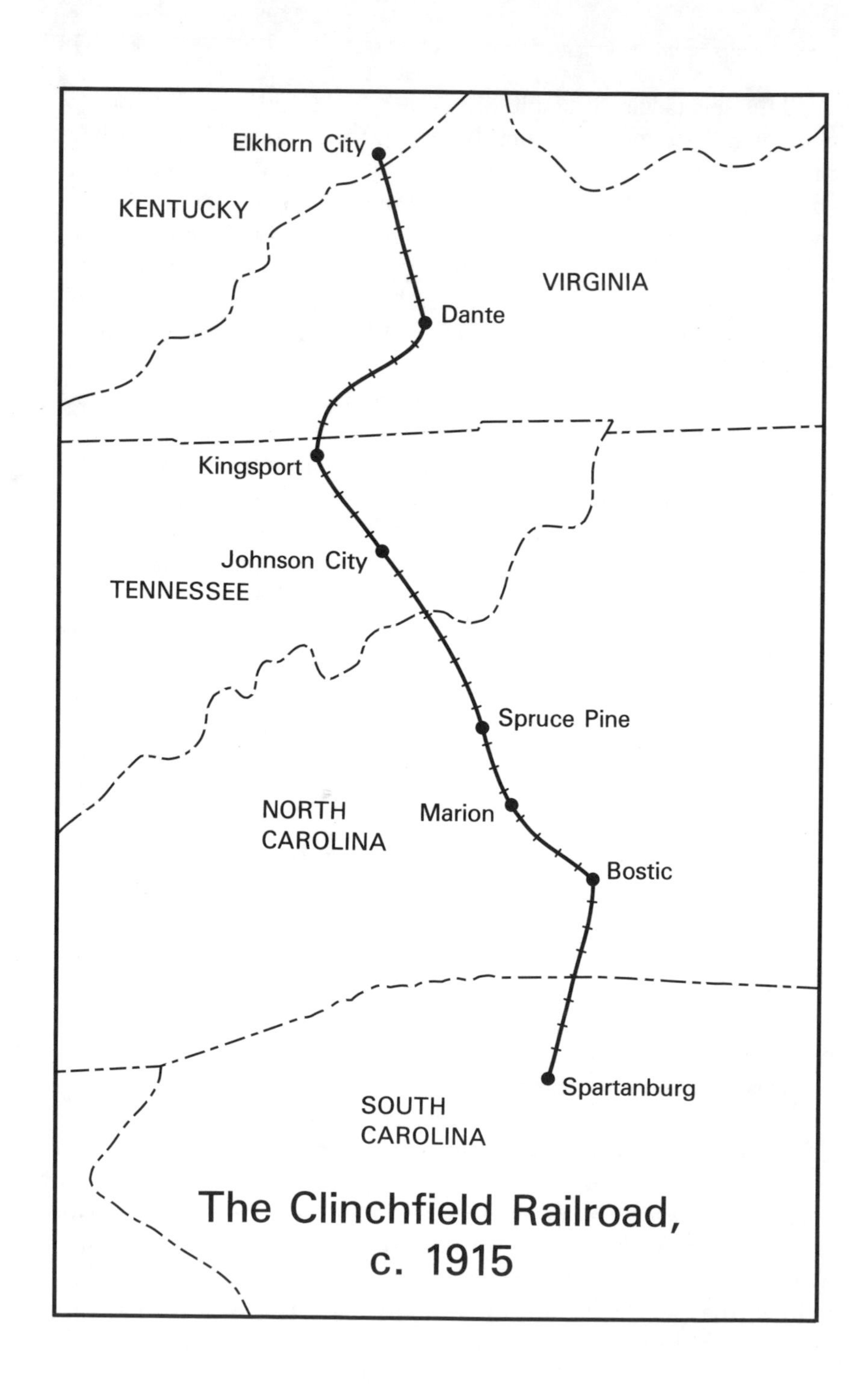

The Clinchfield Railroad, c. 1915

. . . freight and passengers that for more than fifty years had gone over the Great Road down the Holston Valley, then turned by rail over the southern route." After the Civil War, "the small town which had flourished during the first half of the century was left a deserted rural hamlet."[14]

Early railroad construction through East Tennessee followed the valleys, and that which accompanied coal, iron, and timber development in this section of Southern Appalachia during the late nineteenth century offered little more than spur lines. The associate editor of *Railroad Age Gazette* noted in 1909 that "the mountain region of the states crossed by the Blue Ridge is a series of steep slopes, sharp ridges, narrow hollows and valleys and swift mountain streams with very little bottom or tillable ground."[15] No investors had succeeded in putting together the financing to construct a line across the mountains, and few seemed willing to take the risks. In 1911, Mark W. Potter, then president of the Carolina, Clinchfield and Ohio Railroad, explained the consequences: "Because of this mountain barrier commerce between the Central West and the Southeast has swung around through the Virginia gateway at the north or the Atlanta gateway at the south, moving over circuitous routes, affording inadequate service and involving expensive operation."[16] Portions of eastern Tennessee, southwestern Virginia, eastern Kentucky, and western North Carolina were cut off from the major transportation arteries that provided access to national markets.

The construction of the Carolina, Clinchfield and Ohio Railroad relieved that isolation and gave birth to the modern town of Kingsport. Both the railroad and the town owed their existence to George L. Carter, a native son of Southern Appalachia. After Carter's death in 1936, the Kingsport Board of Mayor and Aldermen adopted a resolution remembering him as "our esteemed friend, whose vision and courage is largely responsible for the founding and development of our chosen city."[17] Charles J. Harkrader—the publisher of the *Bristol Herald-Courier* and *Bristol News-Bulletin,* one of the founders of the *Johnson City Press-Chronicle,* and someone who was personally acquainted with Carter—wrote that "the man more responsible than any other person for bringing the industrial age to sections of Kentucky, Virginia, Tennessee, North and South Carolina, was a mountaineer from the hills of Carroll County, Virginia. Often in dire financial straits, struggling against almost insuperable odds, George L. Carter built the Clinchfield Railroad."[18]

The idea of a railroad that would traverse the southern highlands had originated in the Old South. As early as 1832, John C. Calhoun had suggested building such a railroad from Charleston, South Carolina, to Cincinnati, Ohio.[19] Realization awaited the New South's exploitation of untapped resources. George L. Carter, the Clinchfield's promoter, was the embodiment of the entrepreneur of that generation. Daring and sometimes ruthless, he was armed with exceptional vision. Harkrader claimed that Carter "was a mystery while he lived. In spite of his far flung enterprises, few people knew him and almost none knew him with any degree of intimacy. He lived largely to himself, kept everybody, including his employees, at a distance."[20]

In 1902, Carter, then in his mid-forties, with his associates, had purchased the property of the Ohio and Charleston Railway Company. This was the last of a series of companies dating back to the 1830s that had been involved in projects for building a railroad on a direct route from Charleston to Cincinnati. Carter's agents, among them his brother-in-law J. Fred Johnson, took options on thousands of acres along the proposed route from Elkhorn City, Kentucky, to Spartanburg, South Carolina. Carter had also acquired immense tracts of coal lands in southwestern Virginia and eastern Kentucky, known as the Clinchfield Section. This construction project was but one of Carter's many ventures. Earlier he had formed the Virginia Iron, Coal and Coke Company, with assets estimated at $12 million, which possessed coal mines and iron furnaces in Virginia, Tennessee, and Kentucky. This company owned the railroad from Bristol to Appalachia, Virginia, and, in Tennessee, one from Bristol to Mountain City. Carter had already established his reputation as a promoter by 1900, when he moved with his wife and their only child, James, to Bristol from his birthplace of Hillsville, Virginia.[21]

The South and Western Railway Company, Carter's newly incorporated enterprise, established headquarters in the Tennessee-Virginia state-line town of Bristol during 1903; but it later moved to Johnson City. The South and Western extended the line from Huntdale to Spruce Pine, both in North Carolina; but by 1905, according to the Carolina, Clinchfield and Ohio's historical notes, Carter was embroiled in financial difficulties and court battles and had to enlist the aid of northern capitalists to salvage his project. He managed to gain the backing of Thomas Fortune Ryan of New York and Virginia, one of the leading financiers in the country at the time. A syndicate was subsequently organized to complete the railroad. A party of the investors arrived in Bristol by special train, registered at the Hotel Hamilton, and ventured into the wilderness on horseback to survey the magnitude of their undertaking. The exact date of this visit is not recorded, but a photograph taken near Big Stone Gap, Virginia, includes investors Isaac T. Mann, John B. Dennis, W.M. Ritter, Norman B. Ream, Thomas Fortune Ryan, James A. Blair, and H. Ray Dennis, as well as Carter, George B. Kent, the chief locating engineer, and James Hammill, Ritter's attorney.[22] On 7 March 1908 the South and Western Railway Company was rechartered under the name of the Carolina, Clinchfield and Ohio Railroad (CC&O).[23]

Construction proceeded rapidly, the grueling task being borne heavily by Italian immigrants. Labor agents in New York City procured thousands of Italians and members of other national groups, many of whom were just off the boat, unable to speak English, anxious for work, and ignorant of their destination. Harsh treatment of the Italians, even peonage, produced protests form the Italian government, which were lodged with the United States Department of State. After a bloody fight in May 1906 at Marion, North Carolina, which left two Italians dead and five severely wounded, leaders of the attack were indicted for manslaughter, and warrants were issued for the arrest of some agents of the South and Western Company. The company resolved the matter when it agreed to pay indemnities to the families of the dead and to all the Italians who survived the incident.[24] Despite labor difficulties, financial entanglements, and physical obstacles, the line was finally completed in 1912 from Dante, Virginia, to Spartanburg, South Carolina; then the Elkhorn extension into Kentucky was begun. The entire project was finished in 1915.[25]

The Clinchfield Railroad was a remarkable engineering feat. Throughout most of its length, it traversed rugged mountain country, cutting through intervening ridges with a high standard of construction and an easy grade that fitted it for the carriage of immense tonnage. To be profitable, this trade route across the mountains, which had been built at an estimated cost of $40 million, required industrial and urban development along its course. Carter had anticipated all of this when he dispatched his agents and lawyers into the countryside to buy options on real estate. Various sites for developments were considered, including Marion, Altapass, and Spruce Pine, North Carolina; Erwin, Johnson City, and Old Kingsport, Tennessee; and Clinchport and St. Paul, Virginia. According to newspaperman Harkrader, Carter realized that options had to be purchased before news of the construction of the railroad leaked out. Because timing was of the essence, Carter quickly decided "to make the first big strike at Kingsport." The journalist remembered that "some 20,000 German Baptists had just closed a national convention in Bristol and the 'rumor' got abroad that the options were being taken in an effort to relocate several hundred German Baptist farmers."[26] Even if Harkrader's reminiscences were accurate, the *Johnson City Comet* had broken the story on 17 August 1905 of the plan "to boom a town at Kingsport." A week later the same newspaper had reported more details about land options and purchases. According to this account, Benjamin Wexler had sold 483 acres for $17,000; and Dr. Alvin J. Roller, 800 acres for $15,000.[27]

Before they were finished, Carter's agents had obtained options on approximately 7,000 acres "stretching roughly from the western foot of Chestnut Ridge to the Clay Place two miles west of Rotherwood." Harkrader wrote that "almost before the ink was dry on the options, the exciting news of the railroad leaked out." Landowners "cried fraud and refused to convey." Dr. Roller resisted a suit that Carter brought against him in the U.S. District Court at Greeneville for a deed to his 800 acres. The controversy was reportedly settled in a room at the Hotel Hamilton, when Carter's treasurer, Jerry C. Stone, signed a certified check for $80,000. After Roller conveyed his land, other landowners acquiesced.[28] It was about this time that Carter recruited James W. Dobyns, one of his boyhood friends from Virginia, to operate the farms that Carter now controlled at Kingsport. Dobyns, his wife, and their two sons moved into the Rotherwood mansion that had been built by Frederick A. Ross before the Civil War where the north and south forks of the Holston meet.[29]

Harbingers of progress heralded great things for the old town of Kingsport. After having reported a week earlier that the Unaka Corporation, the land company associated with the construction of the CC&O, had plans for a new town, there was another comment from the *Johnson City Comet* on 24 August 1905: "This would mean that Kingsport is to arise from a small country town, located near the intersection of the North and South forks of the Holston River, to become one of the most important manufacturing and business towns in the state of Tennessee." Three years later, the *Bristol Herald-Courier* predicted that Kingsport had "a rosy future," speculating further: "This historic old town, on the Holston River, may become a city of industry, art and manufacture or it may become the metropolis of a region rich in mineral development or a shipping point surrounded by cattle ranches and grazing land unsurpassed for its beauty and fertility."[30] On 9 October 1908 the track-laying force of the CC&O arrived at the north fork of the Holston. With the completion of the bridge across the river, the coal deposits of Virginia were connected with Kingsport.[31] At about this time, a writer for the *Johnson City Comet* reflected elegiacly: "The little farms that have so long lain hidden beneath the shadow of the towering mountains, or snugly tucked away in a little fertile valley between two great hills... will now rouse themselves and rub their eyes and wonder what it all means."[32]

Apparently, by 1911, Carter's relationship with his New York backers was undergoing an alteration. He resigned as chief executive of the Clinchfield Railroad and was replaced by Mark W. Potter, who then served as president as well as chairman of the board.[33] Around 1914 the board of directors of Kingsport Farms, Incorporated, the original company formed in Kingsport by the New York group, authorized Blair and Company, represented by John B. Dennis, to buy approximately 6,355 acres of land in Sullivan and Hawkins counties from the Carter Coal Company for $175,000.[34] At this time, Carter severed his connections with the Kingsport area. He had become estranged from his brother-in-law Johnson—the reason remains a mystery—but he did not forget his friend Dobyns. Without ever having had a written contract or even a precise verbal agreement, Carter gave Dobyns 496.11 acres of the choicest residential real estate in what was to be the new town. According to Harkrader, "This big transfer came in what Mr. Carter liked to call a 'burn book' settlement—i.e., both sides destroying all records." James W. Dobyns's son Flem eventually inherited this valuable property in 1926 and had it platted for the Fairacres subdivision.[35]

Although Carter was not involved in the actual establishment of the planned city of Kingsport, it was he who had recognized the potential of the site, reportedly in 1905, when he "came by train to Moccasin Gap [Virginia], rode in a buggy with R.M. Jones to Kingsport, and spent the night with Jones at his home on the island. The next morning Carter, accompanied by Jones, crossed the sluice and climbed to the top of Kitt's Bluff, whence he, through a pair of field glasses, viewed the country for miles around." Two weeks later, Carter returned with an engineer from Philadelphia and made a survey of the surrounding country.[36] By 1906 a street arrangement, which included the core area with its semicircle, later known as Church Circle, had been drawn, and the names of streets had been labeled on the map.[37]

When Carter removed himself from events at Kingsport, John B.

Dennis filled the vacuum. Dennis, a native of Maine, was the son of a prominent northeastern banker and businessman. He had attended Cornell University for three years and then had transferred to Columbia College, where in 1887 he had earned the Bachelor of Arts degree. After graduation, he had worked for several brokerage firms in Boston and New York City and in 1890 had become associated with Blair and Company. Within three years, he had been made a partner. Dennis's connection with this company led to his initial involvement in Southern Appalachia with the CC&O Railroad.[38] Blair and Company was an underwriter for large-scale speculative ventures. Dennis was a financier, not a corporate businessman, who was reputed to be a financial wizard, a "kind of bird dog" who could sniff out potential profit.[39] Given the snarled nature of his projects in Kingsport, the reputation may have been more glorious than his practices merited. In a report prepared in 1971, William B. Franke, who as a senior partner of the New York accounting firm of Franke, Hannon and Withey had audited the Securities Company in 1938 and 1946, wrote that "the history of the Securities Company [the top holding company of the group associated with Kingsport]...could form the basis of a text book on what *not to do* and what *to do*... in corporate management." A large number of minority stockholders scattered throughout several companies in the group limited freedom of action. Furthermore, as incorporated in the state of New York in 1899, the Securities Company was subject to the personal holding company surtax, which, left uncorrected, might have made it impossible to liquidate the large debt.[40]

Pressure from Dennis's creditor, the New York Trust Company, had forced him to allow Franke's investigation. No reorganization, however, was undertaken until after Dennis's death in 1947. Although financial difficulties were to plague Dennis later, in 1915 he was enthusiastically poised for the Kingsport project. That year, the board of Kingsport Farms, Incorporated, authorized the sale of certain of its properties to Kingsport Stores, Incorporated, and to the Kingsport Improvement Corporation (KIC), newly formed companies. Such transactions made it possible to increase book values substantially at a low cost on income taxes. During 1915 and 1916, the KIC acquired a total of 1,010 acres from Kingsport Farms, Incorporated, as the site for the new town.[41]

When the firm of Blair and Company was dissolved in 1920, Dennis was already deeply involved in the establishment of Kingsport. He had renovated the old Rotherwood mansion and made it his principal residence. Whatever other motivations Dennis had, his prime consideration was the development of an industrial city that would create traffic for the railroad.[42] He recognized the importance of community spirit and the need to promote Kingsport. One report claimed: "Dennis detested publicity. He was never known to make a public speech. He never gave interviews to the press. He tried to avoid public functions. He took little interest in politics and never served on public committees except those dealing with public finance." Dennis's reticence may have stemmed, in part, from his almost total deafness. In any event, he chose to maintain a low profile, and on 31 December 1915 he hired J. Fred Johnson as a promoter, or a one-man chamber of commerce, for the new town.[43]

Dennis's acquaintance with Johnson had begun with Blair and Company's purchase of a controlling interest in the CC&O. The commissaries along the route operated by Johnson and a partner had been included in the deal because they were subsidiaries of the railroad.[44] Although Johnson became the principal promoter of Kingsport, he was not just a front man for Dennis. Dennis was known to the townspeople, he resided in the area, and he was the acknowledged financier of the project. Although Dennis stayed in the background while Johnson was very visible in Kingsport, they were so well matched, such kindred philosophical spirits, that in this task it was almost impossible to distinguish Moses from Aaron. While Dennis envisioned, financed, and directed the establishment of Kingsport, J. Fred Johnson, the native mountaineer, was the man who had the ideas and ideals to make the plan possible. Their expectations for success rested on the availability of raw materials, the completion of the railroad, the existence of an adequate and cheap supply of labor, and the concept of interlocking industries—that is, industries that would cooperate with and complement each other while developing nonlocal markets. With these advantages, Dennis and Johnson expected to create more than just a company town; they anticipated a planned, diversified industrial community.

Dennis and Johnson shared a view of life that had come under attack by this time in America, but an ideological base nonetheless upon which they launched a town. However insipid an American credo of moral values, progress, and culture may have seemed to later generations, it had weathered the nineteenth century; and vestiges of it had carried over into the new one.[45] Self-proclaimed and publicly recognized men of morality used "words like truth, justice, patriotism, unselfishness, and decency...without embarrassment, and ordinarily without any suggestion that their meaning might be only of a time and place."[46] Progress, in keeping with the vanguard of the Progressive generation's thought, "meant an evolution in which men took a hand, a conscious effort to reach a better world which could be glimpsed, or at least imagined, in the future."[47] Culture essentially referred to "polite manners, respect for traditional learning, appreciation of the arts, and above all an informed and devoted love of standard literature."[48] In an address before the Bachmanian Literary Society in 1916, George Bradley, a Kingsport high-school student, urged: "Let us make Kingsport a city of commercial importance, but no less a home of culture in the broadest sense."[49] Although an interest in culture did exist, the initial thrust of activity was toward physical development. Except for expectations of good conduct, regular church attendance, and support of public education, *culture* meant little in the early days of the planned city; but emphasis on *moral values* and *progress* ran high. Because Dennis was such a private person, attributes of America's ideological past are most easily identified in Johnson, the man and his work.

By 1916, when J. Fred Johnson became the principal promoter for the new town of Kingsport, his experiences as a child and a young adult had already forged a character that was heavily imbued with the Protestant work ethic and corresponding middle-class values. Born in Hillsville, Virginia, on 25 June 1874 to J. Lee Johnson and Mary Pierce Early Johnson, he was influenced by the nineteenth-century American value system of which the work ethic was a basic tenet. Nineteenth-century Americans were told (and many believed) that "in a world of pressing material demands it was one's social duty to produce" and that "working also held one back from the sink of idleness." They also harbored a hope for success, as well as the belief that work was a creative act. A final assumption was that "through work men impressed something of themselves on the material world."[50]

The rural Southern Appalachian region offered few economic opportunities to its children. Johnson's native Carroll County, in southwestern Virginia, was poor, but his hometown of Hillsville was the county seat. There, Johnson first heard and participated in civic discussions involving community government, accumulated a knowledge of business principles, and acquired an understanding of people. His father died when the boy was in his early teens, and Johnson had to give up his formal education to rescue his father's general store and to support his mother and two sisters. Setting a demanding pace, he not only managed to pay his father's debts with interest, he also studied after the store closed at 9:00 in the evenings, reciting his lessons to an old schoolmaster. He later read law in Hillsville.[51] Along with considerable ability, Johnson had the good fortune to be in the right place at the right time. He reached manhood as energetic, opportunistic southerners were beginning to subscribe to the New South philosophy, with its emphasis on industrialization, business, and commerce. Embracing an essentially northern value system, southern entrepreneurs began to enter into alliances wth northern capitalists.[52] Johnson's marriage to Ruth Carter led directly to his business association with her brother, George L. Carter, and in turn to contacts with Yankee investors.

The role played by Johnson in Kingsport's history is all the more fascinating because of the complexity of his character. It is often difficult to separate his personal beliefs from the propaganda that was used to promote the town. Even though his professed values and his actions could occasionally be judged contradictory, there is no reason to doubt his sincerity. In correspondence with industrialists, especially George Eastman,[53] and in his speeches to townspeople, Johnson was sometimes effusive. This appears to have been simply a personality trait, but it may have been affected. Whatever the case, Johnson was clearly devoted to the city of Kingsport. He truly believed that a man should leave his mark. When Dennis first offered Johnson the job at Kingsport, Johnson reportedly told his wife that they could either be millionaires or build a town.[54] For the next twenty-eight years of his life, he devoted himself to the development of Kingsport. Although he subordinated his personal interests to those of the town, at the time of his death in 1944, he was associated with two banks, the electric utilities company, and an assortment of other interests, was president of the Kingsport Brick Corporation, and was owner of a department store.

After Johnson's death, friends and associates alluded to his nonacquisitive nature. Newspaperman Charles J. Harkrader once mentioned that "J. Fred could have left her [his wife] far more, if he had chosen to accumulate, but that was not his nature."[55] Perley S. Wilcox, head of Tennessee Eastman Company, once admonished its employees to remember that Johnson "died a comparatively poor man," although "he had been accused of building for his own private interests.... He could easily have been Governor of the State or a United States Senator, or a big businessman commanding a large salary. But he wanted none of these things."[56] H.J. Shivell, one of Johnson's longtime friends, scoffed at the idea of Johnson's relative poverty, however, contending that Johnson had done well enough for himself.[57]

Johnson exhibited no signs of special allegiance to any particular business or industrial group. He answered only to John B. Dennis; but, here, too, Johnson was somewhat independent because of his own success. Dennis obviously recognized Johnson's talents and gave him free rein; and Johnson parlayed his position as president of the Kingsport Improvement Company into that of power broker for the town. A self-proclaimed Democrat, he was not reluctant to cooperate with the Republican politicians of Tennessee's First Congressional District.[58]

Probably a major factor in Dennis's selection of Johnson as promotion agent was the fact that Johnson was a native of the region. As such, he possessed an insight that enabled him to establish a rapport with the local people. Johnson was *of the people* but was *not really one of them.* He respected the inhabitants of the Southern Appalachians, believed they should have opportunities to better themselves, and had no patience with those who failed to use opportunities to their advantage. Conducting a survey among Southern Appalachians during the late 1950s, sociologist Thomas R. Ford found that those who were identified as leaders were generally wealthier and better educated. Holding prestigious positions and wielding influence, they were not typical of the general population.[59] The relationship between Johnson and residents of the Kingsport area just after the turn of the twentieth century was analogous.

Such republican ideals as equality of opportunity, the importance of land ownership, and the virtue of the people surfaced in Johnson's personal philosophy and manifested themselves in the intellectual base of the town. The concept of equality in the United States has been distinguished by its ambivalence, but it has not suggested social leveling; nor did it with J. Fred Johnson.[60] Essentially, it meant equality of opportunity.[61] One of Johnson's closest friends, Colonel E. W. Palmer of Kingsport Press, noted that Johnson believed that a permanent community structure depended on the presence of opportunity for the individual. Those who abused their privileges or failed to make the most of facilities available to them could expect no sympathy from him.[62] Earle S. Draper, who first knew Johnson when Draper himself was an assistant to planner John Nolen, offered another perspective: "Johnson knew the mountaineers and could talk their language. If there was anything to put over such as a land deal, he handled it." Draper described Johnson as "something of a shyster as well as a businessman. He had sympathy with the underprivileged, but he did not think they should be given a price that would go beyond the rightful value. He was a mule trader by nature. He would not give too much."[63]

The permanent community structure to which Colonel Palmer referred depended upon the ownership of property. As a source of independence and as evidence of an enduring attachment to the community, the possession of realty has ranked importantly as a republican ideal.[64] Writing an endorsement in 1933 for a local architect who had applied for a position with the Tennessee Valley Authority, Johnson stated his opinion on home ownership: "I have believed, and have said a thousand times, that one of the greatest needs of this nation is that everybody should have a comfortable home. Of course, I don't mean a big home."[65] This view had been apparent in Kingsport as early as 1919, when a home-and-loan association was organized and took as its slogan "Own the home in which you live." Its guidelines, based on those of a similar organization in Charlotte, North Carolina, encouraged a prospective home owner to buy stock in the amount of the anticipated cost of his home. The entrance fee was twenty-five cents per share, and payments were twenty-five cents per week on each share. These payments, together with the profits of the corporation, were to be applied to shares until they reached a value of $100. For example, a member of the association who bought thirty shares could apply for a loan of $3,000. Such loans carried 6 percent interest and required a lien on the real estate. Although Johnson himself was not among the officers or the directors, some men on the board were subject to his influence, among them James W. Dobyns, the president, and W.W. Hufford, a director of the association, both of whom were managers of Kingsport Stores, which was owned principally by Johnson.[66]

On the issue of landownership, the door swung both ways for Johnson. To be sure, ownership indicated a commitment to the community; but Johnson, in his connections with Carter and Dennis, was a real-estate agent. Johnson's most direct contact with the natives of the Kingsport area during the early phase of the project had involved land deals. Even prior to his association with Dennis, he had been an agent for Carter, buying options for the railroad. Those landowners who later had an inkling of the profits that were made could not have helped resenting Johnson. Their preference for high ground and their indifference to the swampy land that some referred to as "frog level" had led them to sell potentially valuable property for low prices.[67] They were short on capital and ignorant of modern engineering technology that could be used to drain the marshy town site; and Carter, Johnson, and Dennis played their advantage to the hilt. It must be remembered, however, that although the Improvement Company stood to realize significant profits, financial risks had to be taken, physical planning had to be done, and development had to begin before profits could be reaped.

One of Johnson's responsibilities as president of the Kingsport Improvement Company was the profitable disposal of land in line with the overall city design. A major reason for the KIC's engaging a professional city planner was that the platting of lots that had already been done by the railroad engineers did not make the best use of the land—that is, it did not produce the largest possible number of lots for sale. In comparing his first preliminary plan with the old arrangement, John Nolen pointed to the advantage of increased frontage and more lots.[68] H. Ray Dennis, brother of John B., soon informed Nolen that Johnson feared that "the great number of business lots on the new map of the business district will have a depressing effect on sales."[69] Johnson suggested instead that the map show only a portion of the business district. Dennis wrote: "Mr. Johnson thinks that such a map will answer all immediate purposes, and when these sales are well advanced the balance of the business district can be thrown in."[70] All of this soon had Nolen arguing that his plan would yield $100,000 more profit than would the original.[71]

Under Johnson's direction, sales proceeded briskly. In a letter dated 29 April 1922 to Nolen, which carried the postscript "The figures are given for *your personal & confidential* information," Johnson outlined the financial aspects of the Improvement Company's real-estate transactions. The KIC acquired about one thousand acres for approximately $100,000. An estimated one-third of the property went for streets, parks, and other public places, yielding no direct returns. Of the remaining property, about three hundred acres sold for around $1 million. This category included roughly twenty acres of playgrounds donated to the schools and land that was sold cheaply to induce factories to locate in the new town as well as lots deliberately underpriced to stimulate development.[72]

Johnson, while producing such profits for the KIC, personally exhibited the moral values of the era. He contributed to the establishment of several churches in the Kingsport area, but he lavishly supported the First Presbyterian Church, even leaving it a tenth of his estate when he died.[73] The religiosity of Johnson and Dennis and early industrialists was reflected in the rising spires of the four churches on the semicircle, like a halo at the head of the downtown. Johnson was the prime mover of the Community Chest and was personally generous to a fault. He was instrumental in advancing the business careers of young men, by giving them helpful advice from time to time; he was known to have bought wardrobes for poor but deserving students when they went off to college. Having no children of his own, he often treated those of others to ice cream, never failing "to include any stray urchin who was lingering around the soda fountain."[74] He was a patriotic American, and it is not surprising that what was probably the first public Fourth of July celebration on the site of the new town was a flower-decked, mule-drawn float sponsored in 1910 by the Store Department of Kingsport Farms, later J. Fred Johnson Company.[75] During World War II, Johnson kept up a steady correspondence with several of the town's servicemen.[76] While recognizing him as an opportunist, people of the area also knew Johnson as a benevolent patriarch.

The "Kingsport spirit" was not unlike the republican concept of virtue or patriotism in its emphasis on public-spiritedness and self-sacrifice;[77] it was the term applied locally to the sense of community that Dennis and Johnson fostered. The city's inception as a planned industrial center contributed to the pervasive opinion among the early residents of the town that Kingsport was special, unique, and destined for greatness. A publication of the Kingsport Improvement Company in 1920 described the atmosphere and the emerging town as "a large picture puzzle," wherein "the interest and enthusiasm of finding a new piece and fitting it into place has spread from the originators to those who are actually fitting in the new pieces."[78]

Johnson clearly sought responsible industrial citizens for the town. Kingsport never compromised itself with such bait as tax concessions, inordinately cheap land, reduced utility rates, or similar incentives by which some small towns often jeopardized their own finances. The Kingsport Improvement Company did, however, give 200 acres to the Federal Dyestuff and Chemical Corporation in 1915; 35 acres to the Kingsport Wood Reduction Company in 1918; 35.44 acres to the Corning Glass Works in 1919; and 100 acres to Borden Mills in 1924.[79] Johnson believed that if an industry could not afford to pay taxes, Kingsport did not need it. When the city was incorporated in 1917, nearly three-quarters of the tax revenues came from the CC&O Railroad and a dozen of the large corporations.[80] Furthermore, industrialists were expected to exhibit a healthy respect for their employees. Colonel

Palmer of Kingsport Press, who on one occasion had ordered the plant to be shut down out of respect for a female employee who had died, once generalized that the trouble with American industry "has been that many employers didn't give a hang about their labor."[81] The auditor for the KIC told a journalist: "There never has been an inch of ground in Kingsport for a sweatshop."[82] On one occasion, Johnson refused to have dinner with the Borden brothers of Borden Mills, Dennis's friends, because they wanted to construct bungalows without indoor plumbing for their employees.[83] Such attitudes and actions made a lasting impression on townspeople and laborers.

The bustling new town attracted individuals from all over the country to teach, to practice law and medicine, to establish businesses, and to manage the industries. This group, along with a sprinkling of local professional people and members of old established families of the area, provided a nucleus for civic organizations and volunteer work. Most of the early managers and professionals were transplants from elsewhere in the country, but the natives, who will be considered later, provided the bulk of the unskilled labor force.

The launching of the Kingsport project coincided with the wave of bigotry that swept the country during and after World War I.[84] Northern businessmen were tired of union disputes and foreign laborers—and of Bolshevism. Perley S. Wilcox, twenty-five years after the establishment of Tennessee Eastman, commented: "It is only natural that George Eastman and Frank Lovejoy should have been concerned about the kind of people to be found in a new location for the company's business—whether they too should have the quality of thinking for themselves and would not be misled by the flood of Bolshevist propaganda that followed the first world war."[85] Having pure Anglo-Saxon independent-minded nonunion labor appealed to Eastman executives and other industrialists. While cheap labor and raw materials offered incentives, the promoters and early industrialists of Kingsport considered the local people to be the greatest asset.

Dennis and Johnson, who were attuned to such nativistic sentiments of northern capitalists as those expressed by Wilcox, offered them the advantage of a labor supply made up of "pure" Americans who had not yet come under the influence of union organizers. This was a strong selling point for persuading industrialists to locate their operations in Kingsport, and it was a vital part of the propaganda that was used. A tract published by the Kingsport Improvement Company in

1920 boasted that the main body of the population was native-born, with less than 6 percent black and fewer than fifty foreigners.[86] Eight years later, Howard Long, a Kingsport newspaperman, in a book authorized by Johnson and published after his word-by-word approval, devoted almost an entire chapter to the homespun virtues of East Tennesseans. Long noted that "the people of the hill country of East Tennessee" were "of purest American stock, the great-grandsons and the great-granddaughters of those pioneers who wrested the country from the Indians in the eighteenth century, and who turned the tide of the American revolution at King's Mountain." He described them as being of "Scotch-Irish ancestry, most of them, with a sprinkling of German, French and English—sturdy, ambitious, thoroughly reliable, and eager for opportunities of education and industry."[87] Even John Nolen, Kingsport's planner, in 1927 commented on the "Anglo-Saxon stock" and euphemistically wrote of the absence of "inter-racial" and "international difficulties" to complicate "the social and political scheme of the community."[88]

Although it is difficult to laud the nativism that underlay the arguments used in promoting Kingsport or to deny that they made good propaganda, Johnson probably believed sincerely in the virtues of the mountain people, even if cheap labor was the bottom line in southern industrial recruitment. Early managers and supervisors likewise praised the ability of the natives, commented on their willingness to learn, conducted special classes to teach them mechanical skills, and noted their reliability. It must be remembered, too, that Johnson was a native mountaineer; he may have been rankled by disparaging remarks about Southern Appalachians, and he may have felt a bit uncomfortable about his own background while in the presence of wealthy, well-educated outsiders. As one of them, the daughter of a New York City publisher, observed: "He was a country boy, but an awfully nice one."[89] Johnson and the natives probably shared a tinge of "ethnic chauvinism" as they collaborated to lure northern money to Kingsport.[90]

The response of the local people to the advent of industrial capitalism will be explored later, but a part of the "mission" of the industrialists and developers—indeed, a rationalization for low wages—was "to create a method by which these homogeneous independent people of the hills could be acclimatized, as it were, to industrial civilization, trained into craftsmen, producing more and more per unit of time and power and material, and thus raising their own wages, while lowering costs."[91] To a considerable degree, the success of the Kingsport experiment hinged on J. Fred Johnson's ability to nurture myriad, sometimes contradictory, ideological tenets among the industrialists, the professionals and managers, and the laborers. Through strength of personality, Johnson forged the "Kingsport spirit." Its durability would depend on the translation of those ideals into realities.

3

Artifacts of the Planned City

Deeply embedded in the mythology of Kingsport is the story of the town's conception. A popular version relates that around 1910 John B. Dennis was traveling with J. Fred Johnson, his freight agent, when their train stopped in Kingsport to pick up the mail. Leaning against an old boxcar mounted on posts in a muddy cow pasture that served as a depot, they pushed back their derbies, and at that moment, Dennis made the fateful observation: "You know, this would make a fine site for an industrial city."[1] This tale enjoyed such popularity that industrialists and railroad officials subsequently embellished it. In 1959, Walter F. Smith, president of Kingsport Press, claimed that when the railroad was first completed, an arriving visitor would have seen "a meadow rolling down to the banks of the Holston River, a scrawny cow or two, a cornfield, a log cabin on a hillside, the muddy stagecoach road disappearing over the mountain toward Bristol, Virginia."[2] A.L.M. Wiggins, chairman of the board of the Clinchfield and its affiliates, in 1958 pointed to Kingsport as an example of how railroads have benefited the country's interior. According to him, before the advent of the railroad, Kingsport had been a sleepy village with two churches, two stores, and two barrooms.[3] Such quaint stories hit close to the truth, and it would be difficult to exaggerate the importance of the Clinchfield to the town; and while the idea for an industrial city at this location was not original to Dennis and Johnson, they were the ones who transformed a vision into a reality. Between 1915 and 1920, they established the framework for the new town.

Their vision of a planned industrial city at Kingsport carried no guarantee of success. Even with the region's natural resources, virtually untapped labor supply, and newly completed railroad, the remoteness was still a major concern. H.J. Shivell, one of Kingsport's early citizens, in recalling his first trip to the town before 1920, illustrated this point. While working at Long Island, New York, he was sent to Kingsport to look at a leather product being manufactured there. When asked where Kingsport was, his employer replied that he did not know but predicted that the people at Pennsylvania Station in New York City surely would. No one at the information booth or the ticket counter knew the location of the town, but the ticket agent sold Shivell a round-trip ticket to Memphis. Only a few miles out of Johnson City, Shivell happened to meet a resident of that Upper East Tennessee town, who explained that Shivell would have to get off there and take the Clinchfield's Transcontinental to Kingsport. "If you go to Memphis," he advised, "you'll be as far from Kingsport as you were when you started."[4]

Earle S. Draper, the landscape architect, observed: "Kingsport was isolated. If it had not been for the railroad, Kingsport would have been an oasis in the countryside. The river was not navigable. There were no dams for power." Draper's doubts about Kingsport's future were laid to rest when he talked to J. Fred Johnson. Draper recalled: "I had some question as to whether Kingsport would achieve any stature as an industrial city. Johnson sold me on the idea of interlocking industries." The total dependence on the railroad, however, as a lifeline to the outside world placed the infant town in a precarious position. Draper reminisced that in 1916 the South had "the greatest flood ever." After ten days of rain, rail connections between Charlotte and Asheville, North Carolina, were cut for a month. With "practically every dam in North Carolina and East Tennessee" damaged, the CC&O could not restore traffic for four or five months; and Draper had to change his method of getting from Charlotte to Kingsport. Taking the Southern Railroad to Lynchburg, Virginia, he arrived after midnight, took a taxi to the Southern lines west, and finally arrived in Bristol after a broken night's sleep.[5]

Even in the early 1920s, according to Draper, it took from an hour and a half to two hours, over barely passable roads, to travel from Bristol to Kingsport. "In those days," he added, "you figured on changing a tire every twenty-five miles."[6] Not surprisingly, given these circumstances, J. Fred Johnson hustled to get Kingsport placed on the route of the Lee Highway, a national artery from New York to New Orleans. To secure the town's position more firmly, he led a delegation of eleven men, more than that from any other East Tennessee community, to a convention of the Lee Highway Association in 1921 and was himself named one of the directors of the project in the state. When Dr. S.M. Johnson, the general director of the Lee Highway Association, who apparently was not related to J. Fred, announced that the road would pass through the "magic city," the local newspaper proclaimed that "the value of the highway to Kingsport can hardly be overestimated; it will mean arteries of commerce with the surrounding country; it will facilitate shipping by truck; and it will make easily accessible neighbors" of Bristol and Knoxville.[7]

The isolation helps to explain the rather primitive level of development around Kingsport at the time of its mythological conception. Lovedale, a small community whose site now lies within the corporate limits of the planned city, was the business center for the surrounding territory; and Old Kingsport, along the Holston River, was only a short distance away. Lovedale, previously known as Peltier, boasted a few businesses. In 1910 the weekly *Kingsport Sentinel* included the CC&O schedule and the office locations of physicians George G. Keener and N.B. Owens. It also carried advertisements for livery, for the local soft-drink bottling company, and for the general store owned by J.H. Calhoun, W.D. Harmon, and J.N. Ingoldsby. For only $1.50 per day, "traveling salesmen and traveling public" might lodge at the Hotel Howard, which boasted a fine view of the Holston River and the mountain, as well as a convenient location one-half mile north of the railroad station.[8]

The initial development of the new industrial city was not particularly promising. The hasty platting of lots, quick sales, and slipshod construction resembled patterns elsewhere in the Southern Appalachians where the boom-town syndrome had been much in evidence during the 1880s and 1890s. Such towns as New Decatur, Alabama; Middlesboro, Kentucky; Rockwood, Tennessee; and Basic City, Virginia, were born of this era of iron and coal development. Many of the dozens of proposed new towns fell victims to the panic of 1893.[9] Dream cities that had been conjured up for promotional purposes failed to materialize; occasionally, investors built a luxurious hotel to demonstrate their good intentions. The Rockbridge Hotel, erected during the 1890s at Glasgow, Virginia, for example, opened for one gala evening and then went into receivership.[10] At Middlesboro, Kentucky, substantial financial resources of American Associated, Limited, backed by English investors, supported expectations for success. Colonel George E. Waring, an engineer from New York City, planned the town, and considerable development occurred. Nonetheless, the speculative bubble burst with the financial crisis of the 1890s. The Four Seasons Hotel at the Middlesboro suburb of Harrogate, Tennessee, had been practically empty since its grand opening, and within two years of completion, it was torn down, the remains being sold to a Chicago contractor for twenty-five thousand dollars.[11]

Between 1910 and 1915, before Dennis enlisted a professional town planner to bring order to the haphazard development produced by rapid growth, the modern industrial city of Kingsport had its genesis. During this period, at least five significant industries began operations. The Clinchfield Portland Cement Corporation and the Kingsport Brick Corporation were established almost simultaneously in 1910, although the cement plant was purportedly Kingsport's oldest. Brick manufacturing for commercial purposes had been attempted, with little success, in the area as early as the 1880s, when David and William Roller had joined C.N. Jordan to establish a brick and glazed-tile plant.[12] As much as one-half of the stock of the Kingsport Brick Corporation was owned by the Securities Company; the cement factory was a subsidiary of Pennsylvania-Dixie Cement Corporation, established by Conrad Miller of Nazareth, Pennsylvania.[13] In 1912 the Kingsport Extract Corporation began the production of tanning extract. Three years later, a related manufacturer, the Kingsport Tannery, Incorporated, was established.[14] In November 1915, construction began for the Federal Dyestuff and Chemical Corporation, and after two months the plant shipped its first dyes. As of November 1916, it had produced 800,000 pounds of dyestuffs and 350,000 pounds of high explosives. One account claimed that its operations included seven acres of buildings and 350 to 400 acres of land.[15] Kingsport Pulp Corporation, later Mead Corporation, was organized in 1916 and had begun production by the next year. Initially capitalized at $650,000, the company built a $350,000 pulp plant which used the wood waste from the extract plant.[16]

The building of a town and the construction of factories generated a tremendous demand for labor, and a shortage of workers caused delays. In May 1916 the local newspaper reported that two hundred homes were going up; and about a year later, it mentioned five hundred buildings in various stages of completion. Crude, muddy streets and a severe housing crunch gave the new city the character of a frontier boom town. Lots in what would be the downtown business district could be had for as little as $187.50 in January 1916.[17]

The quality of the early housing varied considerably. The cement company had built several wood-and-stucco dwellings for its employees, as well as a clubhouse that provided lodging for newcomers and visitors. Wells supplied water, and the company powerhouse for a while extended electricity to the entire town.[18] Another industry, the Federal Dyestuff and Chemical Corporation, had its own guest housing, a two-story structure with sleeping porches. According to one visitor, this was "the only decent place to stay" around 1915.[19] Photographs of ramshackle structures set on what appear to be blocks or short stilts indicate that it was better to be a guest in town than a permanent resident.[20] Fortunate was the newcomer who could boast of living in permanent accommodations. M.D. Edmonds, reporting for the *Philadelphia Public-Ledger*, observed in November 1916: "So sudden has been the rush of population that the true hallmark of a boom town—the dwelling tent—can be seen on every hand."[21] Charles C. May, writing for the *Architectural Forum*, claimed that although several hundred houses had been built during the year prior to August 1916, "the open meadow land was white with the tents of those who had not yet been accommodated," when he first visited the town.[22] The situation was worse than these descriptions indicated. At one time, a population of 2,870 lived in 286 houses; tents and shacks of every description numbered in the hundreds. According to Dr. T.B. Yancey, who had been recruited to improve public health, open surface toilets "were soon filled to overflowing." "Greek restaurants" were characterized by "filth, carelessness, exposed food and rancid butter, with dishes washed in cold stagnant water." About 250 hogs roamed the town as scavengers.[23]

Although as late as 1918/19 families who had come down from the mountains and in from the surrounding valleys to work lived in tents around what was to be the White City area, Dennis and Johnson were sensitive to comments about a "boom town" and were conscious of the need for satisfactory housing. It was not unusual for Johnson to ride horseback around the encampments, checking on the welfare of the people. Indeed, Kingsport's founders intended to avoid a boom town.[24] Dennis and Johnson were community builders as well as capitalists. Their vision for the model city left no room for the stereotypical company town or mill village. Toward that end, they contrived a physical infrastructure that included a master plan for the city, examples of suitable public and private architecture, and a model charter for an infant municipal government.

As the CC&O's Elkhorn extension neared completion, Dennis and Johnson began to devote more attention to the physical appearance of Kingsport. By September 1915 they had persuaded W.C. Hattan—a native of Virginia and a civil engineer most recently from Meyersdale, Pennsylvania—to become the resident engineer of the Kingsport Improvement Company. Hattan had been working on the Sandy Ridge tunnel for the railroad in the vicinity of Dante, Virginia. His initial assignment in Kingsport was to plan and supervise the building of a small water system.[25] Soon, however, he found himself surveying land, platting lots, staking out foundations of buildings, and working on street profiles. He also located two large ditches on the east and west sides of the town to drain the marshy site. The urgency with which the work was now being pushed was well illustrated by the fact that Hattan and his survey team worked on Thanksgiving morning 1915. The engineer gave his crew the afternoon off while he worked on a lot layout at the office.[26]

On 29 November, as Hattan and his corps began to plat lots on the circle, Johnson and Dennis, along with F.S. Tainter, an expert on water and sewerage systems, and Clinton Mackenzie, an architect—both from New York City—undertook a study of the water supply.[27] Apparently, it was at about this time that John B. Dennis decided that he needed a professional town planner. He communicated this wish to his brother, H. Ray Dennis, who was vice-president of the Securities Company in New York City. One of John's friends, publisher Joseph H. Sears of D. Appleton and Company, put Ray in contact with John Nolen of Cambridge, Massachusetts, who had begun to establish a national reputation as a town planner.[28]

John Nolen's life bears a striking resemblance to a Horatio Alger success story.[29] Born on 14 July 1869, in Philadelphia to John C. and Matilda Thomas Nolen, John was fatherless by the age of two. He was heavily influenced by his mother, and "his background equipped him with a point of view as a planner more characteristic of the young, militant middle-class reformers of the twentieth century than of the more established, paternalistic stewards of wealth and their retinue of the late nineteenth."[30] First educated in the public schools of Philadelphia, he was enrolled as a nine year old in Girard College, a school for poor, fatherless white boys, from which he was graduated in 1884. After working for several years, he had accumulated enough money by 1891 to enter the University of Pennsylvania's Wharton School, with a major in economics and public administration. Examined and allowed to enter as a junior, he completed his Bachelor of Philosophy degree in 1893. For the better part of a decade, he served as executive secretary of the Society for the Extension of University Teaching in Philadelphia, a position that gave him access to public lectures on a wide variety of subjects. Apparently Nolen did some postgraduate work or at least sat in on lectures at the University of Munich around 1900. After a yearlong visit to Europe in 1901/2, he had decided upon a career in landscape architecture. In 1903, with the responsibility of a wife and two children, he left his position in Philadelphia and enrolled in the School of Landscape Architecture at Harvard University, from which he earned the Master of Arts degree in 1905. He subsequently, in 1913, took a Doctorate of Science at Hobart College, in Geneva, New York; but his formal practice as a city planner had been launched around 1905 at Harvard Square, in Cambridge, Massachusetts.

Nolen moved into city planning as it began to take on professional attributes. He had studied under Frederick Law Olmsted, Jr., and other leading figures in the field who viewed landscape architecture as a fine art; but Nolen seems to have been more influenced by New Town planning than by the City Beautiful approach of such designers as Olmsted and Daniel Burnham, as reflected in Chicago. Nolen was apparently impressed by Englishman Ebenezer Howard's Garden City concept, and Nolen "was probably one of the few Americans more overwhelmed by the industrial city of Dusseldorf than the famed gardens of Versailles."[31] "Not a utopian believer in overnight milleniums, he nevertheless sought a broader social order, which, although achieved in the future, could be prepared by continuous replanning in the present," claims one authority.[32] By the time he was engaged for the Kingsport project, he had developed general plans for a few schools and colleges, park systems for several municipalities, an occasional estate, and comprehensive reports for the improvement of several established cities.

At this juncture, Nolen's role as Kingsport's planner needs to be placed in its proper and correct perspective. Enormous credit for the planning of Kingsport has been accorded to him in publications by promoters and civic leaders, by serious students of landscape architecture and city planning, and by his biographer, John L. Hancock. It is understandable that propagandists for the town made use of Nolen's connection because of his reputation as a professional planner. Those devoted to the history of landscape architecture have been influenced by Nolen's own writings.[33] Because Hancock is Nolen's biographer and is virtually the only other historian to date to have made serious use of the planner's papers in respect to Kingsport, it is important that corrections in fact and interpretation be made about John Nolen's connection with the project.

Hancock makes the startling claim that "all of Kingsport's engineering and construction was under [Nolen and his staff's] jurisdiction through the mid-twenties."[34] If careful consideration is given to the correspondence pertaining to Kingsport in Nolen's papers—in which there are numerous references to development having proceeded without plans from Nolen and without his approval—in conjunction with other source material relevant to this period in the town's history, it is evident that Hancock's conclusion is inaccurate. As early as 1919, Nolen exuberantly and prematurely proclaimed that he believed Kingsport "to be the most successful city" that he ever planned.[35] Eight years later, he was just as enthusiastic when he wrote in *New Towns for Old* that his work had resulted in "the development of one of the best-planned industrial communities in the annals of modern town planning."[36] Nolen was a prolific writer, and in his numerous books and articles he trumpeted his accomplishments. Unfortunately and especially obvious in Kingsport's case, he seemed to take all of the credit for the positive elements of the towns with which he was associated and made little if any distinction, in his publications, between plans and implementation.

Nolen, who supposedly operated the largest planning firm in the country between 1915 and 1925,[37] had the reputation among some of his cohorts as a public-relations expert, an outstanding salesman, and a prolific writer who left the actual design to such key members of his staff as Philip W. Foster. Earle S. Draper, who was first employed by Nolen in 1916 after Draper's graduation from Massachusetts Agricultural College (later the University of Massachusetts at Amherst), recalled that the preliminary plan for Kingsport had been completed when he went to work for Nolen. Foster had made one or two visits. Nolen, according to Draper, had nothing to do with the design. He contacted clients, but Foster dominated the office. Foster once told Draper, "We are all very fond of Dr. Nolen, but when he comes to the office to look over the plan, the only comment he ever makes is 'Shall we have white prints or blueprints, and how many?' "[38]

Draper's recollections can be partially corroborated by Nolen's own correspondence, which indicates that he did not submit so much as a preliminary plan until Philip W. Foster had visited Kingsport. Foster telegraphed H. Ray Dennis at the Securities Company in New York

City on 26 February 1916, advising Dennis that he, Foster, planned to accompany Dennis to Kingsport. After the visit, Nolen wrote to Dennis on 9 March, to tell him that the plan would be finished the next day. Earlier, on 7 February, Nolen had expressed the hope that he would have the plan ready for a board meeting of the Securities Company on 24 February.[39] J. Fred Johnson, president of the Kingsport Improvement Company and the man who ultimately had to oversee implementation on the site, had been dissatisfied with Foster and "had almost gotten into a fist fight with him because he refused to listen to Johnson's ideas about some fallacies in the original plan." Nolen then dispatched Draper to Kingsport from Charlotte, North Carolina, where the planning firm was engaged in the development of the Myers Park subdivision for J.B. Duke. "Foster and Johnson were equally stubborn," according to Nolen's young assistant. Draper listened, and he and Johnson got along well—which undoubtedly accounts for the fact that he drew the plan for the Fairacres area during the 1920s after he had left Nolen's office to set up his own practice.[40]

Hancock, true to his contention that "all of Kingsport's engineering and construction" was under Nolen's jurisdiction through the mid-1920s, claims that Nolen was responsible for the decision to use Clinton Mackenzie as the chief architect and Lola Anderson to supervise all plantings of trees, flowers, and shrubbery.[41] Actually, Mackenzie had visited Kingsport as early as 29 November 1915 and had requested information "on lots in [the] vicinity of Broad & Sevier Avenues" as of 20 December.[42] Nolen's correspondence indicated that his first conversation with H. Ray Dennis about the Kingsport project occurred on New Year's Day 1916.[43] Ironically, as of 21 September 1920, the KIC had paid Mackenzie $42,199.37 plus $18,901.87 in expenses, for a total of $61,101.24; Nolen had been paid a total of $12,846.04. Computations of billings for fees and expenses indicate that the KIC paid Nolen and his staff just slightly over $16,000 through 15 January 1921.[44]

Another of the experts involved with engineering in Kingsport—F.S. Tainter of New York City—had first visited the town at the same time as Mackenzie. Apparently, Tainter and Nolen were not associates, for J. Fred Johnson wrote to Nolen on 3 April 1916, asking him to forward a contour map to Tainter that Hattan had provided to Nolen. At the same time, Johnson explained that Tainter needed the map in connection with the extension of the water system and his plan for sewerage.[45] Tainter developed the plan for a water reservoir atop Bays Mountain to supply the town. According to the *Kingsport Times*,

"Large, clear, cold springs" were to "be turned into a huge reservoir," and "cool mountain water fresh from the mountains" was to be piped to the model city.[46] Approximately thirty-five to forty men worked ten hours a day at the going rate of fifteen cents an hour, or about $1.50 per day. They quarried the limestone for the dam at a site on Bays Mountain, using rails for reinforcements. Jerome Pierce, a Union veteran of the Civil War, reportedly provided a wagon and a team of mules to haul the rock and steel. A photograph taken at the scene of construction shows fifteen workers; the one with a necktie seems to be the boss, and the others seem to be ordinary laborers. All are white except for one lone black.[47]

As for Lola Anderson, Draper may have recommended her; but she probably was already an acquaintance of John B. Dennis's. Her father was president of a railroad that connected with the CC&O line, and she later married Dennis.[48] The *Kingsport Times* announced her arrival in town in September 1919, claiming that her presence was in keeping with the City Beautiful idea that had always been a part of the Kingsport plan. Hired by the KIC, she maintained an office in the company building on Shelby and Market streets. A graduate of Cornell University and a Georgia native, she had logged considerable experience, first as an instructor in the Landscape Architecture School at her alma mater and then as an associate in the firms of Earle S. Draper at Charlotte, North Carolina, and of Charles F. Gillette in Richmond, Virginia. Most recently, she had been in charge of drafting and design for P.T. Berkman of Augusta, Georgia.[49]

If Lola Anderson had been brought to Kingsport on Nolen's advice, as Hancock contends, the recommendation came after some failures resulting from his earlier suggestions. E.A. Douglas of Nolen's staff had reported in 1919 that the trees planted the previous year on Watauga Street looked healthy but that the vegetation around the Kingsport Inn showed a lack of attention; he indicated that someone was needed to care for the trees and shrubs. Nolen and Johnson had already been at odds over the types of plantings, because the planner did not concur with the promoter's preference for native plants. Nonetheless, the KIC accepted Nolen's recommendation that Harlan P. Kelsey of Salem, Massachusetts, who had nurseries in Pineola, North Carolina, and Boxford, Massachusetts, be allowed to supervise the work. At the end of the summer of 1919, H. Ray Dennis coolly advised Nolen that he presumed Lola Anderson had arrived. "Mr. Kelsey's trees," Dennis wrote, "were practically a complete failure."[50]

Dissatisfaction with matters pertaining to planting was only the tip of the iceberg. H. Ray Dennis told Nolen on 19 August 1919 that certain plans for housing development had met with such opposition "at the last meeting of the Board and the Directors... that I was at a loss how to write you."[51] Earlier, Johnson had been strongly antagonistic toward Nolen's proposed location for one of the elementary schools. Referring to a letter from Nolen that stated that the planner did not need to offer a special explanation of his preference for school sites, he informed Nolen that he, Johnson, along with men from the Board of Education and the city government, had studied possible locations and had decided that it would be a mistake to accept Nolen's proposal. Johnson curtly concluded his letter: "I have talked with Mr. H.R. Dennis in New York and we are in perfect accord with what should be done and it will be worked out accordingly."[52] Part of this problem, however, stemmed from the KIC's uncertainty about how best to use some of its land in the Lovedale area.[53]

Johnson was also distressed because eight houses in one of Mackenzie's proposed developments faced the rear of dwellings on Walnut Street that, according to him, were "occupied by people of very low character, two or three of them being negroes." He called for the immediate revision of the street plan.[54] In a subsequent letter to Nolen, E.A. Douglas dismissed Johnson's concerns, because "Mr. Dennis, Mr. Mackenzie and others" at a conference had "agreed that it would only be a question of time when the better houses would be built in place of the old ones on the Poor Development. The negroes eventually will all go to the negro village at the other end of the city."[55] The model Negro Village, which is one of the fascinating aspects of the Kingsport plan, will be explored later.

Nolen's plans "did not work out precisely as envisioned," contends Hancock, but "he never received such cooperation elsewhere from business backers."[56] One must conclude, then, that the life of this pioneer professional planner was fraught with difficulties. No control at Kingsport was relinquished to him, and he was confronted by multiple authorities—H. Ray Dennis in New York City, who, while he did not always agree with his brother John, was always loyal to John's wishes; J. Fred Johnson, on site in Kingsport, who had the complete confidence of John B. Dennis (who was also on location, having made Rotherwood his principal residence); and as of 1917, the Board of Mayor and Aldermen and the city manager for the newly incorporated city, who were strongly under the influence of Johnson.

Kingsport's founders, in keeping with the progressive spirit and their own business philosophy, favored a city-manager government with a board of mayor and aldermen. Hugh G. Morison, who once was George Carter's attorney and later was general counsel for the Clinchfield Railroad, in consultation with H. Ray Dennis of the Securities Company, drafted a proposed charter. This document took as its model the charters of Dayton, Springfield, and Ashtabula, Ohio; Jackson, Cadillac, and Grand Rapids, Michigan; Niagara Falls and Newburgh, New York; and nearly a hundred other reform-oriented American cities. The KIC submitted the charter to several southern authorities as well as to specialists at the Bureau of Municipal Research in New York City.[57] Herbert R. Sands, director of the bureau's Division of Field Work, forwarded to H. Ray Dennis a carefully prepared critique of Morison's draft. The Charter of 1917 for the City of Kingsport, Senate bill no. 450, sponsored by J. Parks Worley, reflected the suggested changes. The private bill had passed the Tennessee Senate and House of Representatives, where it was introduced by O.S. Hauk, by 28 February; and Governor Tom C. Rye gave it his approval on 2 March.[58]

The charter, which established the basis for municipal government under a city-manager plan, also included provisions for five departments: Finance, Public Safety, Public Welfare, Public Works, and Education. The names of the first Board of Mayor and Aldermen, all of whom were handpicked by the KIC, were also set forth: James W. Dobyns, mayor, and F.E. Mahan, J.L. Camblos, Thomas C. Warrick, and R.Y. Grant, aldermen. The first city manager, William R. Pouder, a former auditor and assistant to the general manager of a mining and smelting corporation, had been an understudy to two prominent early city managers in the United States—Henry M. Waite of Dayton and Charles E. Ashburner of Springfield, Ohio. Pouder had also been the city recorder of Kingsport's neighbor, Johnson City, before he was invited to collaborate with others in drafting the planned city's new charter. Although Pouder's salary does not seem to be available, his successor's was set at $4,200 per annum in February 1920, a figure that was quite satisfactory for the time and place and is indicative of the value that the founders attached to the position.[59]

Neither the city government nor the KIC remained idle during these early years. Practical men who were caught up in the excitement of building a city, the local leaders were hardly the types to sit still as they awaited the latest drawing from Nolen's office in Cambridge, Massachusetts. They adopted whatever they found feasible and rejected anything they considered foolish or frivolous. They, not Nolen, called the shots; he was at their service. Notwithstanding clashes of personality and differences in opinion, the Kingsport project nonetheless presented a splendid challenge for the professional planner.

Unencumbered with problematic holdovers from the nineteenth century, the Cambridge expert had considerable latitude. Indeed, the relatively uncluttered landscape of the Kingsport site and the surrounding area offered a veritable playground for a landscape architect. Nolen found the prospect of planning a small industrial city very appealing. With enthusiasm befitting the initial stage of a new project, he observed, "The whole thing presents a very interesting situation that is full of possibilities for the application of the best planning principles."[60] He soon confided to H. Ray Dennis, however, that it would have been easier for him had he been able to start afresh.[61] Nolen inherited certain proscriptive conditions, including the location of the railroad; the businesses and industries that had sprung up along the CC & O by 1916; company housing on Cement Hill; and the general scheme of the downtown. William Dunlap, a railroad engineer, had drawn a plan for George L. Carter in 1906. Although it encompassed only a relatively small portion of the land included in the physical design later executed by Nolen's staff, it did include a grid arrangement for a downtown business district; the semicircle known as Church Circle, which has been erroneously credited to the Cambridge planner; and radial streets entering Church Circle from the north. Sufficient implementation had occurred to lend some permanence to the Dunlap rendering, and Nolen was left with little choice but to work with this arrangement.[62]

Another difficulty revolved around the Groseclose property, a tract of nine acres lying near the city center, which the Improvement Company had been unable to acquire, probably because the KIC was unwilling to pay the price being asked. In August 1917, H. Ray Dennis advised Nolen that "Mr. Groseclose is now in the mood to dedicate a portion of his holding in the center of town to the City, and I am wondering if you will send me a little sketch of suggestions as to the proper method of doing this. I don't know that he will follow our suggestions but there is no harm in trying it."[63] Nolen and his staff immediately prepared a blueprint of the property, which included a small park. The planner reasoned that "the property is not very attractive at best. . . . It would be unfortunate if it should in the future develop into anything in the nature of a slum-like area."[64] The National Resources Committee in 1938 observed that the Groseclose property had not been developed in line with the overall plan and that this had "adversely affected the general layout of the street system." The KIC's inability to purchase the Groseclose land led to substandard conditions in certain areas east of Sullivan Street, as mentioned in the same report. On Dale Street, a black section, "slab houses" had been "crowded three on a lot," as lots had "been resubdivided to provide for close rows of one-story cottages."[65]

Given the limitations mentioned above and Nolen's concern about "topographical difficulties"—hilly terrain as well as swampy lowlands—he had, nonetheless, set forth his conditions for H. Ray Dennis on 10 February 1916. Nolen agreed to draft a general plan, showing roads, walks, turf strips, locations of trees, and boundaries of lots. "The usual procedure," he counseled, "is to have the general plan or design plan made by a landscape architect, and when approved, placed in the hands of a local engineer who stakes it out, making slight changes to secure advantages in the lay of the land or for other reasons." For services rendered, he charged according to a schedule adopted by the Fellows of the American Society of Landscape Architects. The client had to assume financial responsibility for alternative or revised plans, traveling and incidental expenses, and blueprints, all of which would be fixed at cost.[66] Nolen also suggested a tentative sequential design program that included a general plan of the entire area, as already covered in the preliminary plan; an extension plan, showing new areas to the east; a center plan at larger scale, with detail of street sections and arrangement; street sections for the area outside of the center plan; a street tree-location plan; a zone map on a black-line print of the general plan; a housing plan for special areas of block and single houses; and detailed plans for parks, playgrounds, parkways, and the hotel site.[67]

Although Nolen's office files indicated that he maintained an interest in Kingsport for the remainder of his life, his firm's connections with the town were strongest between 1916 and 1922. Whatever influence Nolen had on the actual developments was communicated largely by correspondence and through the occasional visits of his assistants. Nolen himself made few trips to Kingsport. After his initial on-site inspections in 1916, he apparently did not tour the project again until 1919, which John L. Hancock attributes to the planner's wartime work.[68] In June 1919 the *Kingsport Times* announced that Nolen was in town and quoted him as follows: "I am delighted with the growth and appearance of Kingsport. It is rapidly attaining every wish I had for it."[69] This optimism contrasted starkly with his comments a few months later.

In a November letter to architect Grosvenor Atterbury, Nolen wrote: "Kingsport keeps moving, although we have never yet been able to get the Improvement Corporation to adopt a good policy and program for the physical development of the town. It looked as if we might do it after the visit in June, but no action of a definite sort was taken."[70] Indeed, neither the city government nor the KIC ever formally committed itself to Nolen's general plan, although both adhered to many of its basic aspects.

The master plan produced in Nolen's office was only a conceptual scheme; the actual construction was left to the KIC engineers who were on location. Nolen's assistants, among them Earle S. Draper, E.A. Douglas, Raymond W. Blanchard, and Paul R. Frost, acted as liaisons between J. Fred Johnson and the local engineers at the site and their boss back in Cambridge, Massachusetts. Nolen meanwhile exchanged considerable correspondence with H. Ray Dennis, vice-president of the Securities Company and chairman of Kingsport Farms, Incorporated. Although an able man who seemed much more realistic than his sibling, H. Ray Dennis operated in his brother's shadow. He was known to say that his duty was "to see that waste baskets were emptied."[71] Always attentive to John's wishes, Ray wrote letters that often contained the phrase, "My brother thinks." Brother John remained aloof from the monotony of detail. Of Nolen's staff, Draper, the first to work on location at Kingsport, developed the best relationship with Johnson. Although young, independent-spirited, and somewhat inexperienced, Draper was also flexible and readily conceded that some aspects of the designs drafted in Cambridge needed modification. None of the other assistants on this project challenged their mentor as he did.

After Draper had been on the project almost a year, Nolen was about to pull him off, which prompted H. Ray Dennis to write: "Unless you have very strong reasons I much prefer to continue using Mr. Draper in Kingsport. He has undoubtedly made a very favorable impression and I know the people there would enjoy a continuance of their work with him." Nolen agreed but observed that Draper did not have much experience in the work about to be undertaken, and Nolen had only wanted them to have the best advice possible.[72] On 15 February 1917, Draper informed Nolen that the street layout was proceeding, "without any sections from the office to go by." "Is it possible," he inquired, "that the preliminary sections which I ratified & checked with slight changes & brought to the office after my trip here in August have never been worked up? Or were they drafted in completed form & sent to New

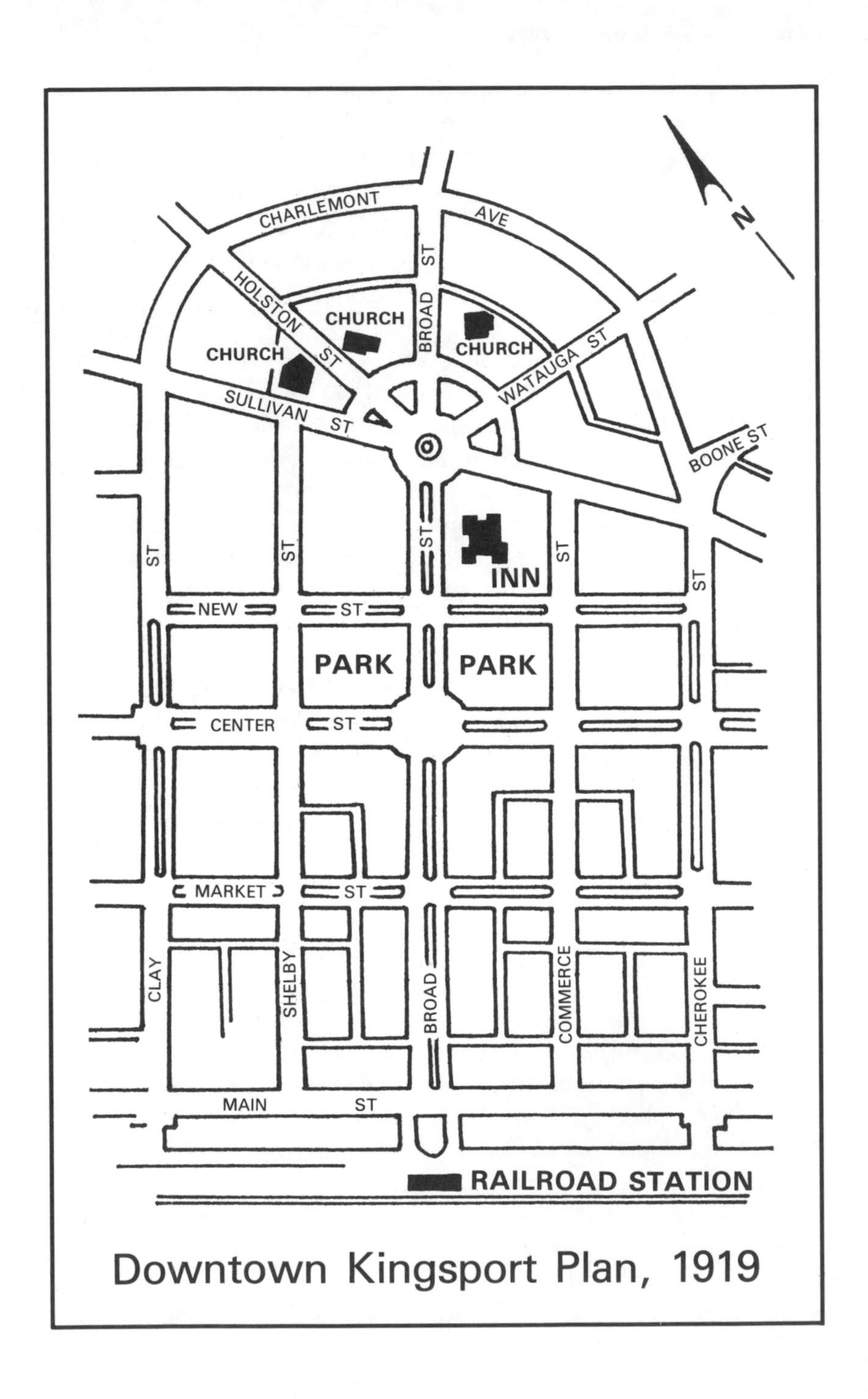

Downtown Kingsport Plan, 1919

York—never arriving here as was the case of the Lovedale development. I call your attention to this as it seems to me most important that they have correct sections to go by before starting construction on any more streets."[73]

In a few days, Draper advised Nolen that he had worked up designs, changing certain features of the Lovedale section, and that Johnson was anxious to have prints of a finished plan because engineers were "waiting to stake it out on the ground and, to that end, he asked if I would urge you to develop this problem as speedily as possible."[74] In early March, Nolen wrote to Johnson that Draper had been to Cambridge and that the two of them had gone over Kingsport matters. "He is now turning it over definitely to us," declared the town planner, "as he has decided to open an office himself, giving his attention to the preparation of plans for private places."[75] Apparently, relations between Nolen and Draper had become strained, but Draper continued to be on friendly terms with people at Kingsport and occasionally worked on independent projects there.

Although dozens of neighborhood and section designs as well as street layouts were drawn in Cambridge, the 1919 General Map of Kingsport, Tennessee, identified as Plan No. 75, is the cumulative expression of the physical ideas generated in Nolen's office.[76] With the Holston River to the south-southwest of the site, the railroad just north of the river, and the rising hills that rimmed the valley to the north, northeast, and northwest, the design had to encompass the intervening lowlands that sprawled from east to west. Nolen's 1919 plan reflected these geographical considerations; it also represented a peculiar blend of the real and the imagined. While showing numerous features that had already been in place by 1919, among them certain industries along the railroad, it also included such anticipated developments as Armstrong Village, the model black community. One of Nolen's principal achievements with the Kingsport plan was to refine the primitive 1906 projection for the Church Circle area and the downtown business district. The model city's first professionally planned residential development, the Shelby Street row houses, appeared in detailed workups of the downtown section, as did the Young Men's Christian Association building and the railroad station.[77]

Only limited aspects of the Nolen downtown schematic were executed. Site choices for a bank and a post office, for examples, were among those not adhered to by the locals, and two blocks for a park bordering the intersection of Broad and New streets were not retained.

Unrealized also was Nolen's proposal for a civic district bounded by parks and drives, churches, and the Kingsport Inn. The Nolen design, known as Plan No. 74, called for a library, a police station, and a city hall facing east on the first block of Broad from Church Circle and directly across the street from the Kingsport Inn. An architectural rendering by the firm of Carrere and Hastings of New York subsequently depicted a compact unit of governmental and public-service buildings on this block, fronted by approximately two hundred square feet of public gardens.[78] A post office, located between New and Center streets and facing west onto Commerce in the Nolen plan, eventually became the home of the public library but was built facing east onto Broad. The only other structure on this block is that of the Kingsport Power Company. Even though this area failed to achieve the grandeur and compactness of the proposed plan, it is nevertheless the section that gives the town its identity.

Along with features already mentioned, the 1919 plan contained substantial amounts of open land, some of which was intended for parks—one reservation was designated as the Oaks, and another expanse on the east was for an eighteen-hole golf course and country club, which was laid out by A.W. Tillinghast, an expert in such matters, who was not associated with Nolen's office.[79] In June 1919, T.H. McCarty, an assistant to Tillinghast, rushed a sixty-man crew that was grading the links. The golf house and the clubhouse, the latter valued at $10-15,000, would be important for the social life of Kingsport, predicted a writer for the local newspaper.[80] A six-acre reserve within twenty-two hundred feet of Church Circle awaited the future community hospital. On the west the plan included an athletic field near the Lovedale tract.

Even death did not preclude participation in the model plan. A cemetery occupied the northwest periphery of the 1919 plan, avoiding interference with industry and housing. Deaths during the 1918 influenza epidemic had made cemetery planning imperative, as H. Ray Dennis explained to Nolen: "Owing to the terrible conditions in Kingsport by reason of the influenza it is essential that we get the plans of the cemetery as early as possible."[81] Influenza flared up in Kingsport throughout 1919, and cases were still being reported in early 1920.[82] Nolen's suggestions regarding the cemetery indicated that he was unfamiliar with local society. Responding to earlier inquiries about arrangements for the dead, he had written to H. Ray Dennis on 8 August 1917: "We have spent a large part of today going over with Mr. Douglas various Kingsport matters, especially the location of the cemetery, or perhaps I should say cemeteries, because I presume we should provide separately for Protestants and Catholics."[83] The residents of Kingsport were overwhelmingly Protestant, and the small number of Catholics hardly justified the allocation of land from the KIC's precious holdings, which, at the outset, amounted to about one thousand acres.

While providing for such features as parks, playgrounds, and a cemetery, the Nolen plan refined and expanded the street arrangement of the 1906 design. Inasmuch as possible, it eliminated the traditional grid arrangement and substituted circumferential and radial lines. Here, Nolan pleased the KIC most, for his arrangement produced the maximum number of desirable lots; and the proposed street widths of sixty, eighty, and one hundred feet lent an air of spaciousness. Lots in the business district had at least twenty-five feet of frontage. The plan provided for twenty-foot alleys, avoided dead-end streets, and enhanced the flow of traffic.[84]

Even though the Nolen plan had several positive aspects, it was geared to the "walking city" and to the railroad and really did not anticipate the impact of the automobile. Nonetheless, the country teetered on the threshold of a transportation revolution, and Kingsport, almost from its inception, benefited from the advent of motor vehicles. Earle S. Draper commented that he did not think that even "Johnson and the engineers had any concept of what the automobile would do for the area" because it "was not considered a reliable vehicle." The plan provided for "adequate parking on the street and for a center strip of greenery for beautification but the... automobile was not considered in street location and design." Even the bus line in town was initially just an extension of "the horse-drawn carry-all that met people at the train."[85] Correspondence between H. Ray Dennis and Nolen confirms Draper's opinion. In February 1917, Dennis wrote: "We have completed one sidewalk, one curb, and one roadway on Broad Street in accordance with your plans. The roadway strikes all of us as too narrow. We should like a revised drawing, allowing a roadway on each side sufficient for teams to readily pass each other. We suppose it was your idea [that] traffic should move North and South. I am afraid in a town like Kingsport it would be very difficult to do this with the limited means of control we shall have at hand." Dennis urged Nolen to reduce the parkway but to leave "sufficient space... for a double track trolley line should the same be built in the future."[86]

Physical considerations of the KIC and of Nolen's staff transcended street layout to encompass neighborhood designs and housing arrangements. Although the Cambridge office had little to do with architecture, an undated general map of Kingsport, bearing the name of Nolen as town planner and Clinton Mackenzie as architect, features Neighborhood Development Nos. 2, 3, and 4,[87] which were known locally as the Fifties, White City, and Armstrong Village (or Borden Mill Village). The Fifties (so named because of their number, which was just shy of fifty), located north of West Sullivan Street, represented the KIC's first major housing project, although the initial residential development had been the Shelby Street row houses. With this project, as with the row houses, English influence on American architecture and neighborhood design was discernible. Hollow-tile construction and stucco, with a little woodwork reminiscent of Tudor styling, characterized the newly constructed dwellings. Here, as well as elsewhere in the town, the influence of the Garden City concept of Londoner Ebenezer Howard operated somewhat. Most of these structures were single units, with some two- and three-family houses mixed in. The six-room dwellings represented a cost of $2,300 to $2,500 each for the developers. Generally, the houses had three bedrooms, and each featured a bathroom and a linen closet. Some had cellars; others had coal-storage bins outside. A small park, flowering shrubs, and rose bushes eventually graced the Fifties.[88] Draper later commented that such houses of stucco and tile as these had nothing to commend them except that they were cheap to construct.[89]

Noting that the company expected to sell a good many of the Fifties houses, Dennis asked Nolen to prepare a set of restrictions before they were put on the market. Nolen responded immediately with three recommendations: a town building code, municipal zoning, and deed restriction. Zoning marked a relatively new approach, having been used first in New York City around 1916; and only the last—deed restriction, which was virtually unenforceable—was employed at this stage in Kingsport's development. This later proved to be a detriment. The KIC, a land company after all, ignored Nolen's advice against selling property.[90]

Clinton Mackenzie, a New York–based architect who once had served as tenement-house commissioner of New Jersey and as a director of the National Housing Association, executed most of the earliest professional designs for the planned city. The ones that reached the construction stage included the railroad station, the Improvement Company's building, the Kingsport Inn, the Shelby Street row houses, the Fifties, some of White City (which was so named because the deeds required that all the houses be painted white), the building of the Young Men's Christian Association, and the clubhouse of the Federal Dyestuff and Chemical Corporation, as well as isolated houses on Broad and Watauga streets. Also, on paper only, he designed dwellings for the ill-fated model Negro Village.[91]

The model Negro Village project at Kingsport provides a fascinating example of the vaporous world of planners and architects. In a 1920 publication, Clinton Mackenzie declared: "It is the first time that an attempt has been made to build a negro village of a high order with their own schools, churches, stores, lodges, etc., providing the same grade of housing and general development as is furnished the white population of the same economic condition."[92] The planned city of Kingsport, like the rest of the country, however, could not break the bonds of racism during this era. After the whole idea of a "separate-but-equal" Negro Village had been abandoned, John Nolen still wrote of it in glowing terms: "The plan gives due consideration to the colored population, which, being uncommonly high-class and industrious, is esteemed accordingly...Kingsport aims to counteract the tendency to migrate to the North, by developing its colored section in marked contrast to the squalid 'Nigger-town' districts so common in Southern communities. Here the colored people have had comfortable, new houses built for them, with modern improvements. In this section the playgrounds, schoolhouses and churches have been planned for in ways commensurate with the advanced standards set for the rest of the community."[93]

The origins of these grandiose delusions can be traced to a September 1916 letter written by H. Ray Dennis to Nolen concerning the Midland Farm layout: "I wish...you could find a place for the negroes."[94] From this point, the idea for a model Negro Village took hold. In March 1917, Dennis asked Nolen to make a trip to Kingsport to consider, among other questions, "the matter of segregation of the negroes." Reference to this aspect of the city plan occurred in 1918 correspondence; then, abruptly on 15 October, H. Ray Dennis halted the project: "I think it might be well to abandon work for the present on the Negro village, as there is no possibility of our doing any of that work now."[95]

Nolen's early designs for the Negro Village situated it in the Lovedale tract on the northwest side of town. The matter surfaced again in correspondence of February 1919, when H. Ray Dennis devoted an entire letter to it. He noted that planning had begun, and he mentioned architectural renderings of three- and four-room houses. Acknowledging Nolen's attention to the black school, Dennis expressed doubt that it would be built until the project was further along. "On the other hand," he reported, "Mr. Johnson and Mr. Grant [R.Y. Grant of Grant Leather Company, i.e., Kingsport Tannery] for whom these houses are being built feel that it is very important to immediately build a Negro church." According to Dennis, "the houses" were to "be built as near the proposed new Gate City Road as feasible in order to give the negroes the readiest access to town." He wondered about the possibility of having deed restrictions in black villages that might forbid the sale of that property to white people. Admitting that this had "caused a commotion," he asked Nolen if it had ever been done.[96]

The choice of a site for the Negro Village soon ran afoul of plans for the location of one of the schools for whites. J. Fred Johnson, obviously displeased with the conflict, advised Nolen in May 1919 that members of the school board, Mayor Dobyns, and he "felt when you consider the proximity of the site which you first selected to the negro village and the fact that the negro village will be approached by the same highway as the school grounds would be approached, it seems evident that another selection would be better."[97] By July of that same year, Johnson and the Board of Education had decided to accept Nolen's choice of site for what would be Andrew Jackson Elementary School; and W.M. Bennett, president of the board, advised the city government accordingly.[98]

This decision did not bode well for the Negro Village. By March 1920 the proposed location had been moved from the Lovedale site to the southeast end of town, opposite the dye plant; and Johnson was insisting that the project be launched immediately.[99] The *Kingsport Times* announced on 2 July 1920 that the construction of a grammar school for black children would begin in a few days, at a cost of about $20,000, and would "form the nucleus, it is thought, for a model village for colored people, as is contemplated in the city plan." A similar notice appeared on 19 October, which mentioned the school again and outlined plans for a sixty-acre development on the southeast side of town, now designated Armstrong Village. Bounded by the railroad to the south and a timbered area, the Oaks, to the east and isolated naturally from the city proper by Mad Branch on the west, the site seemed excellent to those who wanted to confine the black population. The article also described the design of the village, which was highlighted by a common green known as Federal Place, with its very own flagpole. On the west side of the village green, the school would be located; on the north, the church; and on the south, a variety of stores. This description was in keeping with a drawing of the village in Clinton Mackenzie's publication *Industrial Housing*, which also includes a sketch of projected housing, with little black children sitting on the porch.[100]

Nolen's assistants sensed that all was not as it seemed. Paul R. Frost informed his mentor that "Mr. John Dennis has some purpose unknown I think, to either Mr. H.R. Dennis or Mr. Johnson for at least the eastern portion of the village site—towards the woods." Although the school had already been started, John B. Dennis wanted it to be built at another location. "Mr. Johnson sees no objection to a darky village in the somewhat far foreground of his view with Watauga Street," observed Frost. "He has an idea [that] Mr. J.D. may plan to have the darkies here temporarily to meet an urgent need—then use the whole site for this other unknown purpose of his."[101] Raymond W. Blanchard, another Nolen employee, visited the town not long thereafter. With Johnson out of town, Blanchard spent most of his time with S. Phelps Platt, an assistant to Johnson at the KIC, who was a native of New York and a grandson of Senator Thomas Platt, the powerful Republican politician. Commenting on the proposed Negro Village, Blanchard wrote that "the only objection I heard at Kingsport to this site for the Negro Village was that it was too bad to give the colored people such a fine piece of land." About six hundred blacks then resided in the city, and the village was meant to accommodate more than one thousand.[102]

Although a black presence has materialized in this general area in more recent times, it is doubtful whether any blacks lived on this site during the 1920s. Their small number, coupled with John B. Dennis's mysterious dealings, prevented the serious implementation of this portion of Nolen's plan. According to the 1920 census, Kingsport had a population of 5,692, only 454 of whom were black. Ten years later, only 595 blacks were identified in a population of 11,914.[103] Preliminary discussions for the establishment of a new industry were probably taking place as early as 1920, and this may explain Dennis's secretiveness about the possible uses of land in the vicinity of the proposed Negro Village. In any event, Armstrong Village for blacks became Borden Mill Village for whites when that company became the town's largest employer during the 1920s.

Despite such notable dissension as that involving the model Negro Village and other squabbles over physical details in Kingsport, the 1919 plan represented a coherent expression of the principles of town planning in early-twentieth-century America. A reaction had been developing to an approach that emphasized the appearance of the city while almost ignoring other matters. By the 1920s and 1930s, the City Efficient replaced the City Beautiful as the principal objective of city planners.[104] In his voluminous writings, John Nolen clearly distinguishes himself as a pivotal figure in the evolution of professional planning in the United States. In *New Ideals in the Planning of Cities, Towns and Villages*, penned during World War I as potential reading material for the American Expeditionary Forces (the war had ended before it could be printed), he presented his philosophy of town planning: "City Planning... is not a movement to make cities beautiful in a superficial sense. Its purposes are fundamental. It aims consciously to provide those facilities that are for the common good.... it seeks to save waste... for by doing things at the right time and in the right way comprehensive city planning saves far more than its cost."[105]

Nolen also commented on two major misconceptions about city planning: (1) that city planning is concerned mainly with beauty and (2) that professional planning would tend to make all cities and towns alike. "Any city planning that is worthy of the name," he argued, "is concerned primarily with use and only incidentally with beauty"; but with successful planning "utility and beauty are virtually inseparable." Instead of encouraging monotonous landscape, successful planning "should emphasize individuality for a city.... It should unfold and perfect its natural characteristics. It should take account of a city's topography, preserve its natural resources, echo its business purposes, express its wealth, give form to its traditions, ideals and aspirations."[106]

The planner from Cambridge presented his views on industrial cities to the Eleventh National Conference on City Planning at Niagara Falls, New York, and published them in the December 1919 issue of *American City*. Although he made no direct reference to Kingsport, the timing of his remarks and his general comments seemed to stem from that experience. He noted two broad, but not mutually exclusive, problems: those that have to do directly with the economy or efficiency of manufacturing and those that have to do with the contentment and welfare of labor. He added that "the power, growth and progress of a city are limited only by the initiative of its leaders and the united civic interest of its people." He also stated a preference for level land, a condition that he did not find at Kingsport.[107]

Such guiding principles brought a degree of unity and cohesion to the Kingsport master plan, but they suffered considerable erosion as permanent structures were superimposed on the overall design. Proposals for street layouts, the platting of lots, and the location of culs-de-sac could easily be altered on the drawing board; but architecture, once constructed, lent a degree of permanence. Although in its architectural projects the KIC generally established satisfactory examples—single-family dwellings with indoor plumbing—the quick sale of real estate and the failure to establish zoning regulations spelled the absence of effective building control. Clinton Mackenzie was the principal architect, but other prominent figures engaged by the Improvement Company included Thomas Hastings, of Carrere and Hastings, and Grosvenor Atterbury, both of New York; Evarts Tracy, of Tracy and Swartout; and the firm of Electus D. Litchfield. The KIC also enlisted the D.R. Beeson firm of Johnson City to draft plans for schools; and O.K. Morgan, chief engineer of the CC & O, planned and built a freight depot.[108]

Early architecture in the model city ranged from privately commissioned stately residences to the workers' shanties of Pulp Row or Pulp Mill Village, known locally as Chinch Row. Styles included those as markedly different as Georgian-like edifices, which the New York architects seemed to favor[109]—the brick being provided by the Kingsport Brick Corporation, of course—and Spanish-looking bungalows. One particularly bizarre structure, the Tudor-style YMCA, featured a four-columned Greek- or Georgian-rendered courthouse, which was attached during the 1920s to transform it into a municipal building. The city government approved $13,430.70 for the modifications, which were designed by Allen N. Dryden, Sr. Officials had secured permission from John B. Dennis and the KIC, who owned the building, to locate municipal services there for six years. Johnson insisted that the record show that the arrangement was initiated by the city and that no partiality had been shown the KIC.[110] Mackenzie claimed that he only designed what the local people wanted at White City and Little White City, one- and two-story weatherboard houses.[111] In all probability, however, his sketches, which seemed to conform to what historian Gwendolyn Wright has labeled "the minimal house,"[112] were governed more by the wishes of the developers, with construction costs not being unrelated, and the prevailing views of the American architectural establishment of that era than by the expressed wishes of would-be purchasers.

Much of the housing built by the KIC and propagandized as dwellings for industrial workers, the Fifties and White City, for example, initially served managerial-entrepreneurial families, among them the

Shivells and Platts, on their rise to Watauga Street, Orchard Court, and other prestigious locations.[113] A few industries constructed housing for their employees, but the laborers of Kingsport, for the most part, were left to fend for themselves, renting or buying the offerings of independent contractors or choosing to live on nearby farms or in surrounding villages, and using the automobile for transportation. The new town was spared tenements, although John B. Dennis suggested them, much to the consternation of others involved with the town's development. In 1920, Mackenzie advised Nolen that John B. Dennis was "anxious" for Mackenzie "to develop a full block... to provide small stores on the ground floor and cheap apartments on the second and third floors." Dennis also seemed to favor row houses, against the advice of his architectural experts, and had no aversion to cheap, rather shoddily constructed dwellings. At one point, "in a joking way," he told Mackenzie that he, Mackenzie, "had been fighting" Dennis on a particular subdivision for so long "that he was getting tired of it" and that if a plan were not forthcoming, "he [Dennis] would get Tommy Hastings, or some other man, to do it." Mackenzie began laying out the subdivision but confided to Nolen, "It is such a decidedly improper use to make of the land and everyone except Mr. John Dennis is opposed to it."[114]

In some instances, John B. Dennis's ideas on housing died of benign neglect. The experts realized that some of the property on which housing was being built would ultimately be too valuable commercially to remain cheap residential sections. By January 1920 a lot with twenty-five-foot frontage at Broad and Market streets sold for $10,000; and the Kingsport Publishing Company purchased a two-story building with fifty-foot frontage on Market Street for $14,000. Lots on Sullivan Street went for as much as $7,500 during the early days of 1921.[115]

City planners and landscape architects soon began to give the Upper East Tennessee area's model community more than passing attention. In 1922 the Long-Bell Lumber Company of Kansas City purchased a huge tract of timberland north of the Columbia River in Washington State and engaged the firm of Hare and Hare to draft a plan for a new town. According to Earle Sumner Draper, "Kingsport was the prototype for Longview, Washington. The city planner who did that was a close friend of mine, Sid [S. Herbert] Hare of Kansas City, and he came to Kingsport to look it over before he did Longview."[116] A comparison of printed plans and photographs reveals several similarities in street design and architecture, but promotional literature and articles in professional publications pertaining to Longview make no mention of Kingsport. Indeed, in 1926 Hare boasted that the planning of Longview "was perhaps the largest project of this kind" since the planning of Washington, D.C., by Pierre-Charles L'Enfant. Acknowledging that "the opportunity of planning a complete new city of any great extent on undeveloped land seldom presents itself," he claimed that Longview "involved some pioneering in the field of city planning."[117]

Nolen's planning of Kingsport, however, antedated that of Longview by several years. From 1915 to 1920, Kingsport's founders had established the physical infrastructure for the new town. A master plan for its development, which was on the drawing board by 1919, and some of the architecture, which was already in place by 1920, heralded a bright future for the model city and provided convenient promotional trappings. A newly ensconced government with a city manager and Board of Mayor and Aldermen appeared ready to direct the growing municipality. The "Kingsport spirit," however, which rested on the virtue of the founders, the industrialists, the professionals and managers, and the ordinary laborers, would be sorely tried. During the next decade of its existence, one that was fraught with considerable difficulties, Kingsport moved toward a sound economic base as its residents forged a permanent industrial community.

4

Building an Industrial Community

A first-time visitor to Kingsport from another East Tennessee town in 1927 described his approach to the model city in near-mystical terms: "When several miles outside the city I saw rising up to the heavens great volumes of smoke. It was necessary to ask no questions. I knew I was nearing an industrial city and having heard of Kingsport and its marvels, I was greatly impatient to reach this site of human endeavor which has caught the attention of the industrial wizards of the world."[1] Although the new town hardly measured up to what he anticipated, it was a fascinating experiment nonetheless, and the product of more than a decade of struggle.

The Nolen plan, architectural showpieces, and the much-discussed "Kingsport spirit" would have accomplished little had Johnson and Dennis not been able to lure industries to the city. Establishing a firm economic base was difficult, and contrary to the impressions fostered by promotional literature, many years elapsed before the founding fathers could breathe a sigh of relief. John B. Dennis, when he was once asked if he had ever been discouraged enough to quit building Kingsport, replied: "Yes, many times, but never forget, it is frequently easier to go forward in the dark than to stop or to back up, when everything seems lost."[2] Wooing visiting industrialists and would-be investors, nurturing fledgling factories, and highlighting surviving ventures were both an ever-present reality and an ongoing process that occupied not only Johnson and Dennis but also other businessmen who had a vested interest in the town.

Kingsport's early economic history is that of a bootstrap operation. Surviving financial records suggest a tangled web of investors and stockholders. Industries that were established in the town prior to

America's involvement in World War I owed their births largely to the Carolina, Clinchfield and Ohio Railroad (CC&O), whose agents were engaged in a life-or-death struggle to generate industrial development and, hence, traffic for the line. Furthermore, the principal stockholders of the railroad project invested heavily in the infant industries. The brick company, for example, enjoyed the financial blessings of John B. Dennis, J. Fred Johnson, John I. Blair, and Jerry C. Stone, who was once George L. Carter's treasurer and later was with the Kingsport Improvement Company. Stone was also involved in the pulp-mill venture.[3] Mark W. Potter, president of the CC&O, was a voting trustee of the Metropolitan Trust Company of New York when it offered for public sale 300,000 shares of stock in the Federal Dyestuff and Chemical Corporation.[4]

At a crucial stage in its development, Kingsport reaped some benefits from wartime prosperity. Three "war babies" joined the industrial community, albeit temporarily: the Federal Dyestuff and Chemical Corporation, Edgewood Arsenal, and the American Wood Reduction Company. Edgewood Arsenal apparently had been built around 1917 by the War Department to manufacture tear gas, and old-timers vaguely remember what they called "the shell-loading plant." Barracks had been erected for this facility. One source related that "the plant was within a few hours of opening for business when on the morning of November 11, 1918, all the whistles in town opened up and we were told that the war was over."[5] The American Wood Reduction Company, whose accounting offices were in Chicago, directed the construction of a government-owned plant for the production of wood alcohol (methanol). Its weekly payroll for the period ending 31 July 1918 totaled $4,359.11. The plant, however, remained unfinished when the war ended. Lieutenant David R. Scherer, a War Department representative at the construction site, left the military when hostilities ceased and became an unsuccessful candidate for the vacant post of city manager in 1919.[6] The labor shortage, already critical in the town, became worse because of the demands of the wartime industries. In fact, this probably precipitated the resignation of City Manager William R. Pouder. During his two-year tenure, city government had been hard-pressed to obtain satisfactory bids on the various public-works projects that were under way. The Board of Mayor and Aldermen authorized him to establish his own construction force, but the labor gangs that he assembled were frequently commandeered by U.S. Army personnel. When Pouder resigned on 3 July 1919, he hinted that some citizens may have opposed his decisions and that he did not wish to place the city officials in an embarrassing position.[7]

Chemical manufacturing in Kingsport dates from the establishment of the Federal Dyestuff and Chemical Corporation. During the late nineteenth century, chemists had developed synthetics to substitute for natural dyes. Prior to World War I, Germany dominated this industry; but with the fighting, American efforts intensified.[8] The plant in Kingsport addressed this situation. Local residents had high hopes for the new operation, and the newspaper predicted that the plant would employ twenty-five hundred when completed, one hundred of whom would be chemists.[9] Construction began in November 1915 with the arrival of Vice-President and General Manager Dr. John C. Hebden, a graduate of Brown University who had thirty years experience in chemical manufacturing, including work on the continent. On 5 January 1916, the plant shipped its first dyes—$600 worth to the Taubel Hosiery Mills in Riverside, New Jersey. That satisfied customer soon placed an order for twenty tons. The Kingsport company also produced high explosives.[10]

The city fathers tried to discourage notions that their industrial base was geared to a wartime economy, while they cast off attributes of a company town. Effective 15 January 1920, industries abolished the practice of paying in scrip. Heads of industries had conferred and accepted the view of local merchants that the scrip arrangement with Kingsport Stores, Incorporated, placed them at a disadvantage. Although J. Fred Johnson directed the stores and although Kingsport Farms, Incorporated, the parent company, eventually sold its mercantile assets to him in 1923 except for the building and the accounts receivable, he apparently agreed with the industrialists; for it was he, speaking on their behalf, who announced the decision to pay in cash.[11]

Dispelling the effects of World War I and its aftermath on the local economy proved to be more troublesome. Techniques resembled incantation and "whistling in the dark." The *Kingsport Times,* founded in 1916 as a weekly, became the mouthpiece of the Improvement Company, the city government, and the local establishment. Although it would change hands and philosophy more than once in the course of its history and would eventually become a daily, in its infancy it was devoted to civic boosterism. Owned initially by C.H. Lyle and edited and published by R.D. Kinkead and T.L. Anderson—all of whom were connected with the *Johnson City Comet*—the *Times* was "independent in politics" and "devoted to the industrial and moral development of the rapidly growing city of Kingsport," according to a Knoxville counterpart.[12] Somewhat prematurely, beginning in 1917 and then periodically thereafter, the *Kingsport Times* declared that Kingsport was "a permanent town, built on a solid base" and labeled it the "Magic City of the South." In 1919 the *Times* opined that wartime restrictions had actually stymied Kingsport and predicted that with the hostilities ended, the town would "forge ahead more rapidly now." A 1920 Improvement Company tract denied the existence of a "boom" in Kingsport, adding, "There never has been, not even because of the war."[13]

Despite such contentions, the war still had its impact. The dye plant owed its very existence to the military effort, as did Edgewood Arsenal and the wood-alcohol plant. While the latter two apparently had a limited influence on the local economy beyond providing construction jobs, the former, with about one thousand workers, was briefly the town's largest employer. When the war ended, the dye plant fell on hard times. Reorganized in 1918 as Union Dye and Chemical Corporation, it soon suspended operations and laid off workers, pending the settlement of a $2-million claim against the government. A surplus of dyes and the uncertainty of the textile market also figured in the decision. Amidst further reductions and speculations about renewed activity, the company underwent another shake-up, when it came under the direction of B.R. Armour, president of American Aniline Products Corporation. Plagued with these uncertainties and confronted with some injuries and accidental deaths, the company also faced a $30,000 lawsuit after a four year old was electrocuted by a high-voltage fence. For several months, the company remained virtually inoperative; by early 1921, it defaulted on interest-bearing bonds and went into receivership.[14]

The local tanning and extract operations also languished during these years. The extract plant, which dated from 1912, used raw materials from the surrounding area and claimed to be one of the largest facilities of its kind in the South.[15] In 1919, Kingsport Extract Corporation and Kingsport Tannery, Incorporated, combined with Standard Leather Goods of St. Louis to form the Grant Leather Company, under the presidency of R.Y. Grant. Expectations for a 400 percent increase in the capacity of the tannery accompanied the merger.[16] For a while, Grant cut a wide swath in town. Indeed, he had served as one of the aldermen designated by the 1917 charter, but apparently he did not stand for election in 1919.[17] He resided on Watauga Street and had hoped, with J. Fred Johnson, to build cheap houses for the ill-starred

Negro Village. His company erected the Homestead Hotel, "more or less English in design," at the corner of Clay and Sullivan streets, for single male and female employees and planned a housing project to accommodate families that were expected to transfer from St. Louis to Kingsport.[18] Simmons Hardware Company, which had owned Standard Leather Goods, intended to move its harness-and-saddle-manufacturing operations to East Tennessee. A supplier for the army, this company found itself with surplus products when the war ended. The increasing reliability of the automobile and America's love affair with it further diminished possibilities for sales. During the postwar recession, banks called in loans, and the harness operations never made the move to Kingsport.[19]

By the mid 1920s the dismantling of the Grant Leather Company was virtually complete. Local chestnut trees, from whose barks tanning extract had been made, experienced a blight; and cheaper methods were developed for producing extract. At least two unsuccessful attempts were made to sell the company before it was taken over by the Kingtan Extract Company, which was controlled by the Hamilton-Brown Shoe Company of St. Louis. The new owner, however, was interested only in the tannery, not in the belting department or in H.J. Shivell, the young man whom Grant had chosen to run it. Eventually, with the advice of J. Fred Johnson, Shivell, a native of Michigan who with his wife had come to Kingsport from a job in Chicago, founded his own business, Slip-Not Belting Corporation. Before many years had passed, Kingtan Extract Company vanished from the town's industrial landscape.[20]

Glass manufacturing in the model city also had an inauspicious beginning and experienced postwar economic tremors. The principal raw material, white sand, came from Kermit, Virginia, only a few miles from Kingsport by rail. The Pennsylvania Glass Sand Company operated the quarry. Soda ash was procured at Saltville, Virginia, and limestone from quarries at Knoxville, Tennessee. Virginia and Kentucky fields along the Clinchfield supplied the vast amounts of coal required for production.[21] By January 1917 the DeCamp Glass Casket Company had acquired ten acres and expected to spend $150,000 for buildings and hundreds of thousands of dollars for machinery and setup costs. Plans called for three eight-hour shifts per day, engaging 450 men; the projected output was 600 caskets a day, at a cost of $10.00 each.[22] Whether a glass casket ever came off a production line in Kingsport is doubtful. See-through burial containers apparently never caught the public's fancy. Journalist Russell Baker, however, in his autobiography writes about a bootlegger from his section of Virginia who had the dubious honor of being laid to rest in this fashion. "Like most country bootleggers," Sam Reever had "bottled his moonshine in canning jars. When they took him to the graveyard the mourners approved of the fitting way in which Liz [his wife], as a grace note to his life, had him buried in the fanciest Mason jar ever sold in Loudoun County."[23]

In 1919, Corning Glass Works acquired the facilities of Edgewood Arsenal and anticipated operating three shifts per day. By the second week of November, eighty-five construction workers were engaged in expansion that would enlarge the floor space from 41,475 to 165,865 square feet. Management expected to have two to three hundred workers on the site by April 1920. V.V. Kelsey, a former resident of Kingsport and a member of the board of directors of the local building and loan association, became assistant general manager; and the company announced its intentions of employing 250 laborers, 40 or 50 of whom would be women. The plant began operation in December 1920, and reputedly manufactured the first glass cookware ever made in the South. Two months later, because of the postwar depression, the plant was closed. Not until 1926 did glassmaking resume in Kingsport. In 1925, Compagnie de Saint-Gobain of France decided to open a plate glass plant in the United States, and Corning officials suggested a suitable location, their vacant plant at Kingsport. Blue Ridge Glass Corporation of Kingsport, Tennessee, was formed late in 1925 by three firms: Corning Glass Works of New York, Glaceries de Saint Roch of Belgium, and Compagnie de Saint-Gobain of France.[24]

Further complicating the already-bleak economic picture in Kingsport, the pulp mill did poorly from its establishment in 1916 through the 1920s. Clinchfield agents and officials had considered the prospects of pulp production along the line as early as 1910, and industrial agent R.F. Brewer paid a visit to George H. Mead, vice-president and general manager of Mead Pulp and Paper Company of Chillicothe, Ohio, on 24 May. Other overtures followed. Operating out of Columbus, Ohio, W.M. Ritter, a prominent lumberman who had significant holdings in Southern Appalachia, subsequently corresponded with Mead and advised the president of the railroad, Mark W. Potter, accordingly.[25] These feelers stirred George Mead's "civic and professional sensibilities," according to his biographer. A chestnut blight, introduced into the United States in 1906 by shipments of diseased oriental chestnut, had already affected stands of timber in the South. At Kingsport the extract plant discarded "a valuable and vanishing resource"—chestnut chips. In April 1916 Mead's Board of Directors authorized, on George Mead's recommendation, an investment of $100,000, a significant, though not the controlling, stake in the $650,000 Kingsport Pulp Corporation. This was a period of expensive construction, and "the promoters compounded the cost problem by changing construction plans when the plant was half built." Furthermore, "the chestnut chips did not lend themselves satisfactorily to the soda-pulp process: no amount of bleaching could get the pulp clean enough for high quality book paper, and regular woods had to be purchased at prices far higher than those for used chestnut chips." In 1919 the principal owners of the company asked Mead to manage the plant. "Somewhat against our will," George Mead remarked, in 1920 his company purchased the Kingsport operation for $700,000.[26]

Problems with the pulp-and-paper operation were especially pronounced between 1919 and 1926. Although George Mead had financed this venture largely from personal funds, he left the local operations to the plant's manager, John H. Thickens; experts from Chillicothe advised and assisted. Mead himself, for a while, adopted a policy of "benevolent noninterference." Kingsport was the only Mead company to operate at a loss during 1921, and it had not made money the previous year, one that was considered rather good for the pulp-and-paper industry. Losses continued in 1922 and doubled the next year. Nonetheless, the construction of three additional buildings and the purchase of new machines continued. George Mead made regular visits to Kingsport but did not increase their frequency although the situation was dismal; either he did not have a solution, or he preferred that his subordinates come to their senses.

In 1926, the Kingsport operation became a subsidiary of the Mead Pulp and Paper Company. At the president's dinner in Kingsport on 17 January 1927, George Mead accepted his share of the blame: "The lack of success of the Mead Fibre Company up to the present time has been the fault of the President of the Company...I have the responsibility of determining the policies of these companies, and if I cannot determine the policy which makes for success this year or last year or the year before, I think I should be frank enough with myself to acknowledge it." He added, "One of the reasons for our lack of success, in spite of the fact that we have been in the worst period of the paper industry, is our failure to manufacture the best product that could be made in the soda pulp industry." In August 1928, Mead pressed H.P. Carruth, the plant manager of the Chillicothe mills, to involve himself more directly at

Kingsport. "I firmly believe," Mead chided Carruth, "that if you had gone to Kingsport personally and stayed there for six or eight weeks continuously the operation would long since have cleared up, and that it is due to your personal absence that we have lost so much money." Very slowly and for a variety of reasons, the plant in Kingsport moved toward a measure of prosperity.[27] In 1931 it was absorbed by the Mead Corporation.

Between 1919 and 1921, with war industries closing permanently, some manufacturers shutting down, and others losing money, strikes in the bituminous coalfields of Virginia and Kentucky exacerbated already-bad conditions in Kingsport. Cheap fuel had been one of the model city's assets. For the five years preceding the war, industrialists had paid $1.55 a ton. After the war, the cost rose to $2.36, plus 58 cents freight, for bringing coal to Kingsport from the Clinchfield mining district. By November 1919, Kingsport industries were feeling the pinch, and in early December the newspaper predicted that every industry in town might have to suspend operations because of the coal shortage. The Kingsport Brick Corporation, for example, halted work for several days at the end of the year.[28]

A decline in Kingsport's public health accompanied adverse economic conditions during this era. Human misery claimed the attention of city fathers and other concerned citizens. The model city and its hinterland did not escape the global outbreak of influenza in 1918-19, which may have claimed as many as twenty million lives worldwide, including half a million Americans.[29] A group calling itself the Kingsport Hospital Association purchased the equipment of a small privately operated facility in town and offered to turn it over to the city. On 11 October 1918 the Board of Mayor and Aldermen met with about seventy-five concerned citizens and agreed to assume responsibility for the operation of a hospital. This action was spurred by over one thousand cases of influenza in the city and nearby communities. Chairmen of the fire wards received instructions to report families that were rendered helpless by the disease. Teachers in public schools assumed nursing duties and sat with ailing families through nights of crisis.[30]

Health matters continued to attract attention. During the summer of 1919, J. Fred Johnson presented to the Negro Business League of Kingsport a personal gift of $100 and another in the same amount from the Kingsport Brick Corporation for the purpose of erecting a hospital for the black people of East Tennessee. It was also decided during this period to provide health, life, and accident insurance for industrial laborers and city workers, which would supplement workmen's compensation. Described as a gesture of "good will to employees," this coverage was made possible through policies underwritten by the Metropolitan Life Insurance Company of New York at a cost of about seven cents per day for each individual. An employee had $500 in life insurance, no matter how short-term his employment; amounts increased incrementally to $1,500 with five years of seniority. Health coverage became available after one week of illness, and it extended for twenty-six weeks. Metropolitan sent the head of its welfare department, Dr. Lee K. Frankel, to Kingsport to consult with local authorities. Acting on the advice of this prominent New York City reformer, they organized a health center.[31]

The insurance company stationed two public-health nurses in Kingsport, and the city hired Dr. Edna W. Brown, the first female physician in the area, as superintendent of the community hospital. A native of Gilmore City, Iowa, she had recently been surgeon to women prisoners in the alien enemy internment camp at Fort Oglethorpe, Georgia. A few months later, however, two local physicians, C.P. Edwards, Sr., and E.W. Tipton, purchased the Kingsport Community Hospital. The city had purportedly lost $250 to $300 per month on the operation. At the same time, Dr. T.B. Yancey became the municipal health officer. The Metropolitan Life Insurance Company paid a portion of his salary, and the city paid the remainder. The municipal health officer and nurses conducted clinics for prenatal and infant care, nutrition, and dentistry.[32]

New cases of influenza flared up into 1920, and unemployment worsened the conditions of the poor and ill, many of whom lived in tents and shacks. Private charity and local welfare provided food baskets, clothing, and fuel, thus alleviating the suffering of some of the population. During December 1919, for example, the Home Auxiliary Service of the Welfare Federation of Kingsport treated about a hundred children to toys, Christmas dinner, and a movie. Mrs. Jeannette Clifford, who prior to coming to Kingsport with her husband, Dr. J.H. Clifford, had worked for eight years in a Java leper settlement, headed the Home Auxiliary Service.[33] In September 1921, Dr. George G. Keener wrote about the critical financial straits of the unemployed: "When such conditions come to the laboring people, you can always predict a greater amount of sickness with a higher rate of mortality." He cited cases of pellagra, caused by malnutrition and the low vitality of the children. Keener also claimed that the companies in town had "forced their employees to patronize their company physician" during the influenza epidemic, but with the shutdowns, workers had been "unloaded upon the mercy of the people, and the [other] physicians are expected to care for them in case of sickness or accident without receiving, many times, anything for their service." Obviously distressed about having to compete with the nurses of the Metropolitan Life Insurance Company and physicians attached to the industries, Keener nonetheless claimed that he had patients who were "not able to have their prescriptions filled, and some... living on bread and water."[34]

In these times of adversity, Johnson and Dennis stood firm, honed their recruitment techniques, and refined the concept of interlocking industries. They gave no public indication of the dismay that they must have felt, and their promotional efforts showed no sign of wavering. In 1946, however, a civic-club publication recalled the difficult straits of the town during the post–World War I era: "Left with only cement, brick, extract, hosiery and pulp plants and a leather tannery, and those plants faced with heavy curtailment of production, the income-producing employment possibilities were bleak indeed." As for the population: "Thousands of men and women, young and old, in and around Kingsport needed income giving employment. New streets needed paving, there were sanitary and storm sewers to be built, school buildings were required for the already growing child population; morale and incentive were at a low ebb."[35]

Kingsport's developers avoided the textile dependency of the mill villages of the Carolinas but at this crucial stage they welcomed any new factory that seemed to promise sound management, steady employment, and humane working conditions. During the preceding century, Frederick Ross had attempted to establish a silk industry along the north fork of the Holston River, just a few miles from the business district of the future model city. "The only thing I ever had a fancy for in the way of business was the silk culture... I thought I was going to be benefactor to east Tennessee," he confessed. "I built me French reels and made the raw silk and induced many of the farmers to raise and sell me the cocoons." For his troubles, Ross "lost everything" because he overextended himself and was ignorant about the business. He found consolation, however, with "a suit of silk woven in the neighborhood and certainly it was the most enduring substance" that he ever had as his "raiment."[36] After the Civil War the old Ross Silk Mill was sold to Jordan and Son, which converted it into a woolen mill.[37] Some attempt was made later, around 1895, to establish a textile mill on the site of what was to be the new town, but apparently nothing came of this venture.[38] Before the postwar recession, W.B. Davis and Son Company of New York City had agreed to establish a hosiery mill in Kingsport.[39]

Incorporated on 13 March 1917, Kingsport Hosiery Mills owed its birth to the tender heart of a wealthy Yankee. *Manufacturer's Record* reported that a gentleman from New York, being shown around the Kingsport area by Johnson, was moved by the bleak life of the mountain people, particularly the women. " 'What can we do to help these people, Johnson?' he asked. Johnson responded, 'Put up a hosiery mill. I have a man who can run it and an exceptional site. Give these people the opportunity to work, that's all they want.' " The next morning the visitor wrote a check for $250,000 to start this enterprise.[40] Kingsport Hosiery Mills apparently did not experience any shutdowns between its inception and the late 1920s; it continually increased its productivity and its payroll. By June 1919, general manager John H. Baines counted the number of employees at 150 and expected to increase output by 50 percent because of the revival of the hosiery market. For its full-fashioned product, the company, almost a decade later, was using only pure silk from Japan.[41]

This company obviously fared better than its related predecessors in the Kingsport area. By the end of 1919, W.B. Davis, president of the company, had already established a health plan and a nursing service, as well as a rest area and a restaurant for the scores of "girls" who were employed there; and he expected to develop a park close to the plant for the workers' recreation. During the late 1920s the company had 417 employees—121 men and 296 women. The Kingsport Silk Mills and the Rextex Hosiery Mills had appeared by the end of this decade but had vanished from Kingsport's industrial landscape by the 1940s, as had the Kingsport Hosiery Mills. For a while a firm known as Smoky Mountain Hosiery Mills operated on the premises of the former silk mills.[42]

The account of how the hosiery mills originated may be embroidered, but it is probably not apocryphal. Visits by potential investors were not unusual. In July 1919, for example, the *Kingsport Times* mentioned that Johnson was playing host to twenty-five capitalists, manufacturers, and mineralogists from Baltimore. Traveling by rail on a special Clinchfield car, they arrived shortly before noon and expected to leave before nightfall, after inspecting the local plants and investigating natural resources.[43] Not unmindful of outsiders' perceptions of Southern Appalachia and its people, Johnson treated invited guests to an

American sampler and led them on a carefully orchestrated nostalgia trip into the country's past.[44] Historian Roderick Nash has noted that turn-of-the-century America was "ripe for the appeal of the uncivilized on a broad popular basis." The impetus behind what he has dubbed the "American cult of the primitive" rested on "a growing tendency to associate wilderness with America's vanishing frontier and pioneer past that was thought responsible for many desirable national characteristics."[45] Kingsport, as portrayed by Johnson, was the embodiment of the pioneer spirit, southern hospitality, Appalachian distinctiveness, racial and religious purity, and red-white-and-blue Americanism.

Some newcomers to Kingsport have recalled that they thought they had arrived at "the end of the world," but many of them remembered the scenic splendor of its location. Whether debarking from the Clinchfield at the Kingsport depot or from the Southern at the state-line town of Bristol, they could hardly have failed to notice the beauty of the Southern Appalachians. A car met the Bristol travelers, and the twenty-five-or-so mile trip to the model city sometimes involved fording streams. At Edens Ridge they looked out over the lovely valley of the Holston River, in which Kingsport was situated, to see vacant lots, tent dwellings, and newly constructed buildings—the outline of what promised to be a beautiful little city. The more fortunate arrivals lodged at the gracious Kingsport Inn, which featured Georgian architecture and a charming hostess, Mrs. Mahr, the daughter of a Confederate officer named Wilder.[46] Visiting industrialists could anticipate being entertained at Rotherwood, the antebellum estate, owned by John B. Dennis, at the confluence of the Holston River. They might lounge in rockers on the veranda and hear tales of the flatboats that had once left Old Kingsport carrying westward-moving pioneers or regional produce en route to Knoxville or points south. Dinner was served by black waiters bedecked in white jackets, and livelier visitors might get in some shooting the next day. Conversation was sure to include discussions of the needs of the mountain people and how Kingsport's future, already bright, would be ever so much brighter if the guests were to decide to locate plants in the model city.[47] Even the ego of a rational man might swell as he succumbed to visions of leading hillbillies to the promised land of modern industrial capitalism. Occasionally, J. Fred Johnson would encounter a cynic. After touring the town and hearing Johnson chortle about pure Anglo-Saxon children, one disgruntled capitalist, according to local legend, demanded to know the location of the model city's whorehouse.

Full exposure to "the treatment," a term applied to the Dennis and Johnson methodology by some of those who had experienced it, required a lengthy contact. No group ever received a larger dose than visitors from Eastman Kodak of Rochester, New York. Perley S. Wilcox, who eventually headed Tennessee Eastman, was among the first entourage from Kodak Park to visit Kingsport. "If I remember correctly," he stated, "It was January 20, 1920, that in company with two men from Kodak Park and two from the outside, I first met J. Fred at the Kingsport Inn. We spent five days here looking over what little there was of the incompleted Wood Chemical Plant, which was under construction but not finished at the end of the war. We talked with other plant people in town; studied the community and surrounding territory." Returning to Rochester, they wrote their report. Wilcox's portion "bore a rosy tint."[48]

Further consideration was deemed necessary. Charles Flint came and made an independent study. When Dr. D.E. Reid visited, Johnson "could see that he was not impressed to the extent of locating the plant" in Kingsport. At this point, Johnson pulled out all the stops, "asking him to stay longer, saying that he had reserved the best to show him last." A visit to a hillside country school near Kingsport followed, where his host introduced him to the children after this admonition: "There is something which perhaps you have never seen before—42 little children, all pure bred Americans, anxious for something better in life than they can have unless you or some one else will bring it to them from other sections in which the opportunities that these children would like to have are too frequently trampled under foot, without being appreciated."[49] Johnson then asked Reid to speak to the students. Johnson later recalled: "After he [Reid] had finished his remarks a brown eyed mountain boy, about 12 years old—looking as he were inspired, rose from his seat in the rear of the building, walked down the aisle to within two or three feet of the great industrial expert, and gazing up wistfully into his face said, 'Mister, we hope you'll put that plant here.' " With that, Reid was undone and promised Johnson that his report would be favorable.[50]

After several months of negotiations between company officials and the federal government, Eastman purchased the wood-alcohol plant on 26 May 1920 in the name of James S. Havens. On 5 June, at the opening of a Chautauqua program, Johnson announced Eastman's decision to locate in Kingsport, and an editorial in the Kingsport newspaper soon welcomed the "largest manufacturer of photographic equipment in the world" to the town's family of industries. In July, George Eastman, Frank M. Lovejoy, and James Havens came to Kingsport; it was during this visit that Eastman decided to name the new company Tennessee Eastman. As Wilcox commented: "Sort of a pioneer, cow-boy, big open-space flavor, wouldn't you say?" Never one to rest on his laurels, Johnson unleashed his full charm on the Eastman trio.[51] Old-timers maintain that when George Eastman went hunting at Rotherwood, he fired one shot and forty birds fell, so anxious was J. Fred to please.[52] After a few days, George Eastman decided to buy additional property; the initial purchase involved the wood-alcohol plant and its thirty-five acres, plus forty more. He "announced that it seemed advisable to have more plant site, and he proposed to buy all the property east and south of the Horse Creek Road between the CC & O Railroad and the river—a total of 277 acres...and the water rights on Kendricks Creek, and rights-of-way for a pipe line to the plant."[53]

That George Eastman was impressed by the Shelby Street row houses caused John B. Dennis to show a decided preference for that style of architecture, and the impact of the decision to locate an Eastman plant in Kingsport was soon felt in planner John Nolen's office. Within a month of George Eastman's visit to Kingsport, future housing for new Eastman employees merited attention. One of Nolen's assistants suggested that the "20-acre piece between the golf course and the railroad...within easy walking distance of the plant...be kept in reserve for additional Eastman housing." By the end of the year, Eastman had rented a two-story frame barracks as a temporary dwelling for some of its employees. During the 1920s the company constructed Edgewood Village and Beechwood Village for its foremen and workmen. Along the railroad and in close proximity to the plant, the four-, five-, and six-room frame houses, numbering about sixty, featured electricity, indoor plumbing, and hardwood floors.[54]

Kingsport desperately needed Eastman, or a company like it, and Johnson never let down his guard. He courted George Eastman with solicitous messages, invitations, gifts of books, newspaper clippings, and photographs until the latter, suffering from deteriorating health and the vicissitudes of old age, committed suicide. The personal touch may have been all that prevented the demise of Tennessee Eastman around 1924. Although several million dollars had been spent, the plant continued to operate at a loss. The board of directors of Eastman Kodak met to decide the fate of Tennessee Eastman.[55] Johnson recalled the following exchange with George Eastman during a dinner at Rotherwood: "Johnson, it looked as if we would have to stop, didn't it? I answered, yes, Mr. Eastman, but I didn't believe you would...he rather sharply challenged the statement, as he asked, why didn't you think I would? Out of the very depths of my heart and with a profound sense of gratitude and obligation, I said to him, I thought Mr. Eastman you knew that if you stopped it would ruin us. I hope I can always remember as long as I live the kindly, sweet expression that came into his eyes as he softly replied, that was it Johnson."[56] Johnson wrote to Eastman himself after the crisis of 1924: "By the courage and patience you manifested in keeping your plant going, my life's work—the things to which I have consecrated the very best I have had—have been saved and established."[57]

Whatever his motivations, George Eastman kept his plant going at Kingsport in spite of the difficulties, and he made rare visits to East Tennessee, usually in conjunction with trips to Oak Lodge, his retreat in North Carolina. A week or so before his death on 14 March 1932, he reportedly said to Perley S. Wilcox of Tennessee Eastman, "Wilcox, wouldn't it be a wonderful thing if this Kingsport plant of ours turned out to be a great asset to the Company?"[58] Carl Sandburg memorialized George Eastman's suicide in his American poetic panorama "The People, Yes," and Kingsport, according to Johnson, mourned Eastman's passing. As he prepared to end his life, Eastman had scribbled: "My work is done; why wait."[59] Johnson called Eastman "our faithful patient courageous friend and benefactor" and described the mood in town as "a profound spirit of reverential sorrow." "As I walked along the streets," Johnson told Frank M. Lovejoy, vice-president of Eastman Kodak, "laboring men, merchants and professional men, desirous of expressing their respect and affection for Mr. Eastman, took me by the hand and said they were sorry to hear of his death and the way of his going seemed to deepen their understanding and appreciation of him." "The people here," Johnson wrote, "know how he held the life-line for us when it wasn't easy and... they are affectionately grateful... to his memory." In a resolution occasioned by Eastman's sudden death, the Board of Mayor and Aldermen called him "our esteemed friend and humanitarian benefactor" and remarked on the "industrial monument he has left in our beloved city."[60]

The first decade or so of Tennessee Eastman's existence had been filled with difficulties, but George Eastman was not a timid man. Johnson's vision of Kingsport had captured his imagination. During the 1920s the fledgling plant produced methanol, or wood alcohol, by destructive distillation, and other chemicals used in the manufacture of photographic film.[61] The company also ventured into the Charket and granulated-charcoal business. George Eastman was known to have remarked with obvious satisfaction, "Just think, the dining cars on the railroads are now serving meals cooked over Eastman Charkets."[62] To meet its demands for wood, Tennessee Eastman eventually acquired about forty thousand acres of forestland and timber rights in the Kingsport vicinity and elsewhere in the Southern Appalachians, and the company built a thirty-mile narrow-gauge logging railroad from its sawmill at the plant site to the Beech Creek area of neighboring Hawkins County.[63]

At the time of George Eastman's death, major expansion was under way that would make Eastman the bulwark of Kingsport's economy during the Great Depression of the 1930s. It had become apparent to Kodak officials that the Tennessee plant, with its strategic chemicals and nearby source of cotton linters, was the logical site for the production of cellulose acetate to use in film manufacturing at Rochester, New York. Early in 1930 the cellulose-acetate plant began production, and later that same year, a new hydroquinone project was completed. The acetate-yarn plant opened in October 1931. So successful was this venture that work began in 1932 to enlarge the capacity of the yarn plant as well as the cellulose-acetate and acid-recovery units. Tennessee Eastman was within months of completing two production units for the manufacture of a plastic material called Tenite. A new research laboratory, a new power plant, and a new water-filter station were also rapidly nearing completion.[64] Johnson had written to George Eastman in May 1931: "It is really quite astonishing what they have done and the favorable costs at which I believe it is being done. I don't know any better words to express my feelings than to say I was stimulated by the happy faces of men out there at work, grateful for their jobs, and by the atmosphere of enthusiasm and energy that one could feel everywhere about the fine enterprise."[65]

Such industries as Tennessee Eastman that ultimately provided Kingsport with a sound and permanent economic base developed out of the hardships of the 1920s. Whereas heavy reliance on local raw materials and substantial interdependence characterized the emerging factory community, Johnson and Dennis considered diversification a prime virtue; and to the degree that circumstances permitted, they actively encouraged this process. By the 1930s, Tennessee Eastman had taken steps that virtually severed its reliance on local raw materials and had emerged as the largest employer.[66] Such a future was not apparent during the early 1920s, however, and local businessmen and the Kingsport Improvement Company carefully nurtured other possibilities with the same tender care as that accorded to the floundering Eastman facility.

The circumstances surrounding the establishment and success of the Kingsport Press provided the backdrop for the concept of interlocking industries at its best in the planned city. The pulp mill was experiencing considerable difficulty in marketing its product, and stabilizing its operations seemed to be dependent on the manufacture of book paper. Around 1920, John B. Dennis took the problem to his longtime friend the publisher Joseph H. Sears, who once had been the head of D. Appleton and Company. At about this time, Penelope, Sears's daughter, and her husband, S. Phelps Platt, moved from New York to Kingsport, where they resided for the rest of their lives. Sears suggested the publication of a uniform series of literary classics in cloth binding, to be sold for a dime a copy through the chain of F.W. Woolworth stores and the large mail-order houses.[67]

To implement this plan, Sears proposed the formation of a new publishing house that would not only publish this series but also secure contracts from other publishers who had no printing and bookbinding facilities of their own. Colonel Arthur W. Little and his brother, Raymond D., who were the owners and operators of the New York City firm J.J. Little and Ives Company, added their counsel and support. The outcome was the new publishing house of J.H. Sears and Company and a book manufacturer, to be known as J. Little and Company—the Kingsport Press. It had been at this juncture that Mead Corporation was induced to take control of the Kingsport Pulp mill and to build a one-machine paper plant.[68]

During the autumn of 1922 both the Mead paper plant and the printing plant were under construction. The Press settled into a group of connected steel-and-concrete buildings, which had been erected by the Simmons Hardware Company for the Grant Leather Company but had never been occupied.[69] Louis M. Adams, who was then with J.J. Little and Ives Company, became president and general manager. "Equipped with many years of practical experience," according to one source, "he brought to his new field of endeavor an understanding mind and an ability to organize, train the untrained, and create production on a large scale."[70] J. Fred Johnson boasted that "with a leaven of experienced workers to raise the bulk of untrained help to adequate skill, after a couple of years we had here a unit which, on one side of the corporate line fences, was making top-quality book-paper, and on the other side was using this paper in the production of high-grade books."[71]

Initially, Kingsport Press manufactured its own book cloth, because no other firm could meet the specifications of quality, texture, and price for the miniature classics series. By the mid twenties, the company had expanded its operations to include better grades of books. Mead book paper kept pace with the rising standards of the Press, but the Press's in-house operations could not meet the demands for binding fabric. Consequently, the company looked to Holliston Mills of Norwood, Massachusetts, which had been considering a southern location for a bleachery and for the manufacture of certain types of book cloth. Hollis Plimpton, "who regularly flew his own two-seater airplane to Kingsport and landed it in a grassy field" where Cherokee Village was subsequently located, negotiated the deal with the head of the Press, Colonel E.W. Palmer. The Press sold its book-cloth plant, Clinchfield Mills, to Holliston Mills in 1926, and Holliston constructed its bleachery and book-cloth finishing plant on several acres that it leased from Kingsport Press. By January 1927 the Holliston Mills began production in the model city.[72]

Mead, the Press, and Holliston Mills were, during Kingsport's infancy and subsequently to a considerable degree, "functionally interdependent" but "completely independent with respect to ownership, finance and management."[73] The original plants were located directly across the road from each other—Mead and the Press on Center Street, and the Press and Holliston at Clinchfield Street. G.C. McNaughton, a manager of Mead Fibre Company, once said: "This operating arrangement between the Press and ourselves has had a tremendous economic saving on its side.... We save six handlings in the most extreme instance and two handlings in the most direct route possible for paper to take. This means anywhere from two to six freight bills saved, with handling off and on either freight-cars or trucks at each stop, with warehousing and delay, and all the rest." Walter F. Smith, a manager at the Press, agreed: "Get along with the Mead people? We couldn't afford not to, and neither could they. We make money by buying of them and they by selling to us, better money than either of us could make by trading outside. We have just the same sort of relationship, too, with the plant on the other side of us, the Holliston Mills of Tennessee, Incorporated." Other local firms also benefited. For a while, Eastman's sawmill provided book shooks and finished end boards for the Press, as well as box and crate lumber for Mead, the Press, and Blue Ridge Glass Corporation; and pulpwood from Eastman's timber holdings made its way to the Mead operation.[74]

Borden Mills provided another important link in Kingsport's chain of book manufacturing—in the form of gray goods for the production of book cloth—and Holliston Mills became a customer. In 1924 the Borden family, owners of the American Printing Company, one of the largest textile manufacturers in the world, decided to build a plant at Kingsport. Situated just north of the cotton belt and touted for its "100 percent pure American labor," the planned city seemed an ideal location. Some evidence suggests that John B. Dennis was more favorably disposed to this venture than J. Fred Johnson was; the Bordens were Dennis's friends.[75] Later, Johnson commented that he had made a mistake in letting Borden Mills come to Kingsport, because the Bordens wanted a female labor force, the obvious advantage being that women could be paid less. They then encountered difficulty in recruiting enough women workers because the pay in other Kingsport industries was enough to sustain families, and husbands did not want their wives to work outside the home or away from the farm.[76]

All of this had not prevented Johnson's orchestration of homespun gratitude and ceremonial politics. When members of the Borden family arrived in town to launch the project, throngs of pure Anglo-Saxons lined Broad Street, American flags waved, and Model-T's by the dozens rolled into the business district.[77] "Model children" from Andrew Jackson Elementary, one of the "model schools," marched down to the depot to add to the congestion and fanfare.[78] The groundbreaking took place on 16 August 1924, and Tennessee's Governor Austin Peay delivered the keynote address when the cornerstone for the main building was laid on 11 October of the same year. Production began on 26 May 1925. In its halcyon days at the end of the decade, Borden Mills became the town's largest employer at 1,227—758 men and 469 women.[79]

The relationship between the Press, Mead, Holliston Mills, and Borden Mills proved to be a valuable promotional gimmick, as well as an economic godsend for the town's survival. The 27 February 1927 edition of the *Kingsport Times,* commemorating the tenth anniversary of the city's incorporation, boasted that it had been printed on book paper produced by Mead from pulp derived from trees that grew in the region. The entire process from raw wood to finished newspaper had been executed exclusively by local labor. Howard Long, the author of *Kingsport: A Romance of Industry,* which was published in 1928, noted that his book was wholly a Kingsport product. The subject matter, the raw materials for the paper and photographic film, the processing of materials that went into the book, and the actual printing were "made possible by a marvelous coordination of the activities of the group of industries located in the little East Tennessee city—a coordination such as is found, perhaps, no place else in the industrial world."[80]

The benefits of industrial cooperation were not confined to book manufacturing. During the 1920s, Tennessee Eastman and Blue Ridge Glass Corporation shared a water supply. Eastman, which owned the water rights and the pumps, depended on the glass company for filtration. The latter bought an average of 1.5 million gallons a day and sold back 15,000 to 20,000 gallons of filtered water to Eastman for use in its boilers. Kingtan Extract Company sold tanned leather to the Slip-Not Belting Corporation, and almost every industry in town drove its machines with H.J. Shivell's Slip-Not belts.[81] A few years later, Tennessee Eastman relied on the local branch of Southern Oxygen Company for carbon dioxide to clean pipelines and bought a large proportion of its castings from the Kingsport Foundry and Manufacturing Corporation, which was established in 1927.[82]

The nature of some of the industries also aided physical construction of the town. The Kingsport Brick Corporation provided the building materials for the stately Georgian-like architecture that dotted the business and civic sections, and the Clinchfield Portland Cement Corporation lowered the costs of the thirteen miles of paved streets, the thirty-two miles of sidewalks, and about thirty-seven miles of sewer and drainage system that the town possessed a decade after its incorporation.[83] The on-site location of these two plants not only kept down costs of industrial building and municipal construction; it also gave the Kingsport Improvement Company bargain prices on such residential materials as cement, stucco, hollow tile, and brick. Promoters claimed that this kept the cost of living under control. "A workman in Kingsport on the local wage scale," which Johnson acknowledged was considerably below that of the North, was "able to live in extremely comfortable fashion." This, he noted, made for "profitable manufacturing operations...without any oppression of labor."[84] By 1927 the strain of the immediate postwar era had eased, the model city seemed on its way to permanency, and Kingsport's ten industries employed 3,383 workers.[85]

As the industrial base for the model city took shape, the municipal government wrangled over such matters as improving the water supply, establishing telephone service, launching police and fire departments, installing traffic lights, erecting street signs, and assigning house numbers—the last being a condition for securing a local post office and daily delivery of the mail. Each technological development caused celebration and signaled yet another blow for civilization in its confrontation with frontierlike conditions in the raw new town. In January 1917 the *Kingsport Times* had promised that electric lights would be available soon for the principal parts of the city and expressed the heartfelt hope that "the darkness and... the mud" would "soon be a thing of the past." The Board of Mayor and Aldermen granted Cumberland Telephone and Telegraph the franchise for a battery-operated system in June of that year. By February 1921, Rotherwood, Dennis's home a few miles southwest of the downtown, had electricity; lines were being strung to Roller Farm and Riverview Dairy; and White City was about to receive telephone service. In 1920, municipal officials pondered the purchase of a motor-driven garbage-collection vehicle to replace horse-powered contrivances, citing the high cost of horse feed as a major factor. Dr. T.B. Yancey, the city health officer, banished pigs from the town that same year, although cows whose owners obeyed rules and regulations would be allowed to remain because they provided sustenance for the young. The future Mrs. John B. Dennis, Lola Anderson, the town's resident landscape architect and operator of the nursery, was soon in a snit about the bovines that roamed about the town and damaged young trees. Public transportation within the city received a boost with the advent in 1921 of bus lines. Two Mack buses, with a capacity of twenty-nine passengers each, and a Ford bus operated at one-hour intervals between the Clinchfield depot, at Main and Broad streets, and Eastman and Corning Glass, with several intermediate stops. To facilitate this effort, the two companies adjusted their shift schedules by fifteen minutes.[86]

Originating as a planned industrial city, Kingsport fell heir to an industrial-commercial-managerial mentality. Those who shaped the town's destiny shared this outlook, and harmony generally prevailed; individuals who held other views noticed that these fell on deaf ears. Considerable vision tempered this mind-set prior to World War II but was lost or misplaced during the 1950s, 1960s, and 1970s. Singularity of purpose seemed constructive in the early stages, but a monolithic view proved detrimental in subsequent decades.

The Kingsport Improvement Company maintained its paternalistic hold long after the town had a formal government, but because of Johnson's political dexterity and the respect that he commanded, he generally went unchallenged. A controversy between Central High School's Principal H.R. Groat and Superintendent of Schools E.M. Crouch offers one of the few examples of public dissension in the early town. Groat, who resigned, alleged that Crouch spent too much time in J. Fred Johnson's office and that Crouch advocated special attention for children of prominent citizens. In Groat's letter of resignation, a copy of which he provided to the *Kingsport Times,* he stated: "While I believe that Kingsport might prosper under a limited form of dictatorship, the good people of our city cannot and should not continue longer under a monarchy unlimited." Apparently the school controversy created tumult in the town for about two weeks. Finally, when it was hushed, the newspaper featured an editorial entitled "Definitely Settled." "To be more specific," it read, "the *Times* hopes that no more efforts will be made to secure the publication of articles touching on the matter." Lucille Carmack, a student at Central High School at the time, recalled some sixty years later that the principal had really been fired: "Professor Groat was kind of keeping [company] with an athletic teacher. They went to a *dance* at the old Roller clubhouse by the Netherland Inn. The story goes they went to the wrong punchbowl and got a little tipsy. Of course, this was back in the Dark Ages. But, they got fired." Students who liked Groat called a strike, cut classes, and paraded around town.[87]

Although there was no shortage of bootleg whiskey and locally produced moonshine, Kingsport was a dry town in a dry state, and prohibition was the law of the land. Furthermore, Johnson possessed a strong aversion to the consumption of alcohol. A close acquaintance recalled that one of the patriarch's favorite stories, used to extract contributions for the Community Chest, was that of a peanut vendor who, even with modest means and a wife and child to support, always gave generously. In reality, the vendor was also one of the drinking population's best sources.[88]

About as much democracy existed in Kingsport during the 1920s as at any other juncture in its history. City officials adopted the practice of holding town meetings, with the complicity of the KIC, to discuss major community concerns. Not having a formal Chamber of Commerce, Johnson and Dennis solicited advice from "a group of knowledgeable and representative citizens."[89] Property owners had an intimate contact with fiscal policy for the extension of streets, sewers, sidewalks, and curbing. In compliance with the city charter, citizens who petitioned for the creation of improvement districts indicated a willingness to pay a pro-rata share based on the assessed value of their property that abutted on the street under consideration. This included the entire cost of constructing sidewalks, curbing, and lateral sewers and three-fourths of the cost of other improvements and all incidental expenses.[90] Municipal bond issues, among them school construction, were subject to referendum. According to promotional propaganda published in 1926, schoolchildren, "the descendants of English Cavaliers and their followers who settled here before the Mayflower," could "imbibe the Kingsport community spirit" through the educational process; and a head of industry could be found in his office reading a pamphlet on democracy.[91]

Democracy could be set aside, however, for favorites if the situation merited. When the Clinchfield Railroad failed to pay its taxes on time for 1923, J. Fred Johnson wrote to Frank L. Cloud, then city manager, stating that the late payment was an oversight and requesting a waiver of the 2 percent penalty. Cloud responded that the Board of Mayor and Aldermen opposed a waiver, because it would be unfair to other taxpayers whose requests had been denied. City Attorney T.R. Bandy also counseled against such action, but City Treasurer G.D. Black wrote to H.G. Morison, general solicitor for the railroad, on 20 February 1924, to inform him that the penalty had been waived. Black's action had been authorized by the Board of Mayor and Aldermen at its regular meeting on 19 February; George E. Penn had represented the railroad at that time. No explanation was offered in the public record for this reversal.[92]

This was the decade of the twenties, when success was gauged by commercial and industrial development. In a speech to the Society of Newspaper Editors, President Calvin Coolidge declared, "The business of America is business." In 1924 Tennessee native Bruce Barton had published *The Man Nobody Knows*, a biography of Christ written as an analysis of a contemporary executive. Few Americans of this era seemed to disagree with the dictum "The man who builds a factory builds a temple and the man who works there worships there."[93] Kingsport, with its commitment to capitalism, was a municipal cog in the national machine. Conditions in the town during this decade resembled "the urban ethos" to be found in other southern cities, which featured such ingredients as civic consciousness, loyalty and optimism, business efficiency, and social harmony and cooperation."[94]

Recruitment of industries to the town received first priority, but commercial boosterism ran a close second. Kingsport soon challenged neighboring Bristol and Johnson City and set off a three-way rivalry that affected everything from high-school athletics to retail trade. Friendly jousting gave way over the years to some resentment as the model city drew a disproportionate share of shoppers and brought increasing numbers of area residents under its influence because of the jobs that its growing industries offered. As early as June 1919 the *Kingsport Times* had staked claims on the hinterland, proclaiming Kingsport "The Industrial Center of East Tennessee and Southwest Virginia, The Gateway to the Coalfields of Southwest Virginia and Southeastern Kentucky, The Heart of the Rich Mineral, Agricultural and Timber Land of East Tennessee." A 1920 editorial urged Kingsport shoppers to patronize local merchants. Four banks and an equal number of churches complemented the reportedly fifty retail establishments in 1921. "The 'Magic City' of East Tennessee," the newspaper boasted, drew shoppers from a twenty-five- to fifty-mile radius. The local organization of retail merchants, whose president, W. W. Hufford, worked at J. Fred Johnson's "Big Store," had organized trade week that year. Airplanes, a special feature of this occasion, helped to swell the crowds.[95]

The crowning jewel of commercial Kingsport for many years was the "Big Store," operated and subsequently owned by J. Fred Johnson. Originating in 1906 at the confluence of the north and south forks of the Holston River as the Rotherwood Interstate Mercantile Company, it opened a branch store two years later at what would be the vicinity of Hammond Avenue and Compton Terrace. In 1910 the two combined as Kingsport Stores, located on Shelby Street. One of the first employees recalled: "Clerks had to be versatile sales people in the early days of the company. The store was not departmentalized and everything from teaspoons to caskets was sold. We had a general saying among ourselves that we could take a person from birth to the grave." Some employees lived in the building, and if the situation demanded, travelers could be provided overnight accommodations. One female reported that she owed her position as milliner to the fact that she did not use rouge. Johnson hired her after he had canceled his contract with a woman from Baltimore because he had discovered that she indulged in this practice, which he found offensive.[96]

Several firms in Kingsport were offspring of the Big Store, and many prominent citizens had worked there before launching other careers. Dobyns-Taylor Hardware, owned by Flem Dobyns and George Taylor, Sr., dated from 1922. Having secured some experience in the funeral trade while clerks on Shelby Street, L.W. ("Jimmie") Dobson and J.M. Hamlett, Sr., founded the Hamlett-Dobson Funeral Home in 1925.

Longtime employee Sam H. Anderson eventually acquired a Ford distributorship during the 1950s. Tom Warrick became a personnel director at Tennessee Eastman. Other business persons who got their start at the Big Store included H.C. and W.W. McDaniel, V.L. ("Red") Cloud, Walter Bradley, Sam P. Steadman, Mrs. D.R. Pierce, and Mrs. William Wallace.[97]

The introduction of manufacturing and commerce into a predominantly agricultural setting was not without its influence; soon the young town had a significant impact on the surrounding area. Between 1915 and 1925 the rural communities in Sullivan County that were nearest to Kingsport experienced a 24.1 percent increase in population. Newcomers, anxious for industrial jobs but reluctant to abandon the land entirely, clustered on the town's periphery. Those rural communities that were closest to Bristol, the other principal town in Sullivan County, had only a 5.0 percent growth during the same period. Eighty families—from Scott County, Virginia; Hawkins County, Tennessee; a North Carolina location; and a few from Kingsport itself—settled in eight communities just outside of the model city. Thirty-four of the thirty-seven families that left these same eight communities moved inside the incorporation. A 1928 study by the University of Tennessee Extension Service noted that "surplus farm labor" around Kingsport was evidently finding "an outlet in the industrial and commercial activities" of the new town. The survey also cited the efforts of the Kingsport Improvement Company and civic organizations to foster good roads, which had an influence on the following projects: a macadam road to Gate City, Virginia; a concrete road between Bristol and Kingsport, designated as a national highway, which could boost tourism; a planned hard-surface road to Johnson City; macadam or asphalt roads from Kingsport to six outlying communities; and a bridge at the confluence of the north and south forks of the Holston River. Evidence also suggested that area residents were beginning to avail themselves of the dental and medical services. Furthermore, Kingsport was bearing 27 percent of Sullivan County's tax burden as early as 1924.[98]

By the end of the 1920s the planned industrial city of Kingsport, which Johnson called "a laboratory experiment in cooperation," had succeeded.[99] Although some of the industries that appeared during the 1910s and the 1920s eventually succumbed to economic failure, the pillars of the town's economic structure remained firmly entrenched: Tennessee Eastman, Mead, Kingsport Press, Holliston Mills, Blue Ridge Glass, Slip-Not Belting, and Borden Mills (which declined and was later resurrected under the auspices of J.P. Stevens). Two of them, Tennessee Eastman and Kingsport Press, would gain national and even international prominence. Whether labeled "business progressivism,"[100] "the urban ethos," or just "the Kingsport spirit," the dynamics of the Kingsport project served as a magnet, attracting a population from elsewhere in the United States, as well as the people of the surrounding valleys and hill country. The model city quickly became a cultural and economic oasis in the section of Southern Appalachia bounded by northeastern Tennessee, southwestern Virginia, southeastern Kentucky, and western North Carolina and served by the Clinchfield Railroad. The lure of regular cash wages and steady employment cannot be overestimated, but this was not the only attraction, for, as one writer observed early in the model city's history, "the town pays as much attention to humanics as it does to mechanics."[101] In 1937, Johnson wrote in the preface to a civic-club publication that "the humanics are more important than the mechanics." Setting forth what he called "a fundamental truth," he contended that "if it is not good for the community, it is not good for the individual or for business activity within that community."[102] As important to the survival of Kingsport as the philosophy of its founders, the physical plan, and the economic infrastructure were the inhabitants of the town and its hinterland, who determined if and how well its government, social institutions, businesses, and factories would function.

5

The Human Factor

In 1927, on the tenth anniversary of Kingsport's incorporation, an editor of the local newspaper wrote that outsiders considered the town "just an industrial city. . . . However, it is a mistake to believe that a city can be builded of industrial plants alone, just as it is a mistake to believe that brick and concrete and steel constitute a city. It is not buildings that make a city—it is people." Another writer for the *Kingsport Times*, John M. Oliver, pointed to the city's growth during 1926, noting that "marvelous events" had taken place: "Buildings went up over night, new plants located, persons from all parts of the nation found in Kingsport the making of a bright and prosperous future."[1] Natives of the area streamed into town from the surrounding countryside to shop, to seek jobs, or just to gawk. One boy's first visits at about this time remained indelibly impressed on his memory. Later, as a senior citizen, he recalled: "I saw my first electric light burning outside the Mead Corporation and attended a movie at the old Gem Theatre, then known as the Strand and operated by Mr. Harmon who later moved from Main to Broad Street. My first visit to the Theatre was to see Harold Lloyd and Dick Chester in 'Fightin' Fools,' a western. As a child, I was of the opinion that it never rained in town."[2]

During the 1920s the forging of Kingsport's society occurred. Circumstances peculiar to the place, the time, and the cast of players produced the social structure that has retained much of its original character into the 1980s. This fortuitous amalgam, which accommodated outside investors, native entrepreneurs, professionals, managers from elsewhere in the country as well as the homegrown ones, and the local labor force, has been amazingly resilient. As much as any other factor, it accounts for Kingsport's survival and its relative success as a privately planned industrial city. While not having been without exploitive overtones and visible flaws, the arrangement belies the subculture of poverty and colonial models that are so often applied to Southern Appalachia.[3] The Kingsport experiment, for better or for worse, is a case study of American industrial capitalism. Three generations have put it to the test and found its assets greater than its liabilities.

The culture nurtured in the model city was vintage American. The ideals that directed it embodied the social attributes of a mythological Main Street U.S.A. that may have existed nowhere except in the minds of J. Fred Johnson and those whom he converted. Social control rested principally with Johnson, somewhat with John B. Dennis, and to a lesser degree with "a group of knowledgeable and representative citizens."[4] The profit incentive attracted and held the capitalists; the thrill of pioneering on an urban frontier and the expectations for a comfortable life of middle-class respectability lured young adults and married couples who had business and professional interests; and prospects for steady employment and regular cash income whetted the appetites of the area's native population, which had been trapped in a preindustrial time warp as parts of their nation had fervently embraced modern industrial capitalism. All of these circumstances coalesced to produce an aspiring population. Johnson's exhortations and incantations fell on fertile ground, and as the "Kingsport spirit" flowered, it possessed a remarkable ability to exorcise or silence the nonbelievers and the critics and to ignore the unpleasant. H.J. Shivell described Kingsport of the 1920s: "You would have maybe a dozen friends and they would be from a dozen places.... They had to forget where they were from and who their friends used to be—and back the town Mr. J. Fred Johnson was building."[5]

Just as the Kingsport experience fails to conform to the colonial and subculture of poverty models, it also challenges romantic notions about the independent and self-sufficient society, described by Ronald D Eller and others, that existed in the mountains prior to the advent of modern industrial capitalism. Eller writes in his highly acclaimed *Miners, Millhands and Mountaineers* that by 1930 most Appalachian natives had been socially integrated into the new industrial order and had become economically dependent upon it. According to him, "This dependence was not on their own terms—that is to say, it was a product not of mountain culture but of the same political and economic forces that were shaping the rest of the nation and the western world." While this transformation yielded riches for a small number of owners and managers, it brought despair and hardship to many residents of the region.

Elsewhere, he laments: "Suspended halfway between the old society and the new, the mountaineers had lost the independence and self-determination of their ancestors, without becoming full participants in the benefits of the modern world."[6]

While "this dependence was not on their own terms," it was in many instances—and certainly in the Kingsport area—largely by personal choice. Furthermore, there is no reason to assume the workings of an inherently sinister presence if people should embrace or come under the influence of "the same political and economic forces that were shaping the rest of the nation and the western world." What, indeed, may be a less desirable alternative is to be out of step with the modern world and consequently be stigmatized by journalists, politicians, social scientists, and do-gooders.[7] Such commentary as Eller's, which is not without its merits when applied to some places, people, and circumstances, particularly most coal camps, implies that the coming of industrial capitalism blighted a near-idyllic existence. Such was not the case with the people of Kingsport's hinterland, who enthusiastically responded to employment opportunities and such amenities and services as the new town was capable of providing and fostering.

Around 1916, for example, medical services had been very inadequate and, for some area residents, virtually nonexistent. When the editor of the *Kingsport Times*, R.D. Kinkead became seriously ill from appendicitis and complications, he was taken to St. Luke's Hospital at Bristol, approximately twenty-five miles away, over deplorable roads, for an emergency operation. One of Kingsport's elite, who was less than impressed with local physicians, returned to her family's home in New York during the 1920s for obstetrical care.[8] Gradually, the quality of treatment available to area residents improved, largely because Kingsport attracted able physicians and eventually established a permanent community hospital.

The mountains and valleys near Kingsport harbored a preindustrial society. It did not possess the same class delineations as the modern industrial society of the North, but it did have gradations of wealth, characteristic of an agricultural society. There were a few professionals—teachers, lawyers, physicians, seminary-trained ministers, journalists—and a small entrepreneurial class. Even those whose livelihood derived from business activities in small towns found it desirable to own land. The size of the holdings varied, as did the standard of living. Some families owned hundreds of acres in fertile valleys, educated their sons well, and lived in a genteel fashion. Others possessed small farms but worked hard for a meager harvest. Those who were even less fortunate did not have enough property to consider themselves independent farmers, so they labored for their more prosperous neighbors.

The life-style of most of the people, tied as it was to the land, was in harmony with and at the mercy of nature, subject to seasonal changes and fluctuations in the weather. Frank L. Cloud, one of Kingsport's early city managers and the son of a local farming family, once commented on the primitive nature of industry prior to the establishment of the modern city of Kingsport. He referred to fur trapping and also mentioned another turn-of-the-century activity, logging. Whole families sometimes located in the remote, primitive camps to cut a boundary of timber. The nearest market was Knoxville, and flotillas of logs, accompanied by men and boys on log rafts held together by wooden pegs, made the four-day trip down the Holston River. Some loggers ventured on down the Tennessee to Chattanooga, an eight-day sojourn.[9] Customers at the Rotherwood Interstate Mercantile Company, who were usually male heads of households, arrived on horseback or by boat. "When the women did come to town, however, they came by horseback just as the men did," according to one account. "They would bring huge grain sacks to put their purchases in and clerks would fill these with the merchandise, distributing it evenly in either end so that the bag could be thrown across the horse's back, and the shopper would mount and ride off." A clerk of that era recalled that he helped "load their purchases into rowboats tied up at the bank in front of the store. Then they'd pole out from the bank to deep water and row for home." As late as the mid-twenties, some area residents still bartered in produce; and a solitary member from a large family generally came to town about twice a year to make purchases for the entire clan, using lengths of string or sticks to size garments and shoes.[10]

This pattern of existence did not suddenly give way to early modern industrialization; instead, it gradually receded in the face of improved transportation, easier access to markets and suppliers, outside capitalistic interests, and a generation of laborers responsive to fixed hours and regular paychecks. The advent of early modern industrial capitalism lifted natives from a simple agrarian existence and plopped them down into industrial villages and towns; even those who continued to reside on farms could not long remain unaffected by the changing society around them.

At the turn of the twentieth century, Upper East Tennessee and the neighboring portions of other states remained a veritable bastion of white Anglo-Saxon Protestants. Highlanders, like their Deep South cousins, had no reluctance to show their disdain for blacks. Elizabeth Doggett Johnson recalled having been sidetracked in her Uncle George Carter's private railroad car at Altapass, North Carolina, when the black cook got off the train to toss a ball; a local man warned him to get aboard because they did not allow "niggers" to spend the night there.[11] Planner Earle S. Draper concurred: "Up in the mountains in Watauga County, North Carolina, they said the sun never sets on a black person. When we took black servants up there, they stayed home at night."[12] The percentages of native white residents of native parentage for Sullivan County, in which Kingsport was situated, and Hawkins County, within five miles of the core area and the location of John B. Dennis's home as well as other holdings, stood at 93.5 and 92.0 respectively in 1910; blacks accounted for only 5.5 and 7.7 percent. Racism, detrimental as it was, posed but one impediment; ignorance affected both races. Of the population ten years of age and older, 13.1 percent of Sullivan County's people were illiterate in 1910; 17.9, in Hawkins. If, however, only native white voters (male) are considered, several counties of Upper East Tennessee had illiteracy in excess of 20 percent in 1900: Claiborne, Sevier, Hancock, Grainger, Unicoi, Cocke, Hawkins, Johnson, and Carter; but the illiteracy of Tennessee's entire population amounted to 27 percent. At the same time, the illiteracy of native-born whites throughout the United States was 4.6 percent.[13]

Studies of mountain children conducted by Lester R. Wheeler, a professor at East Tennessee State Teachers College in Johnson City, suggested that environment adversely affected their performance on standardized intelligence tests. The advent of industrial capitalism, however, seemed to improve their standings. Wheeler hypothesized that the 1,145 children whom he tested in Unicoi and Carter counties during 1929/30 "under the direct influence of isolated mountain environment... should give a fair picture of the mountain children of East Tennessee.... The environment... [was] strictly rural. Agriculture is the chief occupation of the parents with a small percentage of lumbering and coal mining." Wheeler discovered the median intelligence of the six-year-old children to be 94.7, about five points short of perfectly normal. "As we increase the chronological ages," he wrote, "we have a consistent decrease in intelligence until at the age of sixteen the IQ has fallen about twenty-five points.... With the proper environmental changes the mountain children might test near a normal group."[14]

Ten years later, Wheeler observed that "the average mountain child" had "gained ten points on IQ, or nearly one point a year during the past ten years." Nonetheless, IQ decreased about two points from age six to sixteen. Pointing again to the correlation between environment and intelligence as measured by standardized tests, the professor described what had transpired during the intervening decade: "Our data show [that] about sixty percent of the families in one county and forty percent in another had one or more members working in industrial plants." He elaborated:

> During the past ten years the rapid growth of industry in the area enables the family to supplement its agricultural livelihood with ready cash through employment in the rayon, lumber, pottery and other industrial plants. Farming methods have materially changed; pasture lands now replace many of the corn fields on the rough mountain slopes, and stock raising and dairy farming is proving profitable. Small but modern frame houses located on or near the main highways have replaced many of the log cabins and small rough-board houses. There has been unusual development in the area, and the improvement in roads, schools, agriculture and the economic life of the communities has materially changed the general environment of these people.[15]

In spite of demonstrable liabilities in a confrontation with modernization, this population took advantage of opportunities, however limited, as they presented themselves. "You didn't have to worry about labor supply. If you hired one," exclaimed native Jasper Ketron, a city employee and later an Eastman surveyor, "there was fourteen more out there looking for a job." Nonetheless, as early as 1920, labor turnover received careful attention. According to a report in *Business*, "Each of the industries" in Kingsport used "standardized employment forms and cards" and followed "the same method of figuring and analyzing labor turnover," making it possible "to devise remedies" and "to take practical means of lessening it."[16]

Industrial agents lauded the population for its racial and ethnic purity and its commitment to the work ethic, and they exploited its hunger for regular nonfarm employment in company with its affinity for the land. One representative for the Clinchfield Railroad noted the presence of "12,000 inhabitants [in Johnson City, Washington County] of the best Anglo-Saxon type, who are industrious and willing to work for a reasonable wage; living expenses are very reasonable, in view of the fact that vegetables of all kinds are produced in the valleys surrounding the city." Writing in 1913 to a manufacturer in Pennsylvania who was being plagued by a strike, an agent minced no words: "There is no better help in the world than this mountain type of girl that works ten hours per day for practically one-half the wages that you are forced to pay at this time in Shenandoah. . . . If you want to get away from the annoyance of strikes and the worries of keen competition I would like to tell you something about Johnson City and the relief it offers." Another communiqué the same year, citing statistics based on a recent investigation, described mountain women who were "perfectly willing to work 10 hours per day for almost ½ the same class of wage earners make in the North and East."[17]

Industrial agents for the CC & O encouraged visiting industrialists to see Kingsport. Already typifying the hustle and bustle that they wanted to promote along the line, it was rapidly becoming their showcase town. In 1916, representatives from Villa and Brothers, a silk company on Madison Avenue in New York City, "did not seem anxious to go to Kingsport" after returning to Johnson City from Elizabethton, "but showed enough interest to ask about the labor supply." They had been under the impression that the big industries recruited northern labor, the very thing they were trying to escape. They refused to "consider any town in which they found this class of labor, no matter what proposition was made them." An assistant agent told them that he "did not know what class of labor Kingsport had, but knew that Kingsport had a large native population, and that the surrounding country was thickly settled." Earlier Villa and Brothers had been informed that white female labor in the section could be secured for "a maximum wage of $3.50 per week while learning and $6.00 to $7.00 per week after they are taught."[18]

Despite their possession of traits that were advantageous to capitalists and their much celebrated racial purity, some East Tennesseans, as well as their fellow mountaineers in the region, were crude characters, fiercely independent and sometimes lawless. The struggles of a muddy railroad village to be reborn as a model city and the possibilities for industrial employment offered no immediate panacea. Their presence gave early Kingsport a raw flavor, and only a few miles beyond its periphery, frontier conditions were more ordinary than peculiar. Filth, perversity, ignorance, and criminality occurred too frequently to be ignored. Off the record, early observers commented that an occasional bath could wash ten years off some of the women on Long Island. A few local men seemed to favor adolescent brides. Sometimes, family living conditions could only be described as primitive. While buying land options for George L. Carter, J. Fred Johnson, then a young man, had stopped at a mountain cabin and asked to spend the night. The head of the household told him to come on in; one of the children had smallpox, but the man did not guess that Johnson would get it. Johnson decided to move on down the road. Typhoid, which he contracted during these years, and its accompanying high temperatures, however, may have rendered the father of Kingsport sterile.[19] Jasper Ketron and Karl Goerdel, Eastman surveyors, described one-room mountain cabins where they occasionally stayed during the early 1920s. They went to bed first, and then the family blew out the kerosene lamp and retired; the next morning, the reverse order operated.[20]

Moonshining was an indigenous industry, and neither a statewide bone-dry law nor national prohibition eliminated it. Surveyors who occasionally stumbled upon stills had no difficulty filling their personal requirements. "You could see as many as three stills in one hollow," declared Ketron. He and Goerdel observed one of the largest at Archer Spring, about halfway up Bays Mountain. Strangers at country stores could expect to be interrogated: "What is your name? What are you doing?" When Ketron and Goerdel were summoned before the grand jury at Blountville, the seat of Sullivan County, Goerdel testified: "Our business is not to hunt moonshiners; our business is to survey land and we have to get along with those people. We have to go back." Just outside the courtroom, he encountered "the king bee of moonshiners," who asked "What are you doing here?" "They called us to tell what we know," Goerdel responded. "Did you know anything?" the moonshiner asked. "No," replied Goerdel; "tell your friends to get away when we come along so we don't know them."[21]

Some locals found pleasure in such simple things as digging ginseng and sitting on ridge tops listening to dogs run; others, however, had a propensity for strong drink, which soon spilled into the model city. The town fathers, caught up in a civilizing mission, gradually turned the tide. "Answering the almost unanimous demand of the good people of Kingsport," Police Chief George Barger ordered the owners of a dance hall to leave town in March 1917. The local newspaper gave the following account: "For a few nights this place had the appearance of the days of old, and the young men, eager for any place of amusement, attracted by the pretty girls, the live music and the fascination of being hidden behind the 'Red' windows, danced and drank 'dope' etc. just as near the wee small hours of the early morning as the law and decency would permit." When the owners returned, they were arrested on warrants that charged them with selling soft drinks without a license. A statutory charge was suspended on condition that they leave Kingsport at once and never return. The *Times* editorialized that "all persons thinking Kingsport, because of its abundance of work, its large pay-rolls and its great male population, was a good town for 'suckers' had better just keep traveling."[22]

Local law enforcement left a great deal to be desired. City officials in 1918 found themselves embroiled in a controversy over Chief Barger. Two black prostitutes, one with a criminal record, had made allegations of immoral conduct against him. A third affidavit by a male claimed that Barger had been frequenting black establishments on Sullivan Street. Although cleared of charges, the chief was soon replaced by W.E. Carmack. Later the Board of Mayor and Aldermen authorized a two-week paid vacation for Barger, and in 1920 he served as state fire marshal for East Tennessee.[23] In October 1919, Carmack fell to drinking on a Saturday night, appearing on the streets "in what was described as an intoxicated condition." This conduct reportedly was occasioned by the death of his brother, J.M. Carmack, who had taken a call for the chief and had been shot to death by Jasper Trimble, who was creating a disturbance at the Baptist Church in Old Kingsport. Trimble had recently jumped bond at Blountville and was being sought to answer charges of feloniously assaulting a small boy by running him down with an automobile. With two bullets in his abdomen, Carmack begged Trimble, "Don't shoot me any more, Jasper, I'm dead now." Carmack was taken to the community hospital, where he expired. Trimble hid in an attic of a house at Chocolate Grove on Cement Hill and was captured while sleeping. The city canceled Carmack's hospital bill, and about eleven years later, after much haggling, the Board of Mayor and Aldermen agreed to provide for his widow; the actual amount was not specified. Several months earlier, however, the proposed $4,400 had been slashed to $2,500, and that failed to receive a favorable vote.[24]

Whatever had caused Chief W.E. Carmack's intoxication, it did not go unnoticed. According to the *Kingsport Times*: "Scores of men ...were drunk in the streets last Saturday night and...in many instances police were handicapped in enforcing the ordinances against drunkenness in the city by the moral effect produced by the alleged condition of the chief of police." Carmack was sober enough to resign on Sunday, and the Board of Mayor and Aldermen named Cam A. King as his replacement on 20 October. Acting City Manager Frank L. Cloud warned, "I have told Mr. King to 'go after' the bootleggers and the loafers who are responsible for the violations of these laws in Kingsport"; the Police Department was "expected to make an organized effort to rid the city of the lawless element. Hereafter every able bodied man in this city will be expected to go to work.... and if it is necessary we will find a way to close some of the places where loafers congregate."[25]

Only a few months earlier, two Kingsport policemen, S.P. Dickson and W.M. Lee, had been charged with murder in the shooting death of Jasper Bridwell just east of the Rotherwood Bridge outside the city. The policemen pleaded self-defense and claimed that they had received word that young Bridwell and a companion were coming into Kingsport with whiskey from Kentucky. When they attempted to stop him and his father, who had met Jasper at Waycross, Virginia, Jasper allegedly had aimed a pistol at the policemen. Acquitted by the circuit court on 3 July, Dickson nonetheless submitted his resignation immediately; and Lee was expected to do likewise.[26]

Civilizing some of the people of the Tennessee hill country required diligence and commitment and was not accomplished with undue haste. Walter F. Smith, a president of Kingsport Press, recollected: "We had problems. Old Sam, the town undertaker, stood at the door and collected the guns as the boys came to work for ten cents an hour. In time we learned where strategically to locate the buckets, for we operated in a heavy tobacco-chewing area." In 1921, the *Times* had railed against "promiscuous spitting" and had urged rigid enforcement of the applicable city ordinance. Noting that the Press's management "must have felt the need for divine guidance," Smith remembered that they chose the Bible for their first title. "The customer, however, never saw one [of the first run] because each night the boys took those Bibles home—apparently by the armful." Nonplussed, Louis M. Adams, the president and general manager, commented, "Maybe they'll read them and bring them back."[27]

When George Eastman asked J. Fred Johnson in 1920 what kind of people lived in the area, Johnson had quietly replied, "I am one of them."[28] The nature of local residents ran the gamut of human behavior, remembered Mrs. Johnson.[29] In spite of their crudeness, limited education, and lack of sophistication, natives became able employees. Obviously, they had to be trained for industrial work, but according to one company official, "The people learned quickly." Volunteers offered adult evening classes in town to teach basic reading and writing skills, and "quite a few" took advantage of them.[30] In October 1917 a night school had been organized, allowing those over sixteen who were compelled to work by circumstances to continue their education. As of January 1918, "twenty-nine young men and two young ladies" had enrolled.[31]

Furthermore, education held the key to a brighter future for the young. As early as 1913, Johnson had sought the advice of Sidney G. Gilbreath, president of East Tennessee State Normal School in Johnson City. Gilbreath, although impressed by the brick and cement plants, took a hard line: "The school situation at present in Kingsport is deplorable. I do not know of a more unfavorable situation in the state. To think of two hundred or more children without school advantage in this age could hardly be believed by the more fortunate people of other states. I do not forget, of course, the dilapidated frame house, dirty and filthy, without equipment that is supposed to give educational opportunity, but I count it nothing."[32]

This exchange paved the way for substantial improvements in the immediate situation. The Department of Education at the normal school prepared plans for a three-room building. The cement plant, the brick corporation, and Kingsport Farms each contributed one-third of the $4,000 for the Kingsport Public School at Church Circle, to replace the one-room Oklahoma School that had been built around 1890. The dedication, on 12 September 1913, involved professors from Johnson City, a representative from Nashville, the pastors of three nearby churches, and the Sullivan County Board of Education. This occasion marked the genesis of one of Tennessee's best public-school systems. Professor Fred W. Alexander used the following incident to illustrate the enthusiasm generated by the new facility: "A common laborer—a 'dollar a day man'—stopped an associate on the street and said, 'what do you think? My boy got a grade of 90 in the school. Isn't that great!' Hope comes to the man bound down by common toil because of the chance for his boy, and life was even brighter and his heart was better from the fact that his boy had a grade of 90 from the new school."[33]

When county officials failed to deal with Kingsport's needs, the companies agreed in 1916 to supplement the public term by two or three months. Nonetheless, Gilbreath chided Johnson as the 1916-17 term began: "Unless you develop a first-class high-school, as well as grammar school, at Kingsport, we are going to have to move your big plants from Kingsport to Johnson City. The fact is they ought to have been located here at first!" Ignoring the tinge of jealousy in this comment, Johnson replied simply that a building for the high school was in the works, and "in the meantime we are going to make the very best of our opportunities and difficulties by ripping the partitions out of a couple of residences, organizing the very best business thought of our community into a school board and, despite all the things that hinder us, have a good school this year."[34] By 1920, Kingsport's illiteracy stood just above 10 percent for those ten years of age and older; Sullivan County's, 11 percent; and Hawkins County's, 14.7.[35]

For the first decade or so of its existence, living conditions in the new town remained far from uplifting. Poor housing, even that in limited quantities, and inadequate water and sewerage threatened the public health. In November 1916 a population of 7,260 crowded into 783 houses. "Little regard for sanitation, health and happiness had been shown," wrote the health officer; "with wages high and labor scarce, money was the first thought of all." The highest crude death rate of any year in the history of the town occurred in 1917—26.13 per thousand and 23.1 per hundred births under one year of age.[36] The number of deaths among young adults, children, and infants decreased from 1919 to 1920, but endemic problems surfaced when laborers came into town with their families. An examination of 1,106 schoolchildren in January 1921 revealed that half of them were suffering from malnutrition, 611 had defective teeth, and 591 had diseased tonsils.[37] Dental clinics and compulsory immunizations for students, free of charge, soon became common features of the municipal health program, under the auspices of the KIC, the school system, and the city government. Kingsport, however, remained without a permanent hospital until the 1930s, although physicians and the city government made several short-lived attempts.

By 1916, when Dennis and Johnson began to take firm control of Kingsport's heretofore haphazard development, sanitation became a major concern and garnered considerable attention. During the summer, editorials appeared in the local newspaper, encouraging cleanup efforts. "The time to get busy is now," implored the editorial staff in a piece entitled "Time to Organize and Swat the Fly." "Lime should be used freely in outhouses, alleys, etc. All garbage, manure piles and breeding places should be destroyed. Privy vaults should be made fly proof." Incanting that Kingsport enjoyed "a wide reputation as a health resort, on account of her bracing mountain air, ideal location, pure water and mild climate," the editors suggested that campaigning against flies was precautionary and "in keeping with the sanitary ideas of Kingsport's foremost citizens." By June, "several teams and wagons with a large force of men" were "removing all accumulated trash, filling in depressions and opening up drainage ditches." The newspaper urged cooperation to solve the health menace and for beautification. At the same time, work progressed on the water and sewerage system. In November, Dr. T.B. Yancey, from Somerville, Tennessee, who had been assistant director of rural sanitation for the State Board of Health, resigned his position with Tennessee and the Rockefeller Health Commission to cast his lot with the new town. Known to people of East Tennessee as the "hookworm doctor," he practiced medicine in the model city for the remainder of his life.[38]

Kingsport had a crying need for a pied piper to rescue it from rat infestation, and Yancey led a crusade in 1920. Children were encouraged to kill the rodents and to bring in their tails. Prizes included gold for girls and guns for boys. The burning of city trash pits near Gibsontown flushed out the culprits and aided the competitors. By the third week of July, with almost a month remaining in the contest, 3,800 rats had been exterminated. Neighboring Bristol joined the bounty hunt, and Johnson City, Morristown, and Greeneville were reportedly considering doing so. Johnson, however, made possible "the most successful campaign" another year "by offering $100 cash" as a prize. "Ten thousand rats lost their lives."[39]

The introduction of rural people into an industrial environment involved risks, and the local newspaper occasionally reported accidents; fights, too, sometimes occurred on the job. In 1916 a couple of laborers who were working on the Federal Dyestuff and Chemical plant's new clubhouse became embroiled in a controversy. One laborer, from Montezuma, North Carolina, rendered the other one, from Johnson City, unconscious when he struck him on the head with a pipe wrench. An explosion at the same plant, which destroyed one unit of the facility during May 1917, killed one man immediately and fatally injured two others. The superintendent of the hog ranch at Rotherwood, which was owned by Kingsport Farms, lived only an hour after being caught in the belt of a corn shredder. An employee of the Clinchfield Portland Cement Corporation lost his right leg below the knee after his foot was caught in a crusher. A pipe fitter died in 1919 at Kingsport Pulp Corporation when he came into contact with a high-voltage electrical wire; another man was injured in the same incident. Overcome by aniline poisoning, a worker at the dye plant seemed dead. Acquaintances prematurely started digging a grave, but a physician managed to revive him.[40]

Fires, too, threatened lives and property in the infant town; a fledgling fire department and volunteers fought valiantly, but not always successfully, against a peril that knew no class bounds. The fire whistle sounded in March 1916, and hundreds of anxious citizens rushed into the streets as Kingsport Stores was threatened by a blaze that began in the oil room. A clerk battled the flames with an extinguisher in "a veritable hell of fire" until the fire department arrived. In 1919, two black families, living on the second floor, lost most of their furniture when a frame store building burned. One fireman was badly scorched about the face and neck, and two others were less seriously injured. As the new year dawned in 1921, the Grant residence, a two-story frame structure on Watauga Street that was owned by R.Y. Grant of the leather company, suffered $3,500 to $4,000 damage.[41]

The model city was not without the macabre and the ridiculous. A parade crowd in 1916 saw "the largest elephant in captivity," Big Mary, raise its keeper above its head, hurl him to the pavement, and run one of its tusks through his limp body. It then picked him up and slung him into the huddled townspeople. Tennessee law apparently required that the elephant be put to death. With no weapon to effect its demise in Kingsport, representatives of the Sparks Brothers' Show and the Clinchfield Railroad arranged to transfer it to Erwin, Tennessee. Using a derrick and chain from the railroad's machine shops, they hanged the huge pachyderm.[42] For almost seventy years, the small town of Erwin has borne the stigma of having executed an elephant; consequently, it is only fitting that the model city accept its responsibility for the incident.

Crimes of passion, lust, and violence punctuated the routine of small-town life. During 1919, James C. Whetzel killed his wife, Lillie, at the Kingsport Laundry, where she was working. The whole town was horrified in June 1921 by the rape and murder of an eleven-year-old girl, whose body was found under the bleachers at the baseball field. When a black in his late teens, who had previously been charged with attempted molestation, was arrested for the heinous offense, he was taken to Johnson City under heavy guard because mob violence was feared. Gate receipts from a ball game between the Kingsport community league and a Knoxville team were donated to the family to help pay burial expenses. The father worked at Mead Corporation, and the family lived at the end of Pulp Row. In 1920 local blacks had put up $100 for the arrest of one of their own who had been accused of a statutory offense against a young black girl. In 1928 the Board of Mayor and Aldermen authorized the payment of medical bills for two children, a white girl and a black boy, who were accidentally shot on 20 September 1927, when city and county officers tried to arrest a man who, a few moments before, had allegedly attempted to rob the First National Bank.[43]

A spirit of neighborliness was apparent in the town from its beginnings; J. Fred Johnson was the very embodiment of it. "Everyone gathered at the store and loafed there around the candy and soft drinks counter," an employee recalled. "If a person didn't put in an appearance everyone began wondering if they were ill and Mr. Johnson would start looking around for flowers to send them."[44] If Kingsport were ever to cast off the characteristics of an Appalachian boom town, however, it needed a staunch citizenry to temper the working-class mentality and to establish permanent and sound institutions. When circumstances permitted, Johnson handpicked middle-class professionals for his town. For example, after observing the style and methods of Allen N. Dryden, Sr., a young architect from Chicago who was then representing the Johnson City firm of D.R. Beeson on its Kingsport projects, Johnson urged him to make a commitment to the town. Dryden soon occupied office space in the KIC building and began a successful career as the town's principal architect. His work is reflected, among other places, in the stately residences that were privately commissioned by many of Kingsport's pioneers. Indeed, Johnson likewise was impressed by a Georgian named Lucy McGukin, a classmate of Elizabeth Doggett's at Union Seminary Training School in Richmond, Virginia. When McGukin dined with Johnson, his wife, and Mrs. Johnson's niece Elizabeth, Johnson gave his usual spiel about his town and told Lucy that she should come to Kingsport. A three-year courtship, culminating in marriage, began when Dryden, an elder of the Presbyterian church, met McGukin at the train.[45]

Newcomers joined established families of local gentry—the Grosecloses, Nelmses, Kinkeads, Rollers, and Clouds, along with the Dobynses, transplanted from Hillsville, Virginia—to form the nucleus of the town's elite. To their credit, they made significant civic contributions. Such heads of industries as the Shivells, Wilcoxes, and Palmers established homes and produced progeny. The Platts added a touch of class from New York City. John B. Dennis spent considerable time at Rotherwood when he was a bachelor, as well as after the town's landscape artist, Lola Anderson, became his bride; brother H. Ray Dennis, his show girl-wife Lilla, and their four male offspring were sometimes in residence.

Scores of educators, physicians, attorneys, businessmen, and industrialists joined the throngs who passed through the town; many stayed.

The parents of George Bush, the forty-third vice-president of the United States, lived in Kingsport for six months during 1922. The Simmons Leather Company of St. Louis had sent Prescott Bush, later a United States senator from Connecticut, "to decide what they should do about a leather factory."[46] Karl Goerdel from Laurelton, Pennsylvania, superintendent of the Engineering Division at the time of his retirement and a pioneer builder of Tennessee Eastman, began to work at Kingsport in 1920 as a transit man with a surveying team. James C. White, a native of Solon, Michigan, arrived the same year as a timber cruiser for the company; he became president and general manager in 1945. Walter F. Smith, who hailed from Illinois, joined Kingsport Press in 1923 as general manager of Clinchfield Mills; in 1954, he succeeded E.W. Palmer as president. Edward J. Triebe, from Oswego, New York, came to the Press in 1926 and followed Smith as president in 1960. C.P. Edwards, Jr., a mountain boy from Flag Pond, Tennessee, arrived in Kingsport with his father, a physician, prior to World War I. Attending the Hotchkiss School in Connecticut when the conflict erupted, he went to France as the driver for an ambulance purchased by the student body. In 1918 he returned to Kingsport with $60 as discharge pay, married a Piney Flats, Tennessee, girl, and launched a successful business and civic career.[47] Cofounder of Hamlett-Dobson Funeral Home, Jimmie Dobson of Greeneville, Tennessee, after spending seventy-five days on the front line in France with no relief, claimed "that he just couldn't face going back to planting corn on his family's farm"; instead he came to Kingsport and went to work at the Big Store. W.E. Brown, Sr., one of Kingsport's first elected aldermen, made his way from Letcher County, Kentucky, to the model city. Living with his wife in Bristol, he heard that the American Wood Reduction Company needed an office man, so he hitched a ride over bad roads. Arriving in town, he waded through mud almost up to his knees to get to a boardinghouse on Five Points. Thoroughly disgusted, he was ready to return to Bristol; but a night's sleep restored him. After the job at the American Wood Reduction plant folded, he found employment with the Clinchfield Railroad.[48]

Kingsport favorably impresssed most newcomers. Joseph H. Lewis, twenty-three years old and just out of college, traveled with his bride from Corning, New York, in 1919 to supervise construction of the glass plant. "It was a sparsely populated area with trees 2 inches in diameter planted along the streets, which were paved with mud, mud, mud," he recalled; "everyone wore boots or galoshes." The Lewises liked Kingsport, nonetheless. After the Corning Glass Works closed and they went back to New York, he was enthusiastic about returning to Kingsport. When he learned of efforts to renew glass manufacturing at Kingsport, he convinced Corning to send him back as chief engineer. "I had not lost my love for this little community," he recollected; "the big city was for the birds."[49] During the early 1920s, when Morris Sobel, a Polish-born Jew, first saw Kingsport, he "looked out on [what seemed to be] a midwestern city—empty lots and empty land." But he also saw customers and opportunity, so he established an economy mercantile operation that evolved into one of Kingsport's most prestigious clothiers.[50] Mrs. George Penn, who came from Abingdon, Virginia, in 1921, remembered that her first view of Kingsport was of Bays Mountain and Chimney Top, and she thought it "perfectly beautiful." Mrs. H.J. Shivell, who found "some of the pioneer spirit" useful, recalled fording Steel Creek between Bristol and Kingsport and told about setting a pan of biscuits on the back porch to cool and "watching a rat drag it across the yard, pan and all" when she lived in the Fifties.[51]

For the more cosmopolitan, Kingsport, even with the allure of a novel experiment, seemed a step into the past; but for rural mountaineers, it represented opportunity and hope for the future. One lady recalled her family's move from Speers Ferry, Virginia, to find work: "We brought our furniture on the train. We rented a two-story frame house. I was seventeen years old. My mother and five brothers and sisters came." An elderly man wrote: "I remember how dumb I was. I came from the country—how dumb I was." A resident of Borden Mill Village arrived in August 1929, when he was fifteen: "We moved here from Galax, Virginia in a truck. It was a lot dirtier then." Another "got lost a time or two" in August 1926 because "there were so many circles and curves." Still another had first visited Kingsport as a boy, when he and his father traveled by wagon to sell Irish potatoes and had to ford the north fork of the Clinch River. Selling a load of extract wood brought one youngster to town with his father, and another, age seven, went to Kingsport in a wagon with his father to purchase metal roofing for a barn.[52]

Newcomers from elsewhere in the country and natives of the region attended the same schools and churches. As the town's chief social institutions, they engendered a sense of community. In 1936, when writing to a TVA official, J. Fred Johnson said that a visitor from Washington, D.C., had asked Johnson what he would do in Kingsport if starting again. His reply was: "I would dislike to undertake that, but if I did, it would be to start with the best system of public education of which we were capable, or could learn about, and to encourage the development of churches."[53] Johnson had become a ruling elder in the First Presbyterian Church during 1917 and was for many years superintendent of the Sunday School; his enthusiasm never flagged. He has been credited with assisting in the establishment of dozens of churches of different denominations in the Kingsport area. Dr. Robert King, one of the ministers who officiated at Johnson's funeral in 1944, declared: "The best lots of this city were given to the churches without one dollar of cost.... They labor in vain that build a city except God build it."[54]

Many of Kingsport's elite followed Johnson's lead in the Presbyterian fold, consequently making it perhaps the best financially endowed religious congregation in the town, with Episcopalians in a strong challenging position. Townspeople were also drawn to the Methodist and Baptist establishments in large numbers, although they did not enjoy quite the social status of the Presbyterians and Episcopalians. The Catholics at St. Dominic's had no separate resident parish priest until 1948, but as early as 1914, Father John Callahan, a mountain priest on horseback, had celebrated the first mass in the homes of the few local Catholics.[55] One astute observer commented that in the early days, "there was hardly any social life. Everything centered around the churches."[56] Morning worship, followed by lunch at the gracious Kingsport Inn after it was completed, was the standard Sunday fare for the socially prominent. If "one was invited to dine" at "an exclusive 'family table,' it was proof they'd really 'arrived.' "[57]

Some took issue with Johnson's brand of piety, but no one denied that it was his nature. A friend recalled, "Everybody respected him but not everybody liked him."[58] One person scoffed that Johnson had been known to hold a glass of moonshine at a local celebration, but he did not drink because "he was afraid they'd smell it on him at Sunday School."[59] An attorney, off the record, was less than impressed with Johnson's crocodile tears and his argument, sometimes set forth in a house of worship, that a dollar a day was adequate for a laboring man. A former Tennessee Eastman employee declared: "Kingsport was a good place to live. It was clean enough. J. Fred Johnson was a dirty s.o.b.! He'd let a poor man starve to death." The consensus, however, even among the laboring class, was: "J. Fred Johnson was a fine Christian gentleman who was kind to the poor people of Kingsport."[60]

Only the high regard for public education rivaled the importance of religion in Kingsport. The quality of schools available to blacks and whites—though separate and unequal—steadily improved. City officials, the KIC, and concerned citizens enlisted the help of President Gilbreath at the State Normal School but also looked to Columbia University for expertise. The Gary Plan, or Platoon System, served as a model. William Wirt, superintendent of schools in Gary, Indiana, stressed the importance of work, study, and play as basic components of academic training. Kingsport embraced this concept and devoted attention not only to traditional subjects but also to art, music, vocational training, and physical education.[61] In June 1919 the first graduating class at Kingsport High School numbered 3. During the same summer, 150 boys and girls, grades four through eight, raised gardens on KIC land, and the Board of Education hired a director of music for city schools. In 1920, with white illiteracy for those who were ten years of age or older in the model city at about 9 percent and with that of blacks at more than 20 percent, the school system had a valuable role to play.[62]

The first Board of Education for the City of Kingsport had been appointed on 18 May 1917. Planning for the construction of a high school began within a couple of months, and the bid of the D.R. Beeson architectural firm was accepted on 24 July 1917. Kingsport's first municipal bonds, issued in the amount "of $150,000, bearing 5% interest payable semiannually, with principal maturing serially at the rate of $6,000 annually from 1922 to 1946," were directed toward relieving the school situation; in 1925 an emergency bond issue of $250,000 paved the way for the construction of Dobyns-Bennett High School. Nonresidents soon looked to educational opportunities afforded by the city, and the Board of Mayor and Aldermen decided in 1920 that property owners who paid direct taxes to the town would not have to pay tuition for educating their children, even if they lived outside the incorporated area. From its humble origins at the Oklahoma School, the Kingsport School System advanced significantly within a decade. By 1927 the city boasted five modern school buildings: the elementary schools of Abraham Lincoln, Andrew Jackson, and Central, and the high school, Dobyns-Bennett—all "lily white," in keeping with the standards of the times; Robert E. Lee School, on Wateree and Myrtle streets, served the black school population. In the fall of 1927, twenty-three hundred students were enrolled, and operational expenses for education had amounted to $156,000 in 1926, as compared to $160 in 1913.[63]

Interest in education was not confined to the white community. In February 1919, Robert Clay, state supervisor for schools in Tennessee, had addressed the Board of Mayor and Aldermen, informing its members that the Rosenwald Foundation would match dollar for dollar the construction costs of a school up to $500. He suggested that a meeting be held with the black people before making application. A committee of prominent black citizens, including Professor H.L. Moss, a teacher at the black school in Old Kingsport, was named. Within the month, seventy-five blacks met with city officials to express their interest. In the same year, the Negro Business League, under the leadership of Dr. M.M. Cloud, was organized "to promote the financial and commercial development of the negro and further his educational and social programme."[64]

Black education soon hit a snag. In 1920, when confronted with a labor shortage, City Manager Herbert Kidd recommended that work on a black school to be known as Booker T. Washington be suspended until two white schools under construction could be completed; the Board of Mayor and Aldermen approved this action. When Johnson, representing the KIC, offered to donate all of block no. 90 to the city for a black school, sixty-two white citizens converged on town hall to protest, claiming that the use of the land as a school site would destroy the desirability of their homes and would ruin property values. The board officially remained noncommittal. Six months later, it approved on first reading an ordinance to accept a deed from the KIC for block no. 90 as a public-school site. Architect Allen Dryden began drafting plans, but in February 1925, white citizens continued to oppose the location of the black school. Apparently the resolution of the matter came with the relocation of the old Oklahoma building and its designation as Robert E. Lee School for black children—separate and decidedly unequal. In October 1928 the Board of Mayor and Aldermen accepted a bid from V.L. Nicholson and Company of $32,250 for the construction of Douglass High School near downtown.[65]

Writing about social conditions in Kingsport as they existed in 1945, a resident declared, "For the Caucasian, middle class and upper socio-economic levels, the quality of life...was good."[66] The framework of such a society was already in place by the 1920s. The black population, at 454, constituted only about 8 percent of the official population in 1920, which stood at 5,692; and it posed no serious threat to white supremacy; 5,116 were native white and of native parentage, leaving only 120 whites of foreign birth or foreign or mixed parentage and 2 in the category of Indian and Chinese.[67] About a dozen or so young men of Hungarian (Magyar) descent, who had previously worked for the parent company in Pennsylvania, had come to Kingsport around

1910 as employees of the Portland Cement plant. Some of them found the new town agreeable and settled down with their families.[68] There were a few Jews and Greeks, along with a handful of new arrivals from Syria and Palestine and an Italian-born contractor who occasionally worked on projects in the model city; but the white, Western European strain remained dominant and unchallenged. Males, 2,910 of them, outnumbered females by only 128, although some of Kingsport's "first ladies" labeled Kingsport "a working man's town."[69]

Indeed, it was a man's town; specifically, it was one of business deals, real-estate ventures, engineering feats, backslapping camaraderie at the civic clubs, and enthusiasm for sports.[70] A chain-of-command mentality permeated Kingsport, and deference was paid to those who were perceived to be leaders of the pack. The figure of J. Fred Johnson, who stood approximately five feet ten and one-half inches and weighed in at about 170 pounds, overshadowed all others.[71] With his piercing blue eyes and his attention to detail, he controlled the town. One of the planners observed: "The Kingsport Improvement Company dominated everything. The local government was never thought of. You went to J. Fred." According to the same source, Johnson virtually appointed the city officials.[72] A longtime city employee observed that Johnson kept a close eye on municipal affairs. If something did not please him, the phone rang in City Manager Frank L. Cloud's office; the city manager put on his coat after a brief conversation and hurried up the street to the Improvement Company's offices to confer with Johnson.[73]

Moments of extreme crisis fanned the flames of democracy that were usually banked in the model city. During the mid-twenties, a siege of typhoid fever and several cases of smallpox occasioned town meetings and an emergency bond issue. Physicians were concerned that a revival meeting, which was scheduled to open at a tobacco warehouse in Kingsport on 9 May 1927, would draw crowds from the outlying districts and would effect the spread of smallpox; so the meeting was postponed. Between 30 June and 17 July 1926 the town experienced twenty-five cases of typhoid; so many instances in such a short span spelled trouble. Official commentary blamed the milk from dairies, rather than the water supply. Problems continued through 1927, and in January 1928 the Board of Mayor and Aldermen passed an emergency ordinance to hold a referendum on a bond issue, not to exceed $400,000, for augmenting and extending the waterworks. Voters approved the proposal on 5 May by 236 to 30; 9 ballots were found to be defective.[74]

The guise of town meetings and elections hardly concealed the fact that an oligarchy led by J. Fred Johnson dominated the town. The self-deprecation, to which he seemed given, only enhanced his prestige.[75] His down-to-earth style and his benevolence became a part of local lore. When a silk hat was needed for a talent-show costume, someone thought Johnson might own one and asked to borrow it. His response, "I do not have a high silk hat and I do not like you to think that I am the sort of man to wear a high silk hat," only served to elevate his standing with the common folk. His usual headgear was "a somewhat battered fedora that seemed to land on his head by accident."[76] When a writer for the *Saturday Evening Post* wanted details about Johnson's background for a story, Johnson's "first reaction was decidedly against it." The executive director of the *Kingsport Times-News* attempted to change Johnson's mind, but he remained adamant. "I can't escape the feeling," Johnson wrote, that "when you select one and herald him as having done something extraordinary, if by chance the story of my work at Kingsport should be so considered, it inferentially takes something that belongs to someone else."[77]

Firm in his religious beliefs and personal values, Johnson rarely allowed philosophy to stand in the way of practicality, however; and he seemed less rigid than some of those with whom he had to deal. When one or two men at Kingsport opposed retaining Anna Lee Mitchell as principal at the school in 1916 because they assumed it would be better to have a man, Johnson observed, "I think this is the wrong conclusion myself"; he added that Mrs. James W. Dobyns was also a supporter of Miss Mitchell.[78] When a local real-estate agent informed Johnson that he could settle a right-of-way controversy with the disputing parties for $2,000, J. Fred said, "Settle it, my boy, settle it." Johnson arranged for the same agent to sell some KIC-owned lots to Jews. If anyone complained—and there were hints of anti-Semitism—Johnson could simply say that "Tom did it" and thus escape direct blame. When an acquaintance confronted Johnson with the rumor that Communists were behind a private foundation that had made a sizeable grant to improve health care, Johnson, who was not one to let politics stand in his way, reportedly said, "Would it make any difference if they were?"[79]

Sam Anderson, a longtime employee of J. Fred Johnson and Company, Incorporated, Department Store, when speaking at a Masonic memorial service after the death of the town patriarch, recounted that Johnson "very often wrote little notes about things he wanted done for people or given to them." One such note read: "Please let this poor, little distressed first cousin of yours and mine have a shirt and a pair of overalls. J.F.J." Anderson continued: "The little boy that brought the note was as black as the ace of spades. In talking to Mr. Johnson that night on the telephone he asked me if I had given the little colored boy the things he needed. I replied, 'Yes, I took care of *your* little first cousin.' " Johnson retorted, "Well, Sam, that little negro boy would not have any of the blood of your Father or mine in his veins but as sure as there is a God in Heaven he is your first cousin and mine on the record book up There."[80]

Magnanimous toward the poor and downtrodden and easily moved to tears by the misfortunes of others, Johnson "appreciated a word of thanks from the people he helped";[81] and he generally expected everyone to know and accept his own place. The listing of names and accompanying descriptions in city directories revealed the social stratification: an "employee" of one of the major industries carried more prestige among the working class than a "laborer," a semantic nuance that was reflected in successive compilations. The time and place called for placing an asterisk or a circled c before the names of black people and their businesses in the city directories—a standard procedure. Johnson, who employed a black man as butler and chauffeur,[82] seemed more tolerant of and charitable toward blacks than did many of his contemporaries; the same applied to females.

Women played a vital, albeit subservient, role in shaping the community, and Johnson seemed to appreciate their contributions to public life. He valued his personal secretary, Esther ("Essie") Pfaff, and he bequeathed her $1,000, by the terms of a codicil to his will dated 14 August 1944. Newspaperman W.J. McAuliffe wrote: "In all the conferences about all... things, there was Miss Pfaff and her notebook. Everyone talked freely before her. They knew, if they did not say it, that anyone so wholly trusted by Mr. Johnson, was trusted by them. There was never any talk of leaks from that office."[83] Johnson was devoted to his mother, his two sisters, and his first wife, Ruth Carter, who died during the early 1930s. He left 15 percent of his estate and three pieces of furniture of her choice to his first wife's niece.[84] His second wife, who was also a niece of the first Mrs. Johnson, was a graduate of the University of Tennessee and New York University. She was dean of women at Montreat College at Montreat, North Carolina, at the time of their marriage on 7 March 1936. She later commented that a positive attitude toward opportunities for women existed in Kingsport.[85] On one matter, Johnson did not yield; he refused to countenance women's smoking, and he forbade it in his presence.[86]

Possibilities for active feminine participation and gainful employment seemed somewhat greater in the town's infancy than during later decades. Jobs always existed for female clerks, shop girls, and stenographers; but for the first couple of decades of its existence, a fair number of professional women graced the model city. Several nurses and at least one female physician, Edna W. Brown, served as administrators of Kingsport's hospitals. The KIC hired a woman landscape architect. Lena Barton served as supervising principal of Kingsport Public Schools during 1917, and Augusta Tice, a graduate of Mississippi Woman's College who was also an accomplished musician, became supervisor of public-school music in 1925. Grace Elmore arrived in 1927 from Morristown and taught Latin for the next thirty-five years at Dobyns-Bennett High School. During the 1920s the city hired a school health nurse, and female elementary teachers were ordinary fixtures in the community. Teachers made highly satisfactory brides, and many of the town's early educators soon found prominent husbands. As late as the 1930s, however, married females were not permitted to teach in city schools unless some vested interest of the city or the school system required an exception.[87]

The patriarchy readily accepted the employment of widows and single women and, to a lesser degree, even married women of the laboring classes; they were far less enthusiastic about having middle- and upper-class females earn salaries or wages. As one such woman ruefully put it, "We weren't allowed to work [for pay] so we volunteered."[88] An American pattern, it was magnified in Kingsport.[89] This outlook became even more exaggerated as the town's development stabilized, and some "society" women banded together to protect their sphere. One from the country-club set succinctly stated a prevailing view when she declared that Kingsport would never let a certain female who was suspected of social climbing forget that she had once been a clerk at a local store—never mind that she had a great many personal and professional accomplishments to her credit.

The contributions of a group that a *Times-News* staff writer called "Kingsport's first ladies" lent graciousness and gentility to the town, and they injected a healthy dose of humanitarian sentiment. Mothers' Meetings were held at the Kingsport Public School as early as 1915; among those participating in March were Mrs. James W. Dobyns, Mrs. E.W. Tipton, and Mrs. J.B. Nall. Two women, Mrs. Nall and Mrs. Joseph S. Vance, served on the town's original five-member Board of Education. A few women cast votes in the first municipal election in

1919.[90] The Kingsport Public Library originated with the Kingsport Book Club, organized by such pioneer elite as Penelope Platt and Genevieve Shivell. As volumes accumulated, club members decided that a library seemed desirable, so they established one in the basement of the YMCA building in 1921. It was moved upstairs as it expanded, and in 1932 the book club turned it over to the city. Each year John B. Dennis reportedly donated one hundred books, and during the 1920s, Kingsport Press gave the library a copy of every book that it printed, as well as rebinding old books and magazines free of charge.[91] Nineteen young women met in the community hall at the First Methodist Church and organized the Kozy Korner Klub to aid the church and hospital; four of its charter members survived to witness its fiftieth anniversary.[92]

Although the particular needs of women did not receive top billing in the model city, females did garner a certain amount of consideration. When plans had been formulated for a YMCA building to serve as a community center and when work had begun on it in 1919, Johnson announced that in addition to a dormitory, a gym, a bowling alley, a billiards room, and a swimming pool, "there will be special rooms set aside for young women, since it is intended that they get some benefit from the building." Dr. John Clifford, the YMCA's national secretary, visited Kingsport that year, but the "Y" apparently did not affiliate with the national organization during the 1920s.[93]

For a time in 1929, the National Board of the Young Women's Christian Association thought of expanding the work of its Industrial Department or Town Department into one of the small cities of East Tennessee. Actively promoting union organizing and collective action by female industrial workers, the Industrial Department was especially attentive to the area because of the Elizabethton strike of 1929.[94] According to YWCA records, some person or persons at Kingsport had requested that the organization become involved. "After many letters and interviewing two Kingsport women" who had attended a meeting in Knoxville, representatives visited the planned city. Some twelve to fifteen club and church women met with them and "were most responsive and interested." These women mapped organizational procedure but were surprised at the estimated budget, which included, at their insistence, their own secretary. Recognizing the wisdom of a district association that would share operational expenses, they still could not "see beyond Kingsport" and, although "keenly interested," would not make any commitment.[95] Had Kingsport's industrialists been fully apprised of the YWCA's labor education and organizing, preliminary discussions of this nature would have met with disapproval.

The distance that separated "the ladies" and the working women in Kingsport exceeded the several blocks from Watauga Street to Pulp Row, Cement Hill, and Borden Mill Village. One of the elite first saw "a barefoot child in school" when she came from Oxford, Ohio, to teach music at Kingsport. Young married women of the elite "were able to hire household help"—mostly blacks from Rogersville and Hawkins County for $7.00 a week; a particularly fortunate newcomer brought her maid from Abingdon. "There were no washing machines," they remembered, "and maids scrubbed clothes on a board and cooked on coal stoves."[96] The ladies' fondness for teas influenced residential architecture. According to one source, "They set a formal tea table appointed with sterling silver service, china cups and plates, and open face sandwiches. Guests enjoying this hospitality arrived wearing outfits complete with hats and gloves." Such entertaining required "large rooms, one flowing into another." The traditional design of Allen N. Dryden, Sr., consisted of "a large central hall connecting the formal dining room and living room off which was a solarium and including a spacious kitchen and butler's pantry, [which] comfortably took care of the tea-sipping traffic."[97]

Across town, women lived differently. A daughter of a less fortunate pioneer family remembered that they once had occupied a big tent where her mother cooked for laborers who were building the factories.[98] John Kiss promised his wife that they would not stay long enough at this desolate outpost for her "to use a pound of salt in her cooking." They settled in, however, and Julia Pruszki Kiss found herself presiding over a small house on Cement Hill and becoming "the cook for the whole band of Hungarian workers who had accompanied her husband to Kingsport. At night, the boarders tended the babies, and Julia did their laundry."[99]

Industrialists cloaked themselves in chivalry when they refrained from scheduling women to work at night. Reluctance to pay shift bonuses to females and fears of fraternizing between males and females probably lurked not far in the background. "At first, they didn't work the women on the night shift," an old-timer explained of Tennessee Eastman. "Well, you know, women weren't liberated then. They didn't think it was right to work a woman at night. I mean, she was still treated as a delicate creature." Another old-timer remarked that a woman worker was "still treated as a lady."[100] A teenager, whose right index finger had been severed at the second joint while she was working for ten to fifteen cents an hour at Borden Mills around 1926 or 1927, recalled as a senior citizen, "They were awfully nice to me; I guess they were afraid I would sue them, but Papa had his principles." The company paid her medical bills and covered her loss with approximately $150.[101] A Johnson City woman wrote about what she discovered at one of the factories in Kingsport around 1930, after a girlfriend had helped her get a job there: "When I found out the conditions, I diddnt [*sic*] stay but one day. I talked to several of the girls and they all said I wouldn't make enough to pay my board. The mill pays seven and eight dollars a week. The very best workers make ten. You work ten hours and a half and its night work besides. I don't think I could stand to work at night. So I came back home."[102]

The veneer of self-righteous paternalism in town gave way to old-fashioned horse trading and chicanery in the outlying areas. A local contractor who put in the low bid at Eastman for installing sixty-inch cast-iron pipes that required leaded joints soon found that he was not making costs. No one on the site or in the vicinity had ever worked with such a large waterline before and did not know quite what to expect; spectators came to watch. When Eastman employees informed James C. White that the contractor was losing money, White agreed that the contractor should not only break even but also make a profit. "Trade hard," White advised Howard Wilson, who once worked as a summer laborer and later as a company attorney, "but trade on top of the table so when you walk out of the door everybody knows exactly what the trade is." Around 1930, Eastman paid male laborers twenty-five to twenty-seven and one-half cents per hour, which was five cents more than the prevailing wage in the area.[103]

White had a reputation as a "pretty good trader," better than Perley S. Wilcox. In dealing with the local people, White, as a timber cruiser, arrived at a price that the company was willing to pay per thousand feet or cord on the stump. The amount varied according to the quality of the wood and the lay of the land, but generally he fixed the price at about twenty-five cents.[104] Jasper Ketron, a native of Virginia who grew up in the Arcadia community near Kingsport and worked with an Eastman survey team, provided a rare insight into land deals:

> Back there in the twenties, they wanted to trade a railroad right-of-way down there in Hawkins County and we went down there and looked the thing over

and decided it was going to cost us five or six thousand dollars more to cut through this sandstone and build two bridges. So White says, "See if you can trade with Old Man Lucas." I had the instrument [survey] set up and when it flopped over to turn my angle, Old Man Daddy Lucas [George] came over and looked up there and said, "I want to see through that instrument." "Oh, my God," he said, "It goes right through my tobacco patch." I looked through, I said, "It does, doesn't it, Daddy?" "That's the only cash crop I've got," he says. "Could you move this thing to miss that?" I said, "It's possible," but I said, "You see that shovel back there. He is right on my heels. If you want to put this road around the creek here, why let us have that land and I'll see if I can do some business and swap with you. I don't have time to cut all of that right-of-way out." "Well, I'll put my men in there [tenants] and cut that if you'll run around." I said, "Well, Daddy, how do you want to swap?" He said, "I don't want to give the money back for the right-of-way." He said, "How about swapping even?" I said, "Well, I'll see what I can do." I undone the instrument and took it up.

The next morning we went down and run it out, wrote the description that night, and had it typed up the next morning. . . . Mr. White said, "Give that to Kelly [an attorney] and have him prepare those deeds right now." "Well," he said, "we'll, have to look into the title." I said, "To hell with the title, what we want is the railroad right of way before he changes his mind." Two days later I had the deed down there and had Old Man Lucas sign it. I was in the real estate business for Eastman ever since. They had planned on giving him $2,500. . . . Let them talk themselves into a trap and then close the lid on them, just like they would do to you.[105]

For most area residents, what was happening at Kingsport signaled progress and opportunity. Sociologist Thomas R. Ford conducted a survey among Southern Appalachians during the late 1950s to gauge their responsiveness to industrial society or their reluctance to abandon frontier-agrarian traditions. He decided that "most of the people of the Region . . . have adopted the major goals and standards typical of American society. They, like other people throughout the nation, wish to have larger incomes, greater material comforts, and more prestigeful status." If they cannot "realize these aspirations for themselves, they would at least like to see them realized for their children. In short, the people of the Region have become 'progressive-minded' and 'achievement-oriented' to a surprisingly high degree."[106] The Kingsport experience suggests that such attitudes operated among some Southern Appalachians at least a generation earlier.

Interviews of seventy-one senior citizens, fifty-two men and nineteen women, of Sullivan and Hawkins counties in Tennessee and Scott

County, Virginia, who were employed in Kingsport industries *prior* to 1950 revealed characteristics of a middle-class value system. Some had begun working for as little as fifteen cents an hour, but they shared a common sentiment that industrial employment was a godsend. One wrote that "steady employment—regular checks even though small"—made his existence more pleasant. Another insisted that "life was much easier because I was employed during a depression period." One called his company, Tennessee Eastman, "a good place to work" and said that wages kept improving. One retiree claimed that his life as an industrial worker was "easier and much more interesting" than his years in the United States Marine Corps and the United States Army. Another stated, "I had more money to buy the things that I needed, and I made a lot of good friends." A peer cited "regular hours and equal treatment for all employees." Another one mentioned having "more money, and better health insurance." One respondent commented that "the chiefs of the industries have contributed wisely to the cultural and educational growth of the area," but he said that when he first visited Kingsport, he had not been able to foresee "the amount of industry and the potential for growth and development that later followed." Overwhelmingly, this group considered industrial work easier than farming; few believed that it had been injurious to their health; and women, who earned considerably less than men, seemed pleased with their pay. Their responses were not those of the fatalistic, present-oriented, nonparticipatory human beings described by Presbyterian minister Jack E. Weller and others who have written about Southern Appalachians.[107]

People who earned ten or fifteen cents an hour or a dollar a day during the 1920s obviously could not afford to buy homes in White City that sold for $2,000 to $8,000, and it was not likely that they would rent Improvement Company housing. A 15 percent down payment of $300 to $1,200 was nearly impossible, and many natives looked with distaste on the installment plan. A KIC-owned six-room house rented for $25.00 a month.[108] Renting, however, was not unusual for couples and their children, and many single men and women—general laborers, engineers, and certainly teachers—boarded with families or resided at the Roller Club, the Kingsport Inn, the Homestead Hotel, or less prestigious establishments. Records for 1920, for example, showed 1,302 families in Kingsport and 1,157 dwellings.[109] Neither census reports nor the city directories reveal the apparent magnitude of renting and boarding during the 1920s and the next couple of decades.

The advent of the automobile relieved the housing crisis in the model city, and native landownership in the outlying countryside spared laborers the oppression of a company town. Drawing their identity from the land, they escaped the seemingly helpless plight of laborers in such mountain towns as Marion, North Carolina, and the cotton-mill villages of the Piedmont. By staying on the family homesteads, employing their ingenuity and commonsense know-how to construct decent homes, and sustaining themselves with homegrown vegetables, dairy products, beef, pork, and poultry, area laborers could and did improve their standard of living. Most also remained wedded to such cash crops as tobacco. The regular income of industrial workers, unlike the uncertain return of dirt farmers, made planning possible. A family might look forward to automobile ownership, indoor plumbing, the installation of electricity and telephones as they became available, adequate medical and dental care, high-school educations for their children, and maybe even an outing or vacation.

A 1928 study conducted by the University of Tennessee Extension Service found "no indication of extreme poverty or extreme wealth among the rural people. It is sometimes suggested that manufacturing so upsets the economic equilibrium as to cause these two extremes—wealth and poverty—in the same community. This is not the case in the Kingsport area." The report cited "a more even distribution of wealth" and increased wealth per capita. The Extension Service found that many who worked in the model city drove their own cars to and from work; others contracted with their neighbors for transportation. The passenger rate from Church Hill, a village ten miles southwest of Kingsport, was $2.00 per week.[110] It was not unusual for East Tennesseans and their Virginia neighbors to commute thirty miles or more one way. By the 1930s, bus companies sent their vehicles into the valleys and hollows over dirt and gravel roads. This service for shift workers and shoppers from rural communities survived until the 1950s. For those within walking distance of railroads, particularly the Clinchfield, a day's outing in town began with "catching the train."

Kingsport, for area residents, was not just a place to work. While the elite might reside on Watauga Street or Orchard Court, attend the religious institutions on Church Circle, and take Sunday lunch at "The Inn," many workers and their families lived on outlying family-held land, attended the rural churches, and maintained their ties with kinfolk. Nonetheless, there were still lots of interesting things to see and do in town. When 142 young men left for army training on 20 September 1917, the mayor declared the afternoon a holiday. About two years later, veterans organized an American Legion post and named it for Sergeant Hagan Hammond, "the first boy from Kingsport to lose his life in action." Outlaw Emmett Dalton, of the famous Dalton Gang that robbed banks in Kansas, was scheduled to speak in the model city during 1917; his subject, "The Wages of Sin Is Death." Evangelist Billy Sunday preached at the high school in 1920. Republican gubernatorial candidate Alfred Taylor, who had run a losing race against his brother Robert, a Democrat, in 1886 for the same office in Tennessee's "War of the Roses," and his family quartet appeared in Kingsport during the spring of 1920; he went on to victory in November. The outdoor performances of the Kingsport Concert Band, which was organized in 1907 and reorganized in 1916 and 1920, "became something of a community institution." The Nu-Strand Theater opened at 1:30 P.M. on 1 April 1925 with a showing of "A Thief in Paradise." American Legion block parties attracted huge crowds; in 1926, some twenty thousand attended. Held in November to commemorate Armistice Day, they generally lasted three days and "featured round and square dancing, continuous entertainment and dozens of side attractions."[111]

No event rivaled the week-long summer Chautauquas of the late teens and twenties, featuring everything from scientist-lecturers to Royal Hawaiian singers.[112] "Reflecting its Sunday church-school origins, the Chautauqua glorifed American values, specifically those of domestic fidelity, public morality, clean living, and genuine neighborliness," writes historian Conal Furay. "There was also an abundance of patriotic fervor woven into the lengthy daily programs." It suited Kingsporters, for middle- and upper-class residents exhibited "an optimistic cast of mind" that fostered "a diffuse romanticism" and worked "its way into major experiences as well as the cracks and corners of day-to-day living."[113] Perhaps because it was "a young person's town,"[114] or maybe because of its development as a planned city, citizens had a propensity "to treat reality somewhat more favorably" than it deserved.[115]

Although moonshine whiskey was an adequate substitute for bathtub gin, Kingsport remained unscathed by steamy jazz, violent gangsters, and daring flappers. It had more in common with Sinclair Lewis's *Main Street* than F. Scott Fitzgerald's *This Side of Paradise*, and denizens of the model city more nearly resembled George F. Babbitt than Al Capone. Residents of the town seemed affected by the dichotomous paradox of progress and nostalgia that characterized the American self-image of the 1920s, a kind of "nervousness that induced intellectuals to search for certainty" and "prompted the general public to cling to familiar ideas with nearly hysterical intensity." Historian Roderick Nash writes: "Many Americans felt uneasy as they experienced the transforming effects of population growth, urbanization, and economic change. On the one hand, these developments were welcome as steps in the direction of progress. Yet they also raised vague fears about the passing of frontier conditions, the loss of national vigor, and the eclipse of the individual in a mass society."[116] As an emerging industrial center, Kingsport symbolized progress, but its setting and its development accommodated the pioneering impulse of the frontiersman and the hardy individualist.

The laboring classes in the city and those from its periphery may not have been quite so enthusiastic as were the favored and the elite inside corporate limits. Nonetheless, the former occupied an important place in the plan, retained their sense of self-worth and dignity, and held a personal stake in the town's future. By the end of the 1920s the social dynamics were set: the flow of population and money from elsewhere in the country that filtered through the industries; rising entrepreneurs and professionals from the ranks of newcomers as well as natives; and the Southern Appalachian labor supply. Significant portions of all elements shared J. Fred Johnson's psychic world. This novel experiment—a planned, diversified industrial city in Upper East Tennessee—attracted national attention; more than one hundred inquiries from universities, municipal research organizations, civic clubs, and other cities poured into Kingsport during the first seven months of 1928.[117] Meanwhile, the density of population continued to increase, businesses proliferated, and urban amenities expanded. The 1930s brought the burdens of the Great Depression and made Kingsport, whatever its imperfections, an enigma, an industrial city experiencing growth.

6

The Model City in Depression and War

"Few manufacturing centers have suffered less from the four years of business depression than Kingsport, the planned industrial city of the East Tennessee hills," boasted local journalist Howard Long in a 1933 issue of *Manufacturer's Record.*[1] Weathering economic distress better than many American cities became a mixed blessing as Kingsport beckoned the unemployed and homeless. The Great Depression, the New Deal, and the world war that loomed over these years before unleashing its full fury in the 1940s—all profoundly affected the model city. Although the town continued to enjoy a great deal of favorable publicity, all of the promotional gimmicks of the 1920s and the attention that the region received with the creation of the Tennessee Valley Authority brought criticism. Nonetheless, the years of depression and war marked an extraordinary period of growth and maturation for Kingsport. The influence of the Kingsport Improvement Company declined, extensive construction occurred, city government became more responsible, and industrial development continued. Former leaders aged, some died, and new ones attempted to fill their places. Dyed-in-the-wool capitalists, as it suited their purposes, embraced federal programs that smacked of socialism; and the strong thread of patriotism that had been woven into the social fabric steeled townspeople and area residents as they responded to the needs of a nation engulfed in war. Failure to implement certain aspects of the carefully executed physical plan, coupled with hard times, exacerbated undesirable conditions; but these troubled, challenging years required flexibility. Clearly, the model city assumed an identity shaped more by historical realities than by planning ideals.

In the months just before the stock market collapse of October

1929, Kingsport had experienced significant retail expansion. Such new businesses as Parks-Belk, Charles Stores, and Montgomery Ward began to fill the 200 block of Broad Street. Yet the model city was not unaffected by external forces. The abrupt closing of the Farmers and Merchants Bank during the spring had suggested trouble. On 8 November 1931 the Bank of Kingsport shut its doors, but the First National Bank (precursor of the First American National Bank-Eastern) took over all of its accounts without losses to depositors. The two banks had shared some of the same officers. In 1926, for example, William Roller, the president of First National, sat on the Bank of Kingsport's Board of Directors, and J. Fred Johnson served as a director of both financial institutions, as did Dr. E.W. Tipton. Johnson replaced Roller as president that same year, however. Enjoying a virtual monopoly, First National handled municipal accounts and industrial transactions. Within a few years, payrolls alone exceeded $750,000 monthly. Somewhat defensively, a civic publication admitted that it might "appear a bit strange" that "there should be but one commercial banking institution," but added that the First National Bank "adequately serves, with complete satisfaction, every banking need of the city and adjacent area." Meanwhile, on 4 May 1930, Johnson, Tipton, James C. White, C.P. Edwards, Jr., A.D. Brockman, and Colonel E.W. Palmer had founded the Kingsport Building and Loan Association, which was renamed Kingsport Federal Savings and Loan Association when it received a federal charter in 1935 and was the forerunner of Heritage Federal Savings and Loan Association.[2]

Banking and commerce, although a bit sluggish, did not collapse. The onset of the depression and the tangled finances of John B. Dennis, however, widened the gap between vision and implementation in the planned city and diminished the guiding influence of the Kingsport Improvement Company. H. Ray Dennis wrote to John Nolen in March 1933: "We have, as you know,... assumed the entire burden of making Kingsport bear fruit. The work must continue but in order to do this the time has come when we must broaden our foundations to take in fresh interests." A couple of months later, Clinton Mackenzie reported to Nolen that he had conversed at length with John and Ray Dennis. MacKenzie's verdict was: "Their financial condition is at Low Ebb."[3] A report prepared by William B. Franke confirmed this assessment. Franke recollected in 1971 that the Securities Company and John B. Dennis had been indebted to the New York Trust Company. Mortimer Buckner, then chairman of the board, "was the type of banker who rated integrity above financial standing and sometimes this caused trouble for him and the Bank." Although Buckner seemed unconcerned about the plight of the Dennises, "it was a source of great worry to some of the other officers." They finally prevailed upon the chairman of the board to pursue the matter. As a result, Buckner took Franke to see John B. Dennis and told Dennis that unless Franke "were authorized to make a study of The Securities Company the Bank would be forced to call its loans." "Mr. John Dennis, while making it unmistakably clear to me that he wanted no part of me," declared Franke, "finally agreed to the study, and indeed, he had no choice in the matter."[4]

Franke reported that while he and Dennis "always disagreed on business matters," they became the best of personal friends and saw each other regularly. The report that Franke submitted "did nothing to alleviate the fears of the officers of the New York Trust Company." The group of companies that operated loosely under the auspices of the Securities Company was "insolvent to the extent of approximately $40,000" and possessed a net worth of "slightly over a million dollars," mostly in real estate whose value was subject to many variables. The accountant made several recommendations for remedying the situation and sent a long memorandum to John B. Dennis, outlining possible changes in the corporate and financial structures of the group of companies. "Shortly thereafter while we were visiting the Dennises in Biltmore Forest," Franke recounted, "I asked Mr. Dennis whether he had received the memorandum and he said that he had and pulled it from the bottom drawer of his desk to show me. When I asked him if he had read it he said he had not had time. I knew then it was useless to pursue this further."[5]

The precarious condition of Dennis's finances prevented the continuation of physical development under the control of the KIC. Indeed, following the flurry of activity around 1916 to 1920, the Improvement Company had lost the initiative. If the Dennises had tired, J. Fred Johnson had not. In 1926 he had recruited Earle Sumner Draper to draft a general plan for Fairacres, a beautiful tract of approximately 250 acres that was held by the heirs of J.W. Dobyns, some of which extended beyond city limits.[6] What was to become a lovely residential area began to materialize over the next couple of decades. Draper had maintained his cordial relationship with Johnson and the Dennis brothers after leaving Nolen's employ. Draper had made a trip to Bangor, Maine, to look over the Dennis family's cemetery and had prepared a report for its beautification. On one trip to Kingsport, he brought Henry Kendall of Kendall Mills; they stayed at Rotherwood, and Kendall listened to Johnson's speech on Kingsport. Draper also did some work on Borden Mill Village and the Eastman housing projects. Later, around 1930 or 1931, Draper prepared the Ridgefields plan, which he described as his largest venture at Kingsport, for C.P. Edwards, Jr. Preliminary development of the two thousand-acre spread, which would include a new country club, a golf course, and an extensive residential area, awaited the end of World War II.[7]

Apparently John Nolen resented Draper's involvement in Kingsport after Draper had left Nolen's office, opened his own firm in Charlotte, North Carolina, and established a second office in Atlanta, Georgia. The two had engaged in a brief correspondence during 1920 and 1921. Draper informed Nolen in December 1920 that he had enough work to keep about eighteen men busy, but when he proposed a joint venture between the two firms at Spartanburg, South Carolina, in April 1921, Nolen countered that he was unwilling to enter into such an arrangement because Draper did not have the proper experience for the task at hand.[8] In 1933, after Draper had been named director of the Tennessee Valley Authority's Division of Land Planning and Housing, Clinton Mackenzie, who was also interested in a position with TVA, wrote to Nolen: "I understand that [Arthur E.] Morgan has already offered such a position to Draper who was once in your employ. Johnson had no hand in influencing this appointment."[9] According to Draper, he was chosen because of his experience with town planning, particularly mill villages, in the South. Morgan, he recalled, had "put through a call to me at my Charlotte office. They informed him that I was staying at the Cosmos Club [in Washington, D.C., apparently]. He saw me there. Only one other man had been hired, H.A. Morgan—not even [David] Lilienthal." With offices at the old Department of the Interior building, Draper began selecting personnel for his division. "It was pitiful," he recalled, "to see the talented people—engineers and architects—asking for low-paying jobs to support their families." Draper did not forget Johnson or Kingsport when the TVA town of Norris was under way: "We had to build a large school there and Kingsport Brick Corporation was interested in supplying the brick. They were the low bidder, about 1933-1934. Fred Johnson told me later that this was the largest order they had ever received."[10]

As all of this would indicate, the impetus for continued growth at Kingsport even during the 1920s derived from myriad sources, a pattern that became even more pronounced during the 1930s. That the civic center complex failed to materialize as planned was directly related to the diminishing influence of the Dennises. Federal revenue facilitated the construction of the United States Post Office at the corner of Broad and New streets, and the American Gas and Electric Company, of which Kingsport Power was an affiliate, erected a companion structure on the same block. The library, the police station, and city hall, projected by Nolen for this location, never left the drawing board. Work on the post office, designed by New Yorker Thomas Hastings, began during 1930, one of several public projects that helped to relieve local unemployment. By early November 1931, this building had been completed; the power-company structure, the work of local architect Allen N. Dryden, Sr., opened in September 1932.[11]

Plans for a community hospital had lain dormant for almost fifteen years. Several acres located on one of the most scenic heights of the city had attracted would-be purchasers; but the KIC, true to the original intent, refused to sell. Just seven blocks from the heart of the downtown and protected by ravines that ensured quiet and warded off encroachment, the proposed site seemed almost ideal. After a series of hospitals and clinics at nine different locations had failed, the town badly needed a modern, properly equipped medical complex. Johnson noted that "the owners of the two private hospitals" in 1931 "were anxious to abandon them...by reason of poor construction and inadequate facilities...unfitted for the purposes they are serving."[12]

Citizens gave hospital construction top priority, and in 1931, J. Fred Johnson went to New York City to solicit funding from the Rockefeller Foundation and the Commonwealth Fund. Although the Rockefeller Foundation was not assisting in the building of new hospitals, Barry C. Smith led Johnson to believe that the Commonwealth Fund, which Smith directed, could provide 75 percent of the total cost of a $270,000 facility under certain conditions: (1) the closing of two privately owned hospitals in town and the support of the local medical profession for a new hospital; (2) a construction site; (3) a board of trustees or directors independent of the medical profession; and (4) 25 percent of the cost of construction and equipment. The matching funds concerned Johnson.[13]

In February 1932, Johnson sought advice as well as a contribution from George Eastman. Writing that he was ashamed to admit it, Johnson expressed doubts that the citizenry was able to donate the necessary funds to fulfill Commonwealth's fourth condition. He also clearly outlined the situation: "If I were asked to designate one need for which mountain people suffer more than anything else in their simple lives, I should say it is for modern medical and surgical treatment." Noting that he did not know of a single instance in which the people had not responded generously, he stated his reluctance to impose on them again because of "the strain... of this unusual time." He reminded Eastman that except for "a very few men, who get what we consider good salaries," the town "is made up almost entirely of mountain people who have moved here to work in our industries, buy their little homes and give their families better chances in life."[14] Eastman, preoccupied with his own troubles, committed suicide within a month; but officials at Tennessee Eastman in Kingsport rallied to support the project. Perley S. Wilcox and James C. White were among the nine incorporators representing the community who in July 1933 obtained the charter for the hospital as a benevolent, charitable, nonprofit organization.[15]

Through the Community Chest campaign of November 1933, which helped produce some six thousand pledges, the town raised $76,985 in less than a year. Johnson made another trip to New York City and met with representatives of the Commonwealth Fund, which had been established in 1918 by Mrs. Stephen V. Harkness. Although he had learned since his first visit that plans for the expansion of the fund's rural hospital activities had been suspended, Smith and others agreed to meet with Johnson. According to Sam H. Anderson, a close business associate, Johnson said that he prayed constantly as he went up in the elevator: "Lord let them give us funds so we can have a hospital at Kingsport." He was informed that no money was available, but he told his story anyway and was able to get another appointment for the next afternoon. He claimed that he continued his prayer until he walked into the office at the designated time. He managed to secure a commitment for $192,269. This money from the Commonwealth Fund's Division of Rural Hospitals, plus local donations and numerous in-kind contributions by businesses and industries, paved the way for construction. On 8 June 1934, V.L. Nicholson and Company received the contract; on 27 July 1935 the contractor delivered the buildings to the owners; and on 9 August the dedication occurred.[16]

The construction of the hospital during the depths of depression stands as a remarkable testimonial to the "Kingsport spirit" and to J. Fred Johnson's persuasiveness, but it should not obscure the fact that these years were occasioned by considerable human suffering and financial difficulties. On 7 January 1930, Dr. W.H. Reed of General Hospital and Dr. Thomas McNeer of Marsh Clinic and Hospital, having sustained losses of between $10,000 and $12,000 during 1929, petitioned the Board of Mayor and Aldermen for reimbursement. City government increased its appropriation for the Salvation Army by $150 for February, March, and April 1930 because of the unusual amount of work; transient quarters reportedly overflowed with the homeless. James C. White, who served on the advisory board, wrote the *Kingsport Post* in October 1930 that this agency in Kingsport, as elsewhere, was "reaching people who are in the greatest need, and in many cases are not in a position to secure help in any other way." He estimated that requirements for direct relief would be higher the next year. The city budget for 1931 forecast $2,400 for the Salvation Army. Late in 1930, Johnson, Colonel Palmer, and others persuaded the city to proceed with work on Improvement Districts 70 and 72 "in order to partially relieve [the] unemployment condition in [the] community" and "furnish employment to citizens of Kingsport who are now and have been unemployed for a long period of time." In 1935 the Kingsport Cemetery Corporation, owned by the Dennises, requested reimbursement for the cost of pauper burials, which it had previously absorbed.[17]

Extraordinary measures were taken, although the city itself was forced to borrow from private citizens and to initiate an installment plan for the payment of taxes; some accounts of individuals, businesses, and corporations meanwhile appeared to be uncollectible; and beggars appeared on the streets. Leading citizens, J. Fred Johnson representing the KIC, C.P. Edwards, Jr., Sam H. Anderson, the Dobyns brothers, and J.R. Pecktal, petitioned for the creation of improvement districts on property that they held in order to make work for the jobless; municipally generated public employment continued throughout the 1930s. James C. White repeatedly pleaded for more money for the Salvation Army. Johnson's secretary, Essie Pfaff, was among many who loaned the town thousands of dollars; the city government issued one of the largest of these promissory notes to Mrs. J.W. Groseclose, for $10,000 plus 6 percent interest per annum, and another to the Tennessee Eastman Credit Union, for $25,000 at 4 percent, a few years later. Delinquent taxes amounted to $159,216.31 on 31 December 1935; of this sum, $118,987.98 had been carried over from 1934 and 1935. The latter figure came to approximately $5,000 more than the total of all notes payable by the city at the time. In March 1936, however, the voters remained undaunted when they approved, 566 to 87, a bond issue, not to exceed $300,000, for remodeling and enlarging Lincoln School as a junior high school and for erecting an elementary school. Two months earlier the local American Legion organization, Hammond Post, had voted to buy ten and one-half acres at the intersection of the Bristol and Johnson City highways, now East Center Street and Memorial Boulevard, to establish a recreational area that would include a swimming pool, carnival grounds, a ball field, and a home for the post.[18]

Townspeople responded to natural disasters with the same self-help approach that they used to address financial setbacks. On 14 March 1933, a tornado struck the Cherry Hill section just outside of town during the early evening. Four persons died instantly, an elderly woman expired en route to a hospital, and nine others were critically hurt. The death toll had risen to eight by the next day; and $100,000 worth of farm animals had been lost when the storm touched down in outlying sections. Estimates of total injuries rose to one hundred or more. The injured and the homeless poured into Kingsport; some were taken to the two hospitals, and others were taken to private homes, hotels, and the Salvation Army headquarters. Every doctor and nurse in town reportedly worked through the night. A Red Cross field worker rushed to East Tennessee from Washington, D.C., to take charge of relief. The Salvation Army set up a kitchen in the stricken area and provided temporary shelter. The state legislature appropriated $10,000 in aid, and the American Legion in Kingsport donated $200. Other civic groups also raised funds to help the victims.[19]

Most people during this difficult decade seemed resolved to make the best of a bad situation. The Community Chest drive of 1930 exceeded its $18,000 goal within five days, with pledges totaling $21,328. Although the directors had set no yardstick for contributions, the general chairman, when asked, suggested a day's pay for hourly workers, two days' pay for those who were paid on a weekly basis, and four for people who received monthly salaries. Mrs. T.B. Yancey led a crusade during these times to establish and maintain Faith Home for abandoned children, which functioned for several years through voluntary contributions, hard work, and religious conviction.[20] During the summer of 1934 the city set aside a block on Cherokee Street, between Market and Center streets, for a farmers' market. It foundered, but eventually a market was established on Cherokee between Center and New, which flourished throughout the war years. Townspeople continued to stage Fourth of July celebrations. An estimated four thousand spectators attended the parade in 1934; fireworks, speeches, and an air circus with thirteen stunt fliers and a woman wing walker added to the hullabaloo. A few months later, Christmas sales exceeded those of the three previous seasons. The cost of a doll ranged from 5 cents to $2.98; little red wagons sold for $1.98. In 1935 the Kingsport Merchants Association kicked off the gift-buying season with a parade and a fireworks display. In the same year, Dobyns-Bennett High School won its first Big Six Conference title in football, a cause for considerable celebration in the model city.[21]

The housing situation, which had been acute since the city's inception, worsened during the thirties. The vast expanses of vacant land attracted the homeless. Squatters who had no place to live erected shacks from scrap wood and metal on unoccupied land and created a particularly undesirable area known as Black Bottom. When an attempt was made in 1934 to evict some of the occupants, attorney John R. Todd, speaking on their behalf, appeared before the City Council on 18 September to request that they be allowed to remain on the premises until 1 May 1935. Mayor Glen Bruce appointed a committee to investigate. At the next meeting, the formal report, based on the investigation of eighteen families, concluded that it was not the responsibility of the Board of Mayor and Aldermen to provide housing.[22]

A year later, the problem persisted, and the city government requested an investigation by the Sullivan County Health Department. Dr. F.L. Moore found that eighty-nine persons were living in nineteen shacks that had leaky roofs, twelve outdoor privies, all of inferior construction, and a common water supply from a single tap. One family lived in a tent, and another family—a man, a woman, and a seven-year-old child—were existing in a five-by-eight-foot one-room shack. Practically all of these families were subsisted on Salvation Army relief. Eventually, Todd and several others bought some of the land, subdivided it into small lots, and built inexpensive housing that had low rent. This ameliorated the plight of some but was not able to address the full scope of the problem. Throughout the thirties, poverty-stricken and disabled people clustered in back alleys and on the river banks without heat, electricity, or toilet facilities. In other instances, substandard housing provided some shelter. In one case, eight to ten families shared one commode that was located between their homes. Rotting floors, smelly oil stoves, and dilapidated porches contrasted sharply with better architecture in the model city.[23]

The dimensions of the housing problem, unemployment, and the demand for public services clearly exceeded the KIC's capacity to deliver, which made the townspeople, who were already accustomed to paternalism, receptive to signals from Washington, D.C. Before Franklin Delano Roosevelt took the oath of office, John Nolen had written to J. Fred Johnson that "Kingsport is very soon going to be very much 'on the map.' " Nolen predicted that "Henry Ford's recently expressed opinion in the public press, the proposed development of Muscle Shoals, and the views that are getting currency about the policies of the President-elect, all point to the type of development of which Kingsport is as good an example... as can be found in the United States." Johnson referred Nolen's letter to H. Ray Dennis but remarked that "the President's scheme" seemed "a long ways from accomplishment" and that he was not sure that it was feasible. Johnson added, however, that it might "result in the expenditure of a great deal of money" in East Tennessee, "which would undoubtedly produce local benefits much needed."[24]

On 20 April 1933, leaders in the Tennessee Valley from Bristol to Chattanooga convened at Knoxville under the auspices of the University of Tennessee, where Dr. Harcourt A. Morgan, one of TVA's initial triumvirate, served as president. The conference dealt with the lofty subject "Diffusion, Expansion and Companionship of Agriculture and Industry in the Tennessee Valley." En route to the meeting, federal officials had stopped over in Kingsport to see for themselves the model city which, according to the *Knoxville Journal,* was "recognized as an outstanding experiment in decentralization and diffusion of industry and agriculture." During the afternoon of the one-day meeting, as the newspaper had predicted, Kingsport was "memorialized." Colonel E.W. Palmer, standing in for J. Fred Johnson who had illness in his family, warned against hiring the "dregs of humanity" who would pour into the region as soon as development began.[25]

In spite of all of this, in May, Clinton Mackenzie informed Nolen that John B. Dennis apparently had "no knowledge of the Tennessee valley project except as you have enlightened him"; but Mackenzie noted that Dennis "commences to see how it might help Kingsport." A couple of months later, Mackenzie advised Nolen that he had seen Ray Dennis several times but that John Dennis had "only been in the office for a few minutes each day." Mackenzie added: "They are now sitting. They seem to appreciate slightly some industrial possibilities you mentioned. Otherwise no action I know of."[26]

The Tennessee Valley Authority had little immediate impact on Kingsport's development. Already established, heavily infused with a commitment to private enterprise, and fiercely autonomous, the town gratefully exploited opportunities to do business with the federal agency but made no move to become dependent upon it. Although Johnson and Arthur E. Morgan became good friends, the city patriarch, who was deeply involved with the privately owned local power company, was less than enthusiastic about publicly generated electricity for the city. Like the remainder of the area drained by the Tennessee River and its tributaries, Kingsport ultimately benefited from flood control, recreational facilities, and the industrial and commercial development that TVA fostered in the entire region; the privately owned Kingsport Power Company, however, continued to supply electricity to Kingsport.

The model city and Upper East Tennessee quickly reaped the rewards of yet another federal project: the Tri-City Airport. Made possible by the Works Progress Administration, the airport, which affords the best example of long-term cooperation between Bristol, Johnson City, and Kingsport, was born of necessity. During the early 1930s, Kingsport, like other cities across the country, began to explore the possibilities for air passenger and freight service. What may have been the first freight shipment from the model city occurred on 1 February 1932. When the West Virginia Board of Education placed a rush order on 30 January with the Kingsport Press for some textbooks that were not in stock, no one thought of turning down the business. Within twenty-four hours, the books had been printed, bound, and hurried to Bristol, which had the closest thing to an airfield in the area at the time. At 12:20 P.M., pilot W.L. Small, with the books on board his plane, took off for Charleston, West Virginia, where he landed at 1:30 P.M. Half an hour later, the books were in the hands of the customer.[27]

For several years, barnstorming aviators had used a clearing in the Lovedale section of town for landings when they took people up in open-cockpit biplanes for a view of Kingsport. In 1931 the Board of Mayor and Aldermen observed that there was some community interest in establishing an airport. Ludington Airlines, in January 1933, considered Kingsport as a stopover between New York and Nashville; and the city government agreed to use its equipment to improve the Lovedale field. The idea failed to materialize, however, which placed Kingsport at a disadvantage to Bristol, which had become a landing site for airmail and passenger planes. Johnson City's leaders, bridled by Bristol's seeming superiority, proposed a cooperative venture with Kingsport. As early as December 1933 the Kingsport Board of Mayor and Aldermen considered joining with Erwin, Elizabethton, Jonesboro, and Greeneville as well as Johnson City. Prominent figures in Bristol, realizing that their tiny field would soon be inadequate, agreed to work with Kingsport and Johnson City but rejected Gray Station in Washington County, a site that was then being considered for the airport. Finally, area leaders settled on a location near Blountville, the seat of Sullivan County, which was about equidistant from the three cities. In May 1935, city officials urged State Senator John R. Todd and Representative Brack R. Sams to proceed with enabling legislation for a bond sale to finance Kingsport's contribution to the project.[28]

The three cities formed a joint committee in April 1935 to raise $35,000 locally and to seek $350,000 in federal funds. A three-man committee represented Kingsport, and J. Fred Johnson, as usual, was deeply committed. Federal officials had become aware of the effort by early May. J.E. Moreland, assistant state construction engineer in charge of aviation, advised United States Secretary of Commerce Daniel Roper of the industrial significance of the three cities. Because the area served as a commercial center for approximately two hundred thousand people and home to plants "owned by firms of national importance," Moreland claimed that the venture could result in "a very high-class airport."[29] In July, Johnson made a trip to Nashville to confer with Colonel Harry Berry, state administrator of the Works Progress Administration (WPA). Johnson's plan included a contribution of $25,000 from the three cities and from Washington and Sullivan counties to buy three hundred acres if the WPA would allocate $500,000 to build the airport. Johnson was persuasive, and Berry immediately called Harry Hopkins in Washington, D.C., to set up an appointment. On 24 July Johnson and Berry conferred with Hopkins in the capital and received a favorable response, but Hopkins countered with another proposition: $50,000 from local sources and $400,000 from the federal government.[30]

The applicants justified the construction of the field as a refueling stop for airmail service and passenger traffic, for use by the War Department, and for the protection of national forests. A quarrel between Sullivan and Washington counties over which one would supervise the work temporarily jeopardized the project. Meanwhile, 162 previously unemployed men had been given jobs to clear the land and build a temporary construction road. By 6 September 1935, all preliminary details had been settled, and documents had been signed by local authorities to forward to Washington via Berry's office. Officials in the three cities, however, expressed some concern that the standard contract of the WPA stated that it was under no obligation to complete any project. Work began, however, on 12 October 1935 and proceeded with only minor interruptions. Contributions were as follows: Sullivan

County, $12,000; Bristol, Tennessee, $8,000; Johnson City, $20,000; and Kingsport, $10,000. The ownership ratio was fixed accordingly.[31]

The estimated costs of $555,899.22 in September 1935 escalated to $1,050,136.77 by the time the facility was completed in 1937. Colonel Berry, in January 1937, lamented that his approval of the construction of Tri-City Airport had caused him "grief." A representative of American Airlines "raised quite a howl" when he discovered a 5 percent grade in front of the terminal; he claimed that his planes could not operate under such conditions. The chief engineer for the WPA in Tennessee reported "the existence of a considerable amount of solid rock in the mound upon which the administration building is located, and in the ground leading up to the building" and called for "more money for heavy shooting." Nonetheless, as befitted the final stages of a project, crowds gathered, bands played, dignitaries spoke, and the name of one of Tennessee's politicians, United States Senator Kenneth D. McKellar, was affixed to the airport when it was dedicated on 5 November. At an elevation of 1,520 feet, it actually covered 192 acres of the 323-acre site and featured an east-west runway of 3,584 feet and a north-south one of 3,150 feet.[32]

Authorities in Kingsport rapidly grasped the pork-barrel implications of the New Deal but less quickly recognized the disadvantages of glaring publicity. Journalists, investigative reporters, governmental bureaucrats, and union officials followed federal money into the region. Southern Appalachia was being discovered again.[33] In October 1933 the Board of Mayor and Aldermen authorized the city manager to apply for a loan and grant of $12,500 from the Federal Emergency Relief Administration under the provisions of the National Industrial Recovery Act of the previous June. The blue eagle, the symbol of the National Recovery Administration (NRA), "clutching a gear cog in one claw and bolts of lightning in the other," soon soared over the model city. The codes set minimum pay for office workers at twelve to fifteen dollars per week, depending on the size of the city, and that of experienced factory workers at about forty cents an hour. This occasioned an 11 percent pay increase for hourly employees at the Mead Corporation. Kingsport barbers became the first trade group to display the new emblem, and grocers cut their operations by twenty hours under NRA codes. Foreign visitors, who were usually quite taken with the Tennessee Valley Authority, could easily stop over for a tour of the planned city. In March 1936, two Russians made an inspection visit at Kingsport Press. The chairman and senior engineer of the graphics industry in the Soviet

Union then proceeded to Rogersville to see the International Card and Label Company. Accompanied by an interpreter, they continued their journey toward Norris Dam.[34]

Proponents of big business eagerly contrasted privately planned Kingsport with its East Tennessee counterpart, TVA's development of Norris, approximately twenty miles north of Knoxville. "Instead of spending $1,500,000 on a temporary construction camp for Norris Dam," wrote Charles Stevenson in *Nation's Business,* "the TVA decided to invest twice that amount and solve the world's ills." In 1935, Stevenson reported that a representative of the KIC (Jerry C. Stone), "before the TVA ideals had gone sour at Norris," had commented that "for 15 to 18 years we have been doing in a small way some of the things which the Government plans for the Tennessee Valley." Citing Kingsport as "one of the nation's most unusual cities," Stevenson declared the model city to be "a lesson" to the government whose "publicity agents" launch "into adjectival rhapsodies whenever it evolves a Norris which cannot progress under its original plans" and to industry, especially "to those who might have lost faith in American principles and have come to believe that, after all, collectivism, fascism or communism possibly afford the only way out."[35]

Garet Garrett of the *Saturday Evening Post* was equally spellbound. "The facts, yes," the writer chortled, "a town with no graft or politics, where everything is settled by town meeting; a town where a man who had been cutting wages during the depression was told that he couldn't do that to these hill people." The culprit "then packed up his factory and went away with it, as they wanted him to do." He reflected that "a town where twenty years ago, there was nothing but marginal farming" now has "8,000 people on pay rolls." He had found "a town with a meaning" and now understood why it needed no chamber of commerce. "You do it yourself," he exclaimed to townspeople. "They grinned, and said, 'Maybe Fred Johnson can tell you. He did it to us.' "[36]

Other writers, less susceptible to capitalistic propaganda, found cause for concern. Willson Whitman, for example, published a scathing account in the *Nation.* She noted that *Nation's Business* had explained "in detail how Kingsport was an example of good planning, by private enterprise, while Norris was an example of bad planning, by the government." Lambasting a National Labor Relations Board report that called the town "perhaps the most completely integrated industrial community in America," Whitman exuded venomous commentary on the housing situation. "Within sight of the big beautiful Eastman plant—a ten-story modern building covering a big acreage, all lit up like a Christmas tree with colored lights at night, and looking in general like a Hollywood dream of the future," she reported, lay Long Island, "which the early settlers foolishly took away from the Indians." "Not pampered with fancy schools and churches, . . . their school a little shack so crowded that children attended in three shifts," the Long Islanders, occupying shanties where no self-respecting Indian would live, wallowed in congestion and filth. "The real miracle of Kingsport," she speculated, was that it had not been overrun by typhoid.[37]

What soon became apparent was an enormous credibility gap. Some writers for the national audience, as well as a few federal bureaucrats, readily accepted Kingsport's propaganda; others, like Whitman, went to great lengths—even distortions—to undermine it. Almost all erred in either interpretation or fact. TVA Director Arthur E. Morgan acknowledged that J. Fred Johnson had been "something of a dictator there," telling "the managers to treat their labor decently." Had it not been for Johnson, Morgan claimed, "the same factories might be there, and they might be slaving their labor, and there might be slums in Kingsport."[38] In fact, Kingsport did have its slums and underlying tensions. Town fathers, who had boasted about turning down federal money, the undying loyalty of their workers, and the wonders of participatory democracy, were about to choke on their words.

Federal investigators considered industrial conditions in Kingsport to be superior to the general situation in Tennessee and the South, although there were exceptions. In the 1935 survey made by the Women's Bureau of the Department of Labor, the agent found 30 women and 6 men were working at the Kingsport Laundry. Hourly rates for the women, who worked fifty-two hours per week, were sixteen to seventeen cents during 1934 but had fallen to fourteen and fifteen cents during the following summer. The building was in poor condition, the toilets were especially bad, and the lighting was haphazard. At Miller-Smith Hosiery Mills, 44 women and 32 men were working a five-day, forty-hour week; only males worked on the second shift. Although conditions were described as generally good, the investigator cited unsanitary water fountains, no doors on toilet compartments, and not enough seats for occasional rest periods. Eastman employed 2,987 workers—2,720 white males, 20 black men, and 247 white women. Males worked on all three shifts; women worked a five-day, forty-hour week on shift one only. The investigator, who acknowledged not having toured the facility, nonetheless concluded that it was "a new up-to-date plant with every indication that it is kept clean and in good condition." The 168 women at Kingsport Press, which engaged a total force of 347, labored a six-day forty-eight-hour week and worked on the second shift as well as on the first. No pay differential existed for male operatives, but there were task bonuses. The report described the plant as "exceedingly clean," with excellent housekeeping and lighting, "spotlessly clean" toilets, "a rest room that would be creditable in a hotel, [and] modernistic chairs, with cushioned seats." Indeed, the Woman's Bureau was so impressed with this account that it was published in Bulletin No. 149.[39]

Even Kingsport's admirers recognized that "some things at Kingsport" ran "counter to the present federal idea of a square deal for the laborer"; and "unionism" was "frowned upon."[40] The 1930s brought labor organizations to the town, and complaints against management ran the usual gamut—the intimidation and discharge of organizers and sympathizers, as well as the counteroffensive of attempting to form company unions. Labor disputes plagued the mills that manufactured hosiery, cotton cloth, and silk and attracted the attention of the Industrial and Social Branch of the National Recovery Administration. Investigator J.L. Connor of the NRA answered a complaint against Miller-Smith Hosiery Mills, which had begun operations in 1932 in part of the old Kingsport Hosiery Mills building and a new addition. One of a chain of hosiery mills—others were located at Chattanooga, Etowah, and Dayton, Tennessee—the Kingsport branch knitted a daily output of about two hundred dozen pairs of full-fashioned women's hosiery of three grades, which were shipped to the sister plant at Chattanooga for dyeing and finishing. Some seventy laborers, represented by the American Federation of Hosiery Workers, struck around 13 September 1935 to protest the discriminatory discharge of union members who had allegedly forced a nonunion employee out of the mill. Management agreed to reinstate all workers except the two who were involved in the incident.[41]

In November the United Textile Workers of America charged that Kingsport Silk Mills had refused to recognize the union committee and had staged a lockout involving about 350 workers. Thomas F. McMahon, international president of that union, wrote to Samuel F. McClurd, executive assistant of the Textile Labor Relations Board: "It was an unfortunate mistake on my part—I should have looked where these 'Jews' were going with their silk mills. They are jumping so much from one spot to another seeking reduction of taxes, or exemption entirely, and loans from the Government, that sometimes it is hard work to place them. These manufacturers are the scavengers who are responsible to a great degree, for instability in our industry."[42] Rumors circulated that the local oligarchy was also embarrassed and had pressured the owners to leave town; later, its members boasted about it. In any event, Kingsport Silk Mills closed indefinitely, ostensibly because of poor business conditions but more likely because of the undesirable attention that it was bringing to the model city. By October 1936 a new firm, Smoky Mountain Hosiery Mills, was ensconced on the premises in Highland Park that once had housed the Kingsport Silk Mills. The new company, when in full production, was expected to employ four hundred persons and to operate seventy-six machines.[43]

Local attorney O.W. Huddle, in a 1939 letter to the editors of the *Nation*, afforded some insight into how labor problems involving Fisher-Beck Hosiery Mills had been resolved in Kingsport. Established in 1928 by men of Jewish ancestry, Ray Fisher and Victor Beck, who had come south from the Philadelphia area to work for the Kingsport Hosiery Mills, the company had a monthly output of 1.3 million pairs of seamless men's hosiery and employed about one hundred people on two shifts. Tennessee Eastman provided most of its acetate yarn, although some came from elsewhere in the South. Only the knitting was done at Kingsport; dyeing and finishing work was done at a sister plant in Cranberry, North Carolina.[44]

According to Huddle, Mary Fulton, who was twenty-four years old, had been employed by Fisher-Beck during November 1938. She had worked 132 hours and received $11.48 in compensation, although she should have earned a minimum of $33.00 under the terms of the Fair Labor Standards Act of 1938. Fulton enlisted Huddle's services, and he consulted with agents of the United States Department of Labor. When the case was to be heard in Sullivan County Court, neither Fulton nor other witnesses that she had recommended appeared. Mary reportedly was hiding at her humble residence, and her "aging parents were on the verge of hysterics." Huddle charged that "somebody had forced these people to stay away either by duress or by threats and intimidation that if and when they appeared something would happen to them." Calling J. Fred Johnson "the Great White Father and patron saint of Kingsport" who shed "crocodile tears for the plight of his people," the attorney denounced Johnson's promotion of Kingsport on the basis of cheap labor. "Cheap labor," Huddle argued, means "cheap people, a cheap industry, cheap stores, and a cheap city." Living in shacks, unable to buy clothes, and paid five to seven dollars a week, they were unable "to buy corn meal and fat meat for an ordinary family for a week. But the worst feature of all is that when they want to assert their rights, they are intimidated by threats that their shanties and cheap overalls and the little bit of coarse food which they now have will be taken away."[45] As for Fisher-Beck, it went bankrupt around 1941, finished off by labor unrest and a strike.[46]

Although the local elite had been able to forestall the development of unions during the 1920s and early 1930s, labor organizing had become a reality by the middle of the decade. One study concluded that "Kingsport was kept nonunion not so much by the employers as by the characteristics of the employees." Union organizers had difficulty in recruiting workers from "the outlying hills" because they cherished "the ideal of undivided loyalty to their employers."[47] Hard times and a more sophisticated outlook undermined loyalty somewhat, but threats and intimidation should not be underestimated. It is also true that area labor, for whatever reason—not least of which is a fierce sense of pride coupled with unusual gratitude—has never been particularly susceptible to unionism. Under open-shop conditions that rendered fledgling unions almost impotent, some workers organized all the same. In June 1937 the *Kingsport Times* published a full-page spread in oversized type to caution workers that a labor union did not ensure stable employment, higher wages, or contentment.[48]

At the end of the 1930s, the only closed-shop arrangement existed at Kingsport Press.[49] Supposedly, Colonel E.W. Palmer had invited unions into his plant, believing this would enhance his standing in the publishing industry and would generate business. Some charged that a "sweetheart contract" existed between Colonel Palmer and George Berry, a Hawkins County native and longtime president of the International Printing Pressmen and Assistants' Union, who had been responsible for the establishment of Pressmen's Home—the union's headquarters, trade school, and sanitarium—near Rogersville.[50] In any event, unions were well enough entrenched in Kingsport by the 1940s to stage a strike at Mason-Dixon, a locally owned trucking firm, in 1941 and at General Shale Products Corporation, previously known locally as the Kingsport Brick Corporation, in 1942. Numerous labor disputes during that decade received the attention of the Federal Conciliation and Mediation Service.[51]

Attempts by Borden Mills to discourage unionization had brought representatives from the National Labor Relations Board to the model city around 1937. Many years later, an old-timer at the local newspaper remembered an NLRB lawyer who "came to Kingsport and spent some time digging for something wrong" but who said as he left town, "I just can't understand this place. It is just too good to be true. But I can't put my finger on a thing." At the time of the hearing, however, W.L. Holyoke, the plant engineer of the factory that was being investigated, was also serving as mayor; and the report indicated that "instead of the familiar political bosses," Kingsport had an "oligarchy composed of the 'founding fathers' working with the industrialists."[52]

Because everyone in the city depended either directly or indirectly on the corporations that so enthusiastically embraced civic challenges, the local newspaper editor had been able to remark in 1928 that Kingsport had been unusually free of petty politics. After the onset of the depression, however, some dissent arose, which was subtly reflected in municipal elections. Throughout the twenties and into the thirties, the Board of Mayor and Aldermen and the city manager were little more than figureheads. Real power reposed with J. Fred Johnson, A.D. Brockman, E.W. Palmer, C.P. Edwards, Jr., James C. White, Jerry C. Stone, Dr. E.W. Tipton, and a few other prominent citizens. Behind the scenes, they named the slate of candidates for city offices, who ran neither as Democrats nor as Republicans but as advocates of "good government." The five aldermen served staggered terms of four years. Three were elected at one time and two in the next election. Sometimes they ran unopposed and almost always with only scant competition. The plants urged workers to vote as they chose but, above all, to vote. Foremen offered more explicit advice, and on election day, prominent figures spent several hours at the polls encouraging the voters to cast their ballots properly.[53]

Beginning around 1931, the local power brokers found themselves somewhat on the defensive. In July 1927, Charles F. Lingar, an employee of Borden Mills—at that time the town's largest employer—became mayor. Within four years he had fallen from grace. Although he stood for reelection to the board, he was resoundingly defeated, coming in next to last in a larger-than-usual seven-man race for three vacancies. Shelburne Ferguson, a well-established lawyer, received the most votes (792) and was subsequently named mayor by the new board.[54] Whether the local elite had been temporarily complacent and had allowed an unlikely candidate to win or whether Lingar had become too independent and outspoken for them is not recorded. City directories indicate that between 1926 and 1934, he left the employment of Borden Mills. Around 1935 he was a deputy sheriff for Sullivan County and later was a mechanic with the Works Progress Administration.[55] Ferguson, who was respected and liked by Johnson but was not a member of the Edwards crowd, was less an establishment candidate and more of a populist, according to his son. When he was elected circuit judge of the Twentieth Judicial District in 1934, he resigned the mayoralty; W.L. Holyoke, also with Borden Mills, succeeded Ferguson.[56]

Rumblings of discontent in the town may have made the principal citizens even more attentive to city government. Newspaperman W.J. McAuliffe recalled that "there was in the very early days of the city a small group of malcontents anxious to find fault with the way city affairs were run." After the local newspaper misprinted a figure in the annual financial statement of the city, the group circulated a flyer, according to McAuliffe, claiming that the city was $100,000 in the red and that city officials were covering this fact up with false bookkeeping. City Manager Frank L. Cloud appointed a special committee, composed of the financial officers of the local industries, to audit the books. The committee reportedly found everything in order and the city in good financial condition.[57] Although this rumor was laid to rest, some citizens were watching poll taxes and were questioning other taxation policies that classified KIC land as parks before it was sold to developers for handsome prices. In 1939, attorney O.W. Huddle bought radio time in another town and denounced the local establishment. Karl Goerdel, who was elected alderman that year, recalled: "There was a fellow on the radio, Huddle, who had some candidates he was pushing. The worst thing he could say about me was the way I spelled my name."[58]

By 1939, Goerdel's company, Tennessee Eastman, had moved into a powerful position. The town had grown from an official population of 11,914 in 1930 to an estimated in-town and peripheral population of 18,000 to 20,000 over a five- to six-year period. During roughly the same time, Eastman had expanded and had increased its work force from approximately 400 to 3,700. By the mid-thirties, its payroll included about 53 percent of the town's industrial workers.[59] "I was pushed into being alderman," Goerdel recalled. "I didn't spend one cent for advertising. When the newspaper sent me a bill for advertising, which was very little, I wrote on the bill, 'See my campaign manager, C.P. Edwards [Jr.].' " Nonetheless, Goerdel received the most votes, and the headlines anticipated that he would be elevated to mayor. Eastman officials, however, did not want to give the impression that they were running the town. According to Goerdel, James C. White told him, "We don't want you to be mayor." The official minutes did not record the election returns by vote tallies, which usually were entered. Goerdel obligingly nominated Dr. E.W. Tipton for mayor. A few years before his death, Goerdel recalled: "Russell Stone [who also became alderman in 1939] and I elected the mayor for years."[60]

Voter apathy was a natural by-product of the carefully orchestrated elections. According to a federal survey, there were only thirteen hundred registered voters in 1935. As of 1937, no successful candidate for the board had ever polled as many as eight hundred votes, and no losing candidate as many as four hundred.[61] In fairness it must be stated that the city government performed competently during the 1930s and throughout the war years, an era of unusual expansion and growth. Kingsport's finances fared particularly well. City officials reduced the bonded indebtedness by $700,834.83, from $2,022,269.83 in 1941 to $1,321,435.00 in 1945, using policies established during the 1930s. Projected earnings from the sinking fund seemed more than adequate to meet requirements of the coming years. Unpaid taxes declined from $93,920.39 in 1941 to $38,032.95 in 1945. City expenses rose from $584,900 to $739,000 during the same period; of this, the state and the county provided $107,000 in 1941 and $123,500 in 1945 for education.[62]

The Boards of Mayor and Aldermen that came of age during the late 1930s and early 1940s displayed more vigor than had previous administrations and decisively addressed pressing problems. Self-help and unadulterated capitalism, so much a part of local mythology and boosterism, had lost considerable ground. Confronted with internal as well as external criticism, local power brokers adjusted their approach. Seemingly embracing ideas that were emanating from Washington, they prepared to enjoy the largess of the federal government. One of the first fruits of this new understanding in the model city was the construction of the Civic Auditorium and Armory, east of the business district.

Planning began in the autumn of 1938 during the mayoralty of W.L. Holyoke, ground was broken on 22 December, and the dedication occurred on 9 March 1940. With a seating capacity of 2,032 in the auditorium and with areas for the exclusive use of the 191st Field Artillery of the Tennessee National Guard, the building owed its existence to $125,000 from the city and a grant of $97,510 from the Public Works Administration. Kingsport architect Allen N. Dryden, Sr., executed the arched-dome design, reportedly the only one of its kind in Tennessee and one of only three in the South at the time. Its outer walls, of buff brick trimmed with Indiana limestone, and its interior colors of soft buffs and browns, as well as its design, marked a dramatic departure from the redbrick Georgian style sponsored earlier by the KIC in the downtown.[63] Its site also represented a deviation from the Nolen plan. Given the growth of the city—particularly in residential construction—toward the east and given the parking requirements necessitated by the impact of the automobile, this move seemed prudent. Enthusiasm for additional development in the vicinity of the Civic Auditorium gained momentum. During early 1940 the city acquired a swimming pool, as well as adjacent land, from Hammond Post of the American Legion. Toward the end of that year, the mayor appointed a committee to make a feasibility study for a stadium. The idea blossomed to include a recreational area, which, over his protests, bore the name J. Fred Johnson Park. The city put up $150,000 through a bond issue and secured additional funds from federal grants.[64]

Money from Washington also paid for work on streets and bridges and underwrote a pilot project in regional planning during 1941. Earle S. Draper, who became deputy commissioner of the Federal Housing Administration (FHA), included Upper East Tennessee in the work of the FHA's Land Planning Division. Cooperating with the Tennessee State Planning Commission, the Tennessee Valley Authority, and city governments, the project immediately spurred the formation of municipal planning commissions where none had existed before. The small staff that was assembled for the project also generated a survey of the economy of the Tri-Cities, a review of the governments, and a study of welfare and health services. Each of the cities—Kingsport, Johnson City, and the two Bristols—put up $250 to defray operating expenses.[65]

Disparate interests agreed that the housing situation in Kingsport demanded immediate attention. In 1937, *Architectural Forum* had called Kingsport "a virgin residential market" and had announced that a private New York developer, N.K. Winston, with encouragement from the FHA, had bought land in the model city for development. Finding seven hundred workers who were ready to put cash down on a new home, he engaged architect Lester Maxon, also of New York, to design modest single-story four-room structures and somewhat more elaborate two-story residences of frame and brick. Prices ranged from $3,190 to $4,690. By around 1946, however, this venture, which skirted the old golf course, had produced only thirty-one dwellings.[66] The Kingsport Improvement Company, aided by the FHA, completed Kingsport Gardens, a privately owned project, in 1939. Opposite the city recreation area, the fifty-two apartments and thirty-four single-dwelling units rented for $52.50 and $37.50 per month respectively.[67]

Private ventures at this point had a relatively minor effect on the overall problem. "The same causes that have created slums and decadent areas in our larger urban centers," declared a 1938 report of the National Resources Committee, "may be recognized in their primary stage in Kingsport and may still be avoided in the development which will take place in the future."[68] Gleefully, in 1939, Willson Whitman informed readers of the *Nation* that local authorities in Kingsport now seemed "willing to admit the existence of enough slums to require a federal appropriation for clearance. They think $750,000 would be a nice amount for the United States Housing Authority [USHA] to provide." J. Fred Johnson had reportedly said: "These unsanitary shacks are a disgrace to any place. If you take the cows out of the stalls for any length of time, people move in." A representative of the USHA who visited the town thought the situation "among the worst he had seen."[69]

On 7 February 1939 the Board of Mayor and Aldermen agreed to conduct a public hearing, the initial step toward establishing a housing authority under the Tennessee Housing Authority Law of 1935, as amended in 1937. Two weeks later, 456 residents submitted a petition calling for the establishment of the Kingsport Housing Authority (KHA), and Walter F. Smith was designated as its first chairman. Smith soon informed the elected officials that the city must enter into an agreement with the USHA for the city's slum-clearance project. At the 1 August meeting of the Board of Mayor and Aldermen, with a large number of citizens in attendance, a motion from the floor, which was passed without a dissenting vote, called for the construction of 176 units—128 Robert E. Lee Homes for whites and 48 Riverview dwellings for blacks. Smith and the KHA recommended a segregated fifty-acre site south of the railroad and between the old dye plant property and Kingsport Brick Corporation for black people—a poor substitute but the closest that the planned city ever came to John Nolen's and Ray Dennis's model Negro Village. The total cost of the two projects was $609,000, mostly financed by the sale of bonds, $65,000 of which was held by the KHA and $544,000 by the federal government. After the initial occupancy, the authority launched a program of slum clearance, which by 2 July 1942 had eliminated 218 substandard units.[70]

Even as city officials were moving to address some of the more obvious housing needs, United States entry into World War II and its almost immediate impact on Kingsport made monumental demands on municipal services. On 16 December 1941 at its first meeting after the attack on Pearl Harbor, the Board of Mayor and Aldermen discussed tightening the guard at the waterworks and reservoir because of the war but agreed to leave the matter to the director of public safety as usual. This marked the city government's first official acknowledgment that hostilities might intrude on the model city. By 3 February 1942 the municipal authorities had adopted a formal procedure for ordering blackouts and had put the town on daylight saving time because of "the great emergency... facing the United States of America."[71] Now if not before, the town's destiny and that of Tennessee Eastman Company (TEC) meshed, for "The Eastman" was caught up in a venture that profoundly affected the outcome of the war as well as Kingsport.

The early months of 1942 were dark days for the world, for the United States, and for Kingsport. Fathers, mothers, wives, and sweethearts watched their young men go off to training camps and the inevitable battles that awaited them. Practically every able-bodied male was engaged in defense work of some kind, as, indeed, were many females. So bereft of men was the model city that women found themselves jitterbugging with each other at community dances.[72] German submarines prowled the oceans, exacting a terrible toll on merchant shipping and troop carriers; they sometimes struck so close to the American mainland that their flaming devastation could be observed from the Atlantic beaches. To combat these awesome forces with their seemingly impervious hulls, the British, forewarned by intelligence reports around the mid-thirties, had begun to experiment with an explosive called cyclotrimethylenetrinitramine. By 1938 they had developed the capacity for handling what they called RDX—Research Development Explosive—which carried an explosive effect 50 percent greater than TNT. Because of the volatile nature of RDX, however, which had been a deterrent since it had been synthesized in 1899, the British could manufacture it only in small batches. A Canadian plant near Shawinigan Falls, Quebec, was also preparing to produce limited quantities of RDX, but the total output of the Woolwich Arsenal, the British plant, and the Canadian facility could not begin to satisfy demands. A faster, more reliable method was in the offing.[73]

During 1940 the National Defense Research Committee (NDRC) of the United States Office of Scientific Research and Development joined the British and Canadian scientists in RDX experimentation. Dr. Werner Bachmann at the University of Michigan soon discovered a combination process that involved the reaction of hexamine, nitric acid, and ammonium nitrate, with acetic anhydride being added to remove the water that was formed and to drive the reaction to completion. The Bachmann process still required production in a two-stage process with intermediate drying. Nonetheless, it had the advantages of an 85 percent reduction in the use of nitric acic and a doubling of the yield of RDX from hexamine. The NDRC awarded E.I. Du Pont de Nemours a contract to produce the explosive by batch process at the Wabash River Ordnance Works near Terre Haute, Indiana; the Western Cartridge Company was also enlisted. Acetic acid, a by-product, began to accumulate at the pilot plants, and it had to be reconverted to anhydride.[74]

Tennessee Eastman Company, which was already receiving high visibility in trade journals and national news magazines, had become a major producer of acetic anhydride. During the 1930s the enthusiasm for still photography and home movies and the problem of storing X-rays in hospitals demanded nonflammable film. Cellulose nitrate was highly flammable; cellulose acetate was not. Unfortunately, cellulose acetate, which was made by treating cellulose (purified cotton linters) with acetic acid and acetic anhydride, was expensive because it involved extracting the two acids from wood by crude methods. Eastman chemists found a better way, and in 1930, Tennessee Eastman's first cellulose-acetate unit began to turn out the raw material for safety film. The recovery of acetic acid was an important step in the cellulose-acetate process. Caught up in the strides of the expanding chemical industry, Tennessee Eastman also moved into the fledgling plastics field, beginning production of Tenite I in 1933 and adding Tenite II in 1940. A forty-two-year veteran of Eastman, Perley S. Wilcox (known as "Uncle Perley" to his employees), the president of Tennessee Eastman, had witnessed the growth of his plant from little more than a wood yard and sawmill around 1920 to eighty-two buildings on 372 acres just two decades later. The company, located adjacent to a town of 14,404, as reported by the 1940 census, employed 5,000 workers.[75]

The NDRC solicited the help of Tennessee Eastman officials on 4 November 1941. When a government representative visited Kingsport ten days later, H.G. Stone, TEC's works manager, proposed a method, which was subsequently perfected, for the successful recovery of acetic acid. From this point, the Kingsport company was in the frenzy of the war effort. So impressed were federal authorities by TEC's initial contribution that by January 1942 they had invited the firm to consider pilot plant work on the production of RDX.[76] Indeed, it was in the early days of 1942 that the brilliance, patriotism, and endurance of Eastman employees coalesced to begin one of the many extraordinary chapters of heroic effort on the American home front.

H.G. Stone, Fred R. Conklin, David C. Hull, and Lee G. Davy embarked on a whirlwind trip to learn about the status of RDX manufacture. Around 21 and 22 January they traveled to Washington, D.C., for a meeting with Dr. Ralph Connor of the NDRC and then journeyed to Ann Arbor, Michigan, for a two-day conference with Dr. Bachmann and to witness for the first time the preparation of RDX by the batch process. Either in the laboratory there or on the train leaving Ann Arbor, Hull, in discussions with the others, conceived of the idea for a continuous reactor for RDX, based on the design of the Hershberg melting-pot apparatus, what became known and patented as the Jeep. The next stop was the Western Cartridge Plant at East Alton, Illinois, by way of St. Louis. The official report states: "On January 25-26, working late at night in the Jefferson Hotel [St. Louis], the problems created by RDX were actively discussed. Davy and Hull were quartered in one room while Stone and Conklin were in a connecting room. Davy and Hull were restless and worked into the early hours of the AM calculating the design features for a pilot plant continuous nitrator, embodying the 'Jeep' features. Hull drew up several sketches on Jefferson Hotel stationery, showing numerous modifications of the 'Jeep.' "[77]

Before the quartet left Kingsport, Stone had ordered the construction of a pilot plant for experimentation. When they returned on 27 January, two buildings were nearly finished where there had been open land a few days before. With a new RDX laboratory already prepared, Davy started work on 31 January; by 5 and 6 February he was carrying out the first continuous run in the glass jeep with excellent results.[78] When Dr. Connor came to witness the process and the refinements that were being made hourly, he could hardly conceal his enthusiasm. On 16 February he wrote: "In order to really appreciate the vigor with which Tennessee Eastman moved this program, you should know that my visit last Wednesday was exactly three weeks after I had called them on the telephone to ask if they would consider doing pilot plant work on the production of RDX. The pilot plant is admirably constructed and could be used for training personnel if we care to make it available for these purposes. The pilot plant has been equipped with a large scale metal 'jeep' to allow studies of the continuous process there."[79] In a matter of days, Eastman scientists and engineers had succeeded where others had failed for decades, and they had found a way to manufacture the large quantities of RDX now required to win the Battle of the Atlantic.

Eastman employees could almost feel the Nazis breathing down their necks, and the awesome German submarines were never far from their minds. Feverish efforts were made to improve and perfect methods and to prepare for full-scale production. The initial team of about twenty supervisors and thirty operators at the hastily constructed Wexler Bend pilot plant worked sixteen to eighteen hours a day beside the technical experts. Anyone who had more than five hours of sleep was considered a drone. On one occasion, with almost everything in short supply, Stone made a desperate call to Washington for a particular item. Told that it would take a week, he shouted: "A week! Why the Japs took Manila in a week." The priority was forthcoming that afternoon, and "The Japs took Manila in a week" became the standard rallying cry. Meanwhile, on 6 February, the company had also agreed to start work on Composition B, a combination of RDX and TNT for use in bombs and projectiles, and had begun construction of a pilot plant on Horse Creek Road. By 21 April, Eastman scientists made their first run of an experimental pellet process. E.G. (Ed) Guenther, in collaboration with others, had envisioned a procedure for turning out Composition B in a form that resembled chocolate kisses, the popular candy, thus simplifying what had been a very elaborate time- and space-consuming process of cooling. During the ensuing months, in this familiar form, thousands of Appalachian operators prepared "Jap kisses" for their deadly missions. The first shipment of Composition B left the pilot plant on 25 April, bound for the United States Naval Mine Depot at Yorktown, Virginia; 11,679 pounds of RDX had also been manufactured. So desperate was the navy for explosives that 20,000 pounds of Composition B were shipped as soon as they could be produced, even though a standard boxcar could hold up to 100,000 pounds. Subsequent accounts also indicate that initially only submarine commanders who had the best scores received warheads containing RDX from the precious supply.[80]

Tennessee Eastman filed a progress report on RDX experimentation that simply stated: "As of April 30, 1942, it may be considered that we have completed the semi-works development and have sufficient data for the design of a large commercial installation." Federal authorities were not only pleased but also astounded with what was happening at Kingsport. By early May, bureaucrats in Washington made preparations for the transfer of the pilot plants, under NDRC jurisdiction, to Army

Ordnance. Eastman officials were unwilling to enter into a supply contract for RDX at a definite price per pound because to do so would require that it be furnished at a cost four times the eventual commercial price. H.G. Stone had stated that what would be a reasonable price under present conditions and one that would be readily understood by technicians could be misrepresented after the war and might bring the company much unwarranted, adverse publicity. Because, to a large extent, Eastman Kodak depended on direct sales to the public, it could not risk a hint of scandal. Stone, acting as spokesman for the company, offered to operate the pilot plant for a fixed fee of $1.00 per year.[81]

While financial details were still under discussion, on 6 June 1942, after conferences in Washington between Eastman management, officials from the U.S. Army Ordnance, and the National Defense Research Committee, Eastman received official authorization to design and operate Holston Ordnance Works, or HOW. Sites known as Area A and Area B, about 112 acres in Sullivan County and 5,912 acres in Hawkins County, had already been selected, displacing some residents. Fraser-Brace Engineering Company out of St. Louis received the construction contract, and Charles T. Main, Incorporated, did the site-development and utilities design. Hercules Incorporated contributed plans for the nitric-acid plant.[82] A financial arrangement dated 6 July and approved on 11 July 1942 estimated the cost of the entire plant at $76,930,500 and established fixed operational expenses of $275,000 under one category, an estimated amount of $394,000 in a second, and a fixed fee of $1.00 in yet another.[83]

The model city felt the repercussions of the massive project almost immediately. As early as 17 February, the Board of Mayor and Aldermen had agreed to rent a room at the Civic Auditorium for a Land Acquisition Planning Office for the Kingsport Ordnance Site.[84] This was merely the beginning. The city fathers, indeed most of the solid citizenry, particularly feared the presence of rough construction crews. By the end of June, thousands had begun arriving. Municipal officials discussed enlarging the police force. The *Kingsport Times-News* reported: "As many as 18,000 construction workers were employed on the two areas at the peak of the building program. Barracks were set up for some at Area B, trailer camps dotted the city and nearby countryside, buses of every size, color and condition crowded the highways for 30 miles in every direction bringing workers to their jobs." For eighteen months, in order to accommodate the influx of army personnel and construction workers, Jimmy Vallis, a Greek immigrant, kept the Kingsport Candy Kitchen, a small restaurant at 113 Broad Street, open for nineteen hours a day, from 7:00 A.M. to 2:00 A.M.[85]

The city furnished water and sewer taps for the trailers and tent camps inside the city and for others on the periphery, where many of these hard-drinking and wild-driving individuals lived. The Kingsport Emergency Housing Committee was formed, and the city fathers authorized the construction of temporary buildings adjacent to the Civic Auditorium to meet the demands for office space. During designated hours, portions of streets were reserved for loading and unloading buses carrying HOW workers. Beer joints flourished in the downtown, particularly at Five Points, and drunkenness was common. Cooperation between the construction company and the city in monitoring the behavior of the newcomers ameliorated the situation somewhat.[86]

The winter of 1942-43 was a bad one for construction, but the project was too important to be jeopardized, even by Mother Nature. On 29 April 1943, the first of several lines at Area B began production. Ten days later, Composition B from the main plant rolled off the line. The maiden 100,000-pound carload left the plant on 14 May for a secret destination. The pilot plants had continued to turn out explosives during the interim. On 27 July the United States Ordnance officials authorized a 100 percent expansion. Consequently, construction continued amidst production until 22 January 1944. At that point, Holston Ordnance Works became the world's largest manufacturer of high explosives.[87]

Meanwhile, on 6 December 1943, in an afternoon ceremony, Eastman Company and Holston Ordnance Works received the Army-Navy "E" Award "for outstanding achievement in the production of materials of war." Major General Charles T. Harris, Jr., from Aberdeen Proving Ground, and Lieutenant Commander H.H. Heine, United States Naval Reserve, from the Office of Naval Material in Atlanta, made presentations. Civilian workers in Kingsport also helped to finance the global struggle in which the country was engaged. As early as 4 July 1941 the U.S. Treasury Department honored the Kingsport community by awarding it an Accomplishment Flag for participation in the savings-bond plan. Over 80 percent of employed personnel had enrolled. In 1944 the United States Navy commissioned the USNS *Kingsport Victory,* a cargo vessel, to recognize the enormous success of the city in selling war bonds.[88]

Concomitant to the building and on-line production at HOW, the model city, which had previously been plagued by housing problems, entered years of unprecedented demands. In 1942, with FHA financing, the privately owned Cherokee Real Estate Corporation developed a tract of land along the north side of West Sullivan Street between the Fifties and the Gate City and Bloomingdale highways. Two-bedroom dwellings sold for $4,750 or rented for $44 per month; three-bedroom ones for $5,300 and $52.50 respectively. Kingsport Defense Homes, Incorporated, in which the Dennises had invested, established Baysview, near HOW, with 270 residences; Forest Lawn, with 94; and a Riverview expansion, with 28 units, independent of those rented by the Kingsport Housing Authority.[89] Other residential development southwest of town in proximity to Area B also occurred.

It was not uncommon for local people to take in strangers. Single-family dwellings became boardinghouses, and stories are told about large rooms being partitioned with curtains and sheets to afford a measure of privacy for as many as four newcomers in each. Military brass appropriated John B. Dennis's Rotherwood estate, which bordered on Area B; some of the property was incorporated into the military reservation. Lieutenant Colonel William E. Ryan was commanding officer at HOW from June 1942 to March 1944. He left to serve with the American forces in Europe, and Lieutenant Colonel Francis R. Scherer succeeded Ryan in the post at Kingsport.[90]

Once production was in full swing, employment at HOW peaked at 6,800 and eventually leveled off at 5,000. So successful was Tennessee Eastman and its parent company, Eastman Kodak, in simplifying the various phases of manufacture that area natives from the surrounding hollows, who had little or no training in chemistry and many of whom lacked a high-school education, satisfactorily and relatively safely performed their assignments. This is not to cast aspersions on their intelligence and ability or to diminish their contributions, for their efforts were invaluable to national defense. About 40 percent of them were women. According to one account, dressed in white coveralls and caps, they could have been mistaken for workers in a Fanny Farmer candy kitchen. Having relatives and friends on the battlefronts, they faced their tasks with grim determination and dutiful attention to the maintenance and cleanliness of their work areas. The federal contract prohibited the employment of anyone under sixteen, as well as convicts. Special federal and state regulations governing the hours and working conditions for females also applied. Safety instruction proceeded relentlessly. Workers could expect a standard eight-hour day, with one and a half times the basic pay for extra hours. The wage in munition plants during the war ranged from 50 cents to $1.26 an hour, with $46.36 being about the weekly average. If the workers excelled and if the war reached a successful conclusion, they were in a business with no future. Nonetheless, morale was high at HOW; there was never a lost day of production once it commenced; and there were only three casualties at the plant for the duration of the war—not one of them from an explosion.[91]

Tennessee Eastman's initial success with RDX and the construction of HOW attracted the attention of General Leslie Groves, commanding officer of the Manhattan Project. On 24 December 1942, he telephoned James C. White, vice-president and general manager of TEC, explained that he had a problem, and invited White to come to Washington for discussions. Groves was looking for a company to operate what would be the Y-12 plant at Oak Ridge; Groves wanted practical people, not "long beards," as he put it. He already had the best brains in the country, including most of the recent Nobel Prize winners, working for him. Because of the demands of HOW, Eastman's management was not sure that it was up to the task. Self-effacingly and somewhat naïvely, they explained that they had no experience with the type of work to be undertaken. Groves stressed urgency; Frank Lovejoy pointed out that it had always been company policy to be of any possible help to the war effort; and on 5 January 1943, several officials from Tennessee Eastman and Eastman Kodak agreed, without any dissension, to take on the new assignment.[92]

Secrecy shrouded the massive effort that would produce the first atomic weapons. W.R. Burton opened an Eastman office in Boston to consult and advise with Stone and Webster, the construction company. Eastman scientists and engineers were sent off under cover of darkness to unknown destinations, bearing sealed envelopes that were to be opened at specified times en route. Some found themselves on the way to Berkeley, California. Later, others were told to pack a suitcase and wait at the Civic Auditorium, where they were picked up by chauffeur-driven cars and carried off to Oak Ridge, Tennessee. Dr. Fred R. Conklin from Tennessee Eastman became works manager at the Y-12 plant when the company occupied portions of various buildings that were still under construction at the new town's site.[93]

People who were already on Eastman's payroll formed a nucleus, but more than fifty thousand persons had to be hired. The general labor market seemed to be depleted. Eastman, however, had two advantages:

(1) Clinton Engineer Works, as the plant was known, had "the highest labor and material priorities"; and (2) "within a reasonable distance of the area lived" what was purportedly "some of the most 100% Americans in the nation—in Tennessee, Kentucky, Virginia, Georgia, and adjoining states." Independent but loyal to their employers and devoted to their country, they made excellent workers. One woman commuted from Chattanooga, arising at 3:00 A.M. and returning home at 11:00 P.M. One man walked six miles to catch a bus for a fifty-mile one-way trip to his job. Clinton Engineer Works of Tennessee Eastman Company (CEW-TEC) advertised in newspapers and national magazines and sent interviewers "to the four corners of the United States." Furthermore, "young women recruiters were sent away from the Knoxville area to [such] diverse points as Arkansas, North Carolina, Kentucky, and others. As much as three months were spent on the road in the spring of 1944 and 1945 talking to high school girls who would soon graduate." These Eastman employees, too, received the Army-Navy "E" Award.[94]

Eastman operated the Y-12 facility from 5 January 1943 to 4 May 1947, when the company asked the federal government to be relieved. Works manager Conklin noted the feeling of regret because the association had "been so pleasant" and "had endured for so long." World War II had ended almost two years before, in August 1945, with the atomic bombing of Hiroshima and Nagasaki, the awesomely successful handiwork of the Manhattan Project. The first bomb that was dropped on Japan contained U-235 from the Y-12 plant; therefore, Eastman immediately received widespread publicity. Entering the atomic age made the once-exciting explosive of Holston Ordnance Works at Kingsport merely conventional.[95]

After the bombings of Hiroshima and Nagasaki and all that led to their destruction, neither the world nor Kingsport would ever be the same. Tennessee Eastman Company had played a major role in the transformation of both. The relatively innocuous small-town life of the twenties in Kingsport had given way to the doubts, suspicions, and occasional despair of the 1930s, but the old "Kingsport spirit" soared during wartime. "The people of Kingsport," a postwar civic publication declared, "notwithstanding the problems and inconvenience thrust upon them by the advent of Holston Ordnance Works in their midst, have a distinct sense of pride in having had a hand in a great achievement, accomplished by one of its own great industries."[96] Confidence had been restored. In the months immediately after the atomic devastation of Japanese cities, the townspeople, who were always more practical than philosophical, gratefully accepted the end of the war with little if any serious thought about the possibilities for nuclear proliferation.

Reconversion to peacetime conditions occupied center stage. Area residents needed time to adjust—to welcome home the survivors of faraway battles, to grieve for the lost, and, when possible, to arrange for the exhumation and return of their men's bodies from foreign soil. Tennessee Eastman Company had made Kingsport the subject of national and international attention. Whether playing host to the distinguished members of the RDX Committee or to British scientists, the town had put on its best face. Robert St. John of the National Broadcasting Company lectured in the model city and subsequently made it the subject of two consecutive programs, aired from 10:15 to 10:30 A.M. on 31 October and 1 November 1944. "The other day," St. John warbled, "I dropped in on what I consider THE *ideal* community. It's a place called Kingsport, Tennessee." The words that closed his first broadcast were: "And I want to tell you that over in EUROPE, plans are ALREADY being made, to use Kingsport as a MODEL, in rebuilding cities which have been left in RUINS, as WAR has swept over them! In a way THEY'RE lucky! Bombs and shells have made it possible for THEM... to start from scratch... just as Kingsport did!"[97] With words like these ringing in their ears, the citizens of Kingsport faced the future with optimism.

Above, the "Big Three" of Kingsport, about 1940. Left to right: Perley S. Wilcox, first president of Tennessee Eastman Company; J. Fred Johnson, the town's principal promoter and one-man chamber of commerce; and John B. Dennis, financier. Below, a panoramic view of the city they built: Kingsport during the 1920s. Both courtesy of the late Mrs. J. Fred Johnson.

Right, John Nolen of Cambridge, Massachusetts, Kingsport's town planner. Courtesy of the Department of Manuscripts and University Archives, Cornell University Libraries.

Below, an aerial view of contemporary downtown Kingsport, which still reflects the plan drafted by railroad engineers and refined by Nolen. Courtesy of *Kingsport Times-News.*

Grading work for construction of the Clinchfield Railroad was done by human muscles battling difficult terrain. Courtesy of the late W.A. Starritt, Sr.

The Clinchfield depot in Kingsport, designed by New York architect Clinton Mackenzie. Photo from the Kingsport Improvement Company's promotional album, courtesy of Allen N. Dryden, Jr.

J. Fred Johnson's "Big Store," about 1910. Courtesy of Tom Yancey III. The store was then owned by Kingsport Farms, parent company of the Kingsport Improvement Corporation, and was later sold to Johnson. The Kingsport Improvement building (below), like many in the city, was designed by Clinton Mackenzie. Photo from the KIC's promotional album, courtesy of Allen N. Dryden, Jr.

Above, a portion of Broad Street as it looked in the late 1920s or 1930s. Below, the Kingsport Inn, designed by Mackenzie. Both courtesy of the Kingsport Public Library.

A view of the confluence of the north and south forks of the Holston River as seen from John B. Dennis's home, Rotherwood, shown opposite as it looked in the 1920s. Both from the KIC promotional album, courtesy of Allen N. Dryden, Jr.

The Hunting Wagon used to transport visiting industrialists, shown at Rotherwood. Courtesy of the late Mrs. J. Fred Johnson.

Below, John B. Dennis, man of vision, on the front porch at Rotherwood. Courtesy of Kingsport Public Library.

J. Fred Johnson's home on Watauga Street. From the KIC album, courtesy of Allen N. Dryden, Jr.

A section of White City, designed by Clinton Mackenzie. Courtesy of the late Mrs. J. Fred Johnson.

Above and below, the Fifties development, designed by Mackenzie. Note the cows grazing in the foreground and the large drainage ditch. Above, from the KIC album, courtesy of Allen N. Dryden, Jr.; below, courtesy of Kingsport Public Library.

The Shelby Street row houses, like the Fifties, were designed by Mackenzie. From the KIC album, courtesy of Allen N. Dryden, Jr.

Three houses designed by Allen N. Dryden, Sr., the first architect to establish a firm in Kingsport. Below, the house designed for Mr. and Mrs. H.J. Shivell, Dryden's first Kingsport design. Opposite top, the house designed for Mr. and Mrs. S. Phelps Platt, Jr.; bottom, the log home designed for Harvey and Ruth Brooks. Photos courtesy of Allen N. Dryden, Jr.

Kingsport Press worker Gaines McGlothin was one of the subjects of a 1933 photographic essay by Lewis W. Hine, illustrating the mix of industrial and rural life in the Kingsport area. He is shown cutting index tabs for a dictionary and working on his farm three miles from the plant. Courtesy of the National Archives, Washington, D.C.

Ruby Hilton was another of Hine's subjects, on the job at Kingsport Press, above, and at home on the outskirts of Kingsport, below. Courtesy of the National Archives, Washington, D.C.

The remains of Frederick Ross's mid-nineteenth-century silk mill, later the Jordan Woolen Mill, on the north fork of the Holston, with the Big Elm in the foreground. Courtesy of Kingsport Public Library.

The Kingsport Brick Corporation (later General Shale Products), the city's second oldest industry, as it appeared in the 1920s. Note the pollution over the plant and surrounding landscape. From the KIC album, courtesy of Allen N. Dryden, Jr.

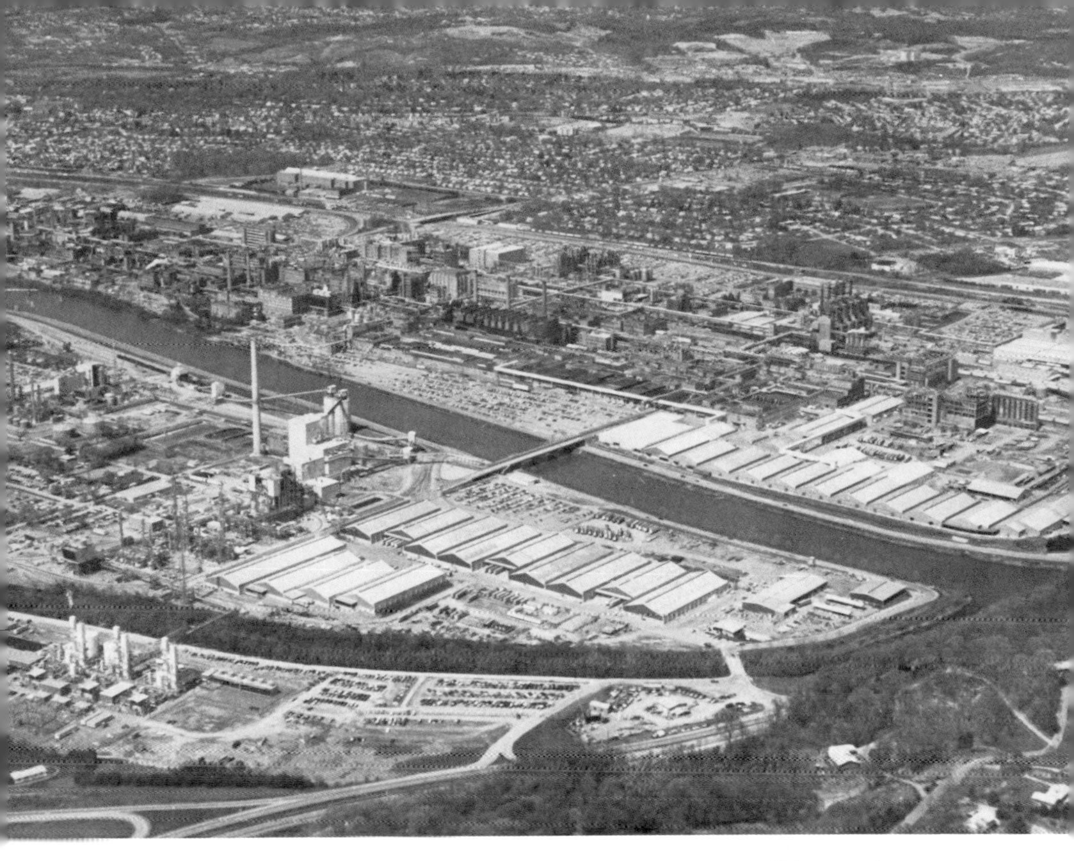

Above, an aerial view of the sprawling Eastman companies, one of Tennessee's largest employers, in the 1980s. Courtesy of Tennessee Eastman Company. Below, Kingsport Press's facilities in Hawkins County are part of the company's 40 acres of work and storage space. Now owned by Arcata Graphics, the company is one of the largest book manufacturing operations in the United States. Courtesy of Arcata Graphics/Kingsport.

A 1986 aerial view showing Church Circle, a principal feature of Nolen's original plan for the city, and a portion of downtown Kingsport. Photograph by Ken Murray.

7

Kingsport in Transition

War-weary residents of Kingsport and the surrounding area "turned out by thousands upon thousands to throng Broad Street" shortly after the Japanese surrender.[1] They were relieved to have an end to the deadliest, costliest, and most devastating struggle known to recorded civilization. The confidence with which they faced postwar adjustment was laced with some degree of uncertainty. The model city was about to embark upon an era marked by previously unprecedented growth through annexation; significant residential, business, and public-service-oriented construction; some developments that would irrevocably alter the downtown; and others that would bring social tensions that would help to undermine the "Kingsport spirit." Although the residents of Kingsport could not foresee all of this in 1945, the more astute of them sensed that their community was teetering on the precipice of disconcerting change. Just as World War II marks a watershed in world history, the passing of much of Kingsport's pioneer leadership serves as a milestone in the life of the planned city.

On 4 October 1944 the lead story of the *Kingsport Times* announced: "Death brought to a close today a career that has not only paralleled but led the destinies of Kingsport and neighboring counties of Upper East Tennessee for the past 30 years." J. Fred Johnson, affectionately known as the "father of Kingsport," had expired. Having been in ill health for a year or more, he had prepared accordingly. He had made a new will in January 1944 and had added a codicil a few months later, increasing the amount of cash bequeathed to two faithful employees. Expressions of sympathy arrived at the home on Watauga Street for weeks from public officials and private individuals throughout the city, state, and nation and from servicemen at faraway battle stations. The funeral service was conducted on 5 October at the First Presbyterian Church; city offices were closed; burial followed in the city cemetery;

and the will was probated two days later. Thus, the customary religious and legal rituals marked his passing while a small vibrant city in Southern Appalachia served as his monument. His friends arranged two additional memorials to honor him: an endowed chair in chemistry at King College in Bristol and the J. Fred Johnson Memorial Library, a project that culminated with the relocation of the Kingsport Public Library to the old post office building at the corner of Broad and New streets; it was finally dedicated on 19 November 1961.[2]

Johnson's was the first of a series of deaths that marked the end of an era for the model city and erased the leadership of the founding generation. Several former aldermen and business leaders passed away during the late forties and early fifties. As 1946 dawned, longtime city manager Frank L. Cloud expired; John B. Dennis died in February 1947; and the end came for Perley S. Wilcox in 1953.[3] Prominent citizens of that era, when asked who became the town's power broker after Johnson's death, found it difficult to settle on a single name. Some of them, including H.J. Shivell and Howard Wilson, mentioned C.P. Edwards, Jr., a prominent businessman. Shivell observed, however, that although his friend Edwards would have liked to fill Johnson's shoes, it was an impossible goal for him or anyone else; Johnson was unique to the town's experience. Karl Goerdel quickly mentioned James C. White of Tennessee Eastman Company. Both Edwards and White wielded considerable influence; neither of them seemed interested in elected offices.[4]

Edwards was a banker, insurance broker, and real-estate developer who during the early 1960s served as chairman of the board of the First National Bank of Sullivan County, president of the Kingsport Federal Savings and Loan Association, and chairman of the board of the Bennett and Edwards Insurance Agency, which he and a partner had founded. He was also the developer of Ridgefields subdivision. A highly successful entrepreneur, he functioned as a business and civic promoter who at one time was active in thirty diversified operations.[5] For several years he also owned the Kingsport Publishing Company, which printed the morning *News* and the afternoon *Times*. He headed a group of civic leaders who bought the *Kingsport Times* from T.H. Pratt and Howard Long in 1938. According to Edwards, they had "originally purchased the newspaper with the idea of keeping it a conservative, constructive, civic paper, dedicated to helping Kingsport progress in a positive, favorable manner." In 1962, Edwards sold the company to the Sandusky Papers of Sandusky, Ohio, much to the chagrin of many of the town's citizens.[6] The passing of the newspaper publishing company from local ownership has continued to be a source of irritation to some.

James C. White, whose formal education did not include a high-school diploma, was a man of considerable ability.[7] When he died in 1973 at the age of eighty-three, the newspaper proclaimed that he had been associated with Tennessee Eastman Company longer than any other man. He had risen from timber cruiser to the presidency of the company by 1945, at which time he also became a member of the executive committee of Eastman Kodak Company. He was a fellow of the American Society of Mechanical Engineers and had received honorary degrees from King College in 1947 and Brown University in 1953. Known as a powerful leader in his church and the community, he was especially noted for his connections with the hospital, where he served as president of the board as well as in various other capacities.[8] The story circulated that the hospital was at one time outfitted with stately white columns because White decided that it should be so and found the money to pay for them.

No one man possessed all the qualifications to replace Johnson, and while a few like Edwards and White could assume some of his functions, they did not bring to their tasks the same energy and comprehensive vision or public stature that had made Johnson a dynamic leader. Kingsport had only one father, and surrogates did not measure up to the challenge. With the town's "one-man chamber of commerce" gone, businessmen, industrialists, and civic leaders quickly organized the Kingsport Development Commission and later the Kingsport Chamber of Commerce. These institutions, for a while, fostered capitalistic development and sustained civic consciousness; the nurturing and refurbishing of community spirit exceeded their capabilities. Smug and comfortable with Kingsport society as it was, the commercial and industrial elites accepted the socioeconomic attributes of Johnson's legacy with complacency. Whatever change they supported had to conform to their narrowly drawn definition of progress, of which the profit incentive was a major, if not the overriding, consideration.

Reflecting on Kingsport as he, a newcomer, found it in 1945, James Welch, a retired Eastman executive who was also president of Appalachian Management Assistance, observed in 1983 that "some of us have outdone Pygmalion in creating an image of Kingsport. Through our rose-colored glasses we have viewed and dreamed of the 'model city'... believed it...loved it...to such an extent that—in our minds, anyway—it is real. Sadly and realistically, we must admit that our model spiritual creation of the perfect community is as unreal as the life Aphrodite was capable of giving Galatea." At the same time, Welch admonished citizens not to "focus all... attentions on the sore fingers of the community."[9] The postwar public rhetoric and promotional tracts of the Chamber of Commerce as well as other groups were of the Pygmalion genre. They described a near-perfect industrial community, replete with medical facilities, excellent schools, and civic and cultural activities for Caucasian middle- and upper-class citizens. Characterized by public meetings, civic clubs, churches, and volunteer services, democracy not only worked but also reportedly flourished in the town.[10]

Local civic leaders prepared propaganda in response to a flood of requests for information, and journalists made Kingsport the subject of articles, after Robert St. John's broadcasts. The stories that both groups cranked out described a close-knit white Anglo-Saxon community in which the number of foreigners was negligible and blacks constituted only 4 percent of the population.[11] A visiting writer noted that "many Kingsport workers believe a man achieves greater dignity, independence and security by owning a small farm" and gave credit to a local building-and-loan association for the "homesteads" that dotted the countryside.[12] Some laborers, however, owned property in the surrounding countryside that had been willed or deeded to them from family-owned holdings dating back for several generations. They raised vegetable gardens, hogs, poultry, and a tobacco patch in their spare time and commuted, by automobile or bus, to their factory jobs, where they gave their employers an honest day's work.[13] This pattern of existence, which had been apparent from the town's infancy, produced a growing concentration of people on the town's periphery who were not and did not choose to be participants in the rather closed social life of the town, paid no municipal taxes, and owed no particular allegiance to the Kingsport community. Although the 1940 census registered only 14,404 residents within the incorporation, almost 30,000 people lived within two miles of the city limits. When the first registration for ration books had been held during the war, the Kingsport office issued 50,993; and annual payroll lists of industrial employees for 1943, for example, had numbered 19,672.[14]

External attention also encouraged Kingsport residents to believe that they had found the American way. A study that was sponsored by the National Housing Committee and was published in 1944 praised the town for having had a unified planning approach that had been attentive not only to economic considerations but also to human needs.

Nonetheless, "the appearance and integrity of the character of the development is rapidly lost," observed the researchers, "in the towns which reverted to 'normal' municipal practices such as Kingsport and Longview."[15] In August 1945 the *Monthly Review* of the Federal Reserve Bank of Atlanta recognized the town as a demonstration case for "certain important principles of sound industrial growth" and hailed "intelligence, hard work, and careful planning" as "the true foundations of Kingsport's success."[16] Charles Stevenson, managing editor of the *Washington News*, writing for the *National Municipal Review*, praised local citizens for the orderly fashion in which peacetime economic reconversion had been achieved.[17] His article, which subsequently appeared in *Reader's Digest*, reported that over the tranquil scene of neat homes and Georgian churches and public buildings "rose the coughing of steam shovels, the noise of building, of expansion of jobs" accomplished by "private enterprise with real community spirit." For Kingsport, it was "not *back* to peace but *forward* to peace."[18]

The United States Information Agency considered the Kingsport of the late forties and early fifties "the model city" and its vice-mayor, Sam S. Benedict, so typical of the "American way of life" that they were featured as part of a Cold War propaganda film for overseas consumption. Benedict, who took his starring role in stride, was photographed at a City Council meeting and on a family camping trip.[19] Kingsport also participated in the Exchange of Foreign Leaders Program of the International Exchange Service, sponsored by the U.S. Department of State. In 1955 a German cooperative-action team, which included the lord mayor and four others from Singen, visited Kingsport. Kingsport subsequently sent representatives to Europe.[20]

Some reminiscences suggest that growing up in Kingsport was nearly idyllic. John Palmer of the National Broadcasting Company, who was a scion of Colonel E.W. Palmer of Kingsport Press, recollected how as a schoolboy he had looked forward to April and May—his favorite months—which meant "the Legion pool, frog-gigging on Bays Mountain, snaring crawdads in Reedy Creek, badminton in the back yard, softball games in the field across the street, the 4th of July parade and picnics at Stoney Creek, the American Legion Carnival and fishing trips with Dad to Cherokee and Boone lakes." Palmer also remembered "the high school band parading down Broad Street late Friday afternoons before football games and farmers on Saturday morning standing in front of the granite bank building on the corner, comparing watches ... the State, Strand, Rialto and Center movie theaters" where he stood "in line on Saturday mornings" and paid "9 cents to see Roy Rogers and Hopalong Cassidy."[21] Elizabeth Dudney, a veteran science teacher in the city school system, enthusiastically recalled the first Girl Scout Troop, Kiwanis Kapers, and how "everyone in town knew everyone else."[22]

Those on the town's periphery, beyond the pale of the elite, shopped downtown, frequented the movie theaters, trooped into the professional offices, and turned out for Fourth of July celebrations, Christmas parades, and week-long preaching missions. Many postwar "baby boomers" became the first of their Appalachian clans to be born away from home as young mothers availed themselves of the services provided by Holston Valley Community Hospital and as physicians became less likely to make house calls. Embracing the chrome-and-enamel world of the fifties, area housewives bought their Maytags, Frigidaires, and dinette sets from merchants in the model city; and many a farm-boy-turned-industrial-worker bought his first Chevrolet or Ford pickup from the town's automobile dealers. During that decade it was estimated that at least 90 percent of the young people left neighboring Hawkins County to find work; but many of them went no farther than Kingsport.[23]

Children of the town's industrial workers were more likely than not to be enrolled in a county school system, not in Kingsport, where Superintendent Ross N. Robinson "kept his teachers the highest-paid and best" and Dobyns-Bennett High School's Principal C.K. Koffman "ran a tight ship with a heart of gold."[24] Classroom registers for all enrolled students in Tennessee then called for the fathers' places of employment, not the mothers', because the majority of the latter did not work away from home. Proud was the child who could respond to the teacher's inquiry that his papa worked at "The Eastman," "The Press," "The Mead," or any other major company in town. Such a reply symbolized family security. Many fathers and mothers expected their sons to "get on" at one of the plants, and some hoped that their daughters—until marriage—might blossom into bank tellers and stenographers in town after a stint at Whitney Business College or on the basis of high-school typing and shorthand classes.

The surprisingly highly developed public-transportation system of the late forties deteriorated quickly during the 1950s as more residents of the region found that owning an automobile was within their reach. While the former situation lasted, however, it contributed to the social cohesion of Kingsport and its hinterland. The Clinchfield Railroad was still providing passenger service, making whistle-stops in rural communities, and carrying people into town throughout the 1940s. The City Transportation Company scheduled 500 bus runs daily, and 125 buses passed through Union Bus Terminal en route or providing connections to points beyond Upper East Tennessee.[25] The home-owned newspaper, with its morning and afternoon editions, and WKPT-AM and FM radio, which controlled the printed news and dominated the local airways, also engendered a sense of unity and community spirit.

By the 1940s, air traffic and trucking had lessened the town's dependence on the railroad; but Kingsport was still the CC&O's best customer, providing it with 125 to 150 carloads of freight per day. American Airlines, Pennsylvania Central Airlines, and Twentieth Century Airline made passenger stops at Tri-City Airport. Capital Airlines also briefly served the facility during the fifties, but these companies withdrew, and Piedmont Airlines came to enjoy a dominant, if not monopolistic, grip on air passenger traffic in the region. By the late 1940s, local industries were relying heavily on air transport, and at least one local company owned its own plane. Trucking firms, too, eased Kingsport's isolation. Locally owned and operated, Mason and Dixon Lines kept approximately 500 trucks on the roads between Atlanta and New York. The Silver Fleet Motor Express and Rutherford Freight Lines shared a terminal in Kingsport. The East Tennessee and Western North Carolina Transportation Company, as well as Associated Transport and the Super Service Motor Freight Company, also accommodated Kingsport.

As Kingsport industries reached out for domestic and foreign markets in the years after World War II and tied into national transportation arteries, more immediate considerations also beckoned the citizenry. The distance that separated the quality of life for the races as well as the classes remained substantial.[26] Around 1939, according to an application made to USHA, an estimated 22,500 residents, or about 5,500 families, had crowded into 2,741 dwelling units. Public-housing projects in the meantime had ameliorated the situation somewhat, only to have desperate shortages burgeon again when local industries received defense contracts. The nation's postwar housing problem was likewise felt in Kingsport.[27] Finding satisfactory residences presented problems for newlyweds of modest means. One couple laughingly recalled that anything and everything was offered as an excuse for apartments. They recollected having been shown a unit in which the commode was almost thronelike in appearance because of the jerry-built plumbing in the upstairs of a structure intended to be a single-family dwelling.[28] The KHA, in conjunction with federal agencies, operated a trailer camp for veterans in an attempt to meet the temporary needs of former soldiers and their families.[29] James H. ("Jimmy") Quillen, who became a very popular U.S. congressman from Tennessee's First District, established the Kingsport Development Company after the war, which catered to would-be buyers who were eligible for Veterans Administration home loans and FHA financing. For a thirty-year loan, the Veterans Administration required no down payment; the FHA, 3 percent. Quillen quickly developed Garden Drive and the Belmont area off Wilcox Drive, Kingsley Hills in the Bloomingdale area, and some housing on the west end of town beyond Sevier Terrace.[30]

When promotional literature boasted that Kingsport had "an adequate number of schools in a well integrated system,"[31] *integrated* referred to program, not to race. A color line divided the model city as surely as it did other southern towns, as well as most of those elsewhere in the country during this era. Few blacks could expect to rise above janitorial service in business and commercial employment, although a sprinkling of them owned businesses, classified themselves as musicians, followed the ministry, or practiced their professions within the black community. Black teachers had a lower pay scale than their white counterparts, and the money spent to educate a black student was considerably less than for a white child.[32] The Reverend C. Everett Edge, who moved to Kingsport during the early 1950s, "thought this was far enough north to get away from [the] kind of treatment" that he had experienced in Montgomery, Alabama; but "the first thing" he saw was "a sign at Johnson Stadium reading 'Whites Only.' "[33]

Public accommodations were limited and rigidly segregated. A black could not expect to eat at the Kress or Woolworth lunch counters.[34] When the new Strand Theater, built to replace an earlier one that had burned, opened in July 1947, it had seats for 1,040 patrons; 164 were reserved for blacks. The blaze that had destroyed the old structure had been "discovered in the floor of the Negro balcony, only 10 feet from the highly inflammable projection room."[35] The Gem Theater seemed almost self-congratulatory in offering a special showing of Walt Disney's "Song of the South" for blacks only. The local newspaper, in a story entitled "Uncle Remus Picture Runs for Negroes," unabashedly announced the special midnight show on Thanksgiving eve and provided a description of the highlights of the movie.[36] The manager of the Kingsport Inn refused to let "niggers" eat in his hotel, even in a back room. That also applied to the members of Duke Ellington's orchestra, who were in town for a Jaycee-sponsored dance for whites at the Civic Auditorium.[37] When two black ministers had appeared before the Board of Mayor and Aldermen in October 1944 to request that a swimming pool for black people be included in the 1945 city budget, the town fathers informed them that this would require a referendum on a bond issue and that such action was not advisable at that time. In August 1945, "a group of colored people" appeared before the board to state that they had purchased eight lots in the Riverview section for a recreation area and wanted to turn the property over to the city. The council agreed to review and consider the matter, but no immediate decision was forthcoming.[38] Several years later, however, the black community had its own park and pool.

The paternalistic elite that often recited the virtues of their workers could just as easily quell any sign of labor independence. When City Manager D.W. Moulton, fresh from Chattanooga and newly instated at a salary of $7,500,[39] was approached by representatives of a local union representing firemen, police, and public works employees, the Board of Mayor and Aldermen took a hard line, unanimously declaring: "The City of Kingsport will not recognize any demands made on it by any Union. Any City employee who participates in a strike will forfeit his job automatically."[40] E.F. Dean, the spokesman for the American Federation of State, County and Municipal Employees Local No. 1034, submitted a letter to the board on 6 August. He informed them that their city employees, many of whom were veterans who had "recently seen active service in a war to uphold these rights granted to them under the Constitution and left many of their buddies dead on the battlefield" had "exercised their God given right to organize into a union." The local requested a 20 percent increase in pay for policemen and firemen and a 48-hour week. Other employees wanted a 20 to 30 percent raise and a work week of 44 to 48 hours. After the city manager had found that municipal workers received less than the general average paid by local industry for similar work and that their work days were extremely long, the board accepted Moulton's recommendation for pay increases, shorter hours, and a vacation plan, at the same time asserting that it would not recognize any labor or trade union. By 3 September it had passed an ordinance that called for the discharge of any policeman who engaged in a strike.[41]

Ever sensitive to rising unionism, the mayor and the aldermen also rallied when local attorney Howard Wilson, representing the

Clinchfield Railroad, appeared before them in April 1955 to request additional police and fire service. He stated that the railroad was willing to pay the costs but noted that it was the duty of the city to protect the lives and property of its citizens. With a vague reference to "this emergency," which was recorded in the minutes, they agreed to place on duty as many additional policemen as necessary for twelve to sixteen hours per day. The "emergency" apparently arose from strikes throughout the South, which involved railroad and communications workers and which affected the Louisville and Nashville Railroad, of which the Clinchfield was then a subsidiary.[42]

City government seemed to grow bolder and certainly more independent after Johnson and Dennis had been laid to rest. On 3 June 1947 the board had instructed the city manager to write a letter to the Chamber of Commerce, asking that it establish a committee to consider using TVA power for Kingsport.[43] In 1925 the local operation had been sold to American Gas and Electric Company and had become a subsidiary of the Appalachian Electric Power Company; Johnson, however, continued to retain a substantial financial interest. The power company's building, which had "the only large assembly hall in the city" before the construction of the Civic Auditorium, "was given over for the free use of the ladies." Civic clubs of all types met there, as well as book clubs and garden clubs. During World War II, more than one million bandages were made on the premises. All of this, according to a local publication, afforded "another link in the splendid relations existing between the Company and the people of Kingsport."[44] Whatever the intent of the Board of Mayor and Aldermen, the privately owned utilities company remained entrenched.

While Johnson's demise left the town bereft of a particular type of leadership, Dennis's passing occasioned the dismantling of the Kingsport Improvement Company and severed any remaining tenuous connections between the public incorporation and the private company. After John B. Dennis's death in February 1947, his brother, H. Ray, became president of the Securities Company. Ray quickly sought the advice of William B. Franke, which had been calculatingly ignored by John. An audit was begun of all of the family's holdings, and H. Ray Dennis and Franke "agreed on all matters and, together... proceeded to do what was necessary to clean the corporate house and to place the Company in a sound financial condition." It took several years and considerable effort, but the mergers and liquidations turned the family's interests from real estate to marketable securities. In 1955, "for the first time in many years the accumulated deficit had been liquidated and at December 31, 1955 there was a surplus of $82,000," according to Franke. "During the year substantial investments were made in marketable common stocks and the common stock portfolio at year-end showed an appreciation of over $300,000."[45]

The Dennis family, by the early 1950s, was well on its way to divestiture of its real estate in Kingsport. Before John B. Dennis's death, he had enlisted Olmsted Associates of Brookline, Massachusetts, to undertake some landscape refinement of the cemetery. Carl Rust Parker of that firm continued to correspond with H. Ray Dennis. For a while, there was some discussion of a mausoleum or vault section, which Parker assumed would be "urgently needed" if John B. Dennis were "to be finally buried in Kingsport." By 1950, however, the family was considering the possibility of selling the cemetery, which they did in 1955.[46] Eventually, the Dennises disposed of all of their Kingsport real estate, although they retained reversionary rights to alleys and similar bits of property that might cease to be used for their initial purposes as originally conveyed to the city. In 1958 the city rejected H. Ray Dennis's offer to sell the property on which the Kingsport Inn was located as the site for the proposed new city hall, mentioning adverse public reaction to the idea of destroying the inn.[47] Nonetheless, the property was eventually sold by the Dennises, and the once-gracious Kingsport Inn was razed. The last significant real-estate transaction of the Securities Company in Kingsport occurred on 17 December 1977, when it sold a section of Maple Street between Oak and East Center streets to the Kingsport Housing Authority for $3,150, the appraised value. As of the end of that same year, the company chose not to remain franchised in Tennessee.[48]

For better or for worse, city government in the Kingsport of the late 1940s and early 1950s enjoyed an autonomy that it had not previously known or possessed. In the post–World War II history of the model city, this materialized as structural reform, flow charts, and regulatory specificity. The establishment of the Municipal Planning Commission, which was composed of representatives from the Board of Mayor and Aldermen and prominent citizens, signaled this new initiative. Kingsport's first zoning ordinance became effective in January 1946; subdivision regulations for the city and for the surrounding Eleventh, Twelfth, and Thirteenth civil districts of Sullivan County took effect in August 1948. The creation of the Zoning Appeal Board accompanied these developments. The building code was revised in 1952, and two substandard-housing ordinances, which included most of the elements of a complete housing code, became operational in August 1954. Subdivision regulations and the building code applied to new residential, business, and industrial development and to the remodeling and expansion of existing buildings and their uses. The housing code not only affected new construction; it also set forth methods for improving housing to meet standards and procedures for the gradual demolition of substandard dwellings.[49]

According to a report prepared by the Upper East Tennessee Office of the Tennessee State Planning Commission in 1956, the zoning ordinance proved "particularly effective in eliminating the building of more than one house on a lot and in minimizing population density and overcrowding through the requirements for minimum lot area per family in residential areas." The regional planning staff also suggested that it was in the interest of the city to have the county administer the building codes and zoning ordinances beyond the incorporated area. Otherwise, Kingsport residents might "ultimately have to pay a share of the costs for bringing any annexed areas up to reasonable standards."[50] Prevailing wisdom on land-use planning in Sullivan and Hawkins counties, however, upheld the residents' view that a man had a God-given right to do as he wished with his land, even if this meant establishing a hog pen next door to his neighbor's new split-level house. Zoning regulations, in the city where they existed, were not worth the paper on which they were written unless they were rigidly enforced. In Kingsport, enforcement rested with the Division of Building Inspection;[51] but the work of the building inspector could be adversely affected by a lack of commitment from elected officials or a disinterested citizenry.

Air-pollution control, which was referred to as smoke abatement, received its first serious attention from city government during 1946. The Board of Mayor and Aldermen arranged for a study of existing conditions and the preparation of an ordinance. A year elapsed as due consideration was given the risk of killing "the goose with the golden eggs"—the industries that employed thousands of people. Finally, the board decided that a public referendum was in order. The vote on 9 September 1947 showed that 829 favored smoke-and-dust control and 346 opposed it.[52] The City Council subsequently passed the ordinance and established the Department of Air Pollution Control as well as an appeals board. The 1948-49 biennial report of the city government cited some outstanding accomplishments over the previous eighteen months "in spite of some impressive handicaps," which included "the reluctance of one plant [the cement company] to comply fully with the ordinance." Another obstacle arose when an extended coal strike began in September 1949, producing a shortage of "low volatile coal." The ordinance was challenged but was upheld by the Tennessee Supreme Court.[53] Despite an important beginning, air pollution in Kingsport was far from being eliminated.

With the newly ensconced zoning ordinance, subdivision regulations, and housing codes, as well as a polite bow to air quality, the city government girded itself for an aggressive annexation program. Progress required growth for this generation, which frequently manifested itself as geographical expansion and the redrafting of the boundaries of the incorporation. The old leadership, personified by Johnson and Dennis, had directed its energies toward the improvement of the initial town site, and prior to their deaths, only two minor additions had been made: a small thin strip in the vicinity of the intersection of Center Street and what later became Wilcox Drive, and another piece of property near what would be J. Fred Johnson Park. Both of these additions, in 1937 and 1939 respectively, were accomplished by legislation in the Tennessee General Assembly. In 1951 a small area north of the stadium, known as Stadium Court, and a large section north of Radcliffe were also attached to the city by state legislation, the last annexation to be accomplished in this manner.[54] A state constitutional amendment of 1953 limited this practice. The principal remaining method of territorial acquisition required a petition from fifty resident freeholders in the area under consideration, although subsequent legislation offered additional options.[55]

The deaths of the founders may have been less relevant to Kingsport's expansion than were the emerging patterns of aggressive real-estate development and urban imperialism that characterized American cities of the 1950s and 1960s.[56] In any event, beginning around 1949, the city embarked on a course that within approximately fifteen years would more than double its land area, would strain and sometimes exceed its capacity to provide services, and would somewhat undermine the unity and cohesion of the community. During the last days of the forties, the Board of Mayor and Aldermen, upon petition, prepared for the annexation of the remainder of Fairacres Addition and the old nursery tract. This was accomplished by ordinance, effective 10 January 1950.[57] By the procedure of ordinance and referendum, the city in March 1950 added Forest Lawn, a 550-acre area on the east side of town, taking in what became designated as Green Acres and the

Konnarock Road vicinity.[58] In January 1951 the Board of Education reminded the people of Kingsport that unless an elementary school was constructed for the Forest Lawn section, an emergency situation could develop in two or three years that would necessitate the use of the old Douglass building, previously used for black education.[59]

The years from 1951 to 1955 witnessed a virtual whirlwind of improvement-district activity in the planned city as it extended services, constructed and upgraded sidewalks and streets, and looked to the educational needs of its young population. During 1953 and 1954, with due consideration to the effects that this would have on industrial processes, city officials decided to fluoridate the water supply—a decision that came after they had been duly advised that industrialists did not think it would have an adverse effect.[60] Christine Triebe, "a registered nurse by profession and a public servant by choice," and wife of Edward J. Triebe, a high-ranking executive at Kingsport Press, led the crusade for fluoridation.[61] The city also acquired a new site for the post office on Center Street and exchanged it for the old federal building; provided for the enlargement of Holston Valley Community Hospital; authorized the construction of more low-rent housing units and the preparation of plans for remodeling the old post office as a library; and proceeded with the construction of a new elementary school and the renovation of a part of Dobyns-Bennett High School.[62] Kingsport had hardly witnessed the completion of the first junior high school around 1954 when the citizenry was advised that another one might soon be needed. Indeed, a referendum for this purpose was held on 25 September. Characteristic of Kingsport's commitment to education, the voters approved the bond issue 607 to 15.[63]

Up to this point, annexation had not created any serious divisions in the community or any conflict with the environs. The majority of the population retained a unified view of what constituted progress. Although hostilities half the world away interfered intermittently with the somewhat monotonous rhythms of middle-class respectability during the early 1950s, adults who had weathered not only the severest depression in the American experience but also the world's most awesome war settled comfortably into family life on what historian Kenneth T. Jackson has dubbed the "crabgrass frontier." Folk singer Malvina Reynolds called these homes "little boxes on the hillside...made of ticky-tacky...and they all look the same," but for occupants of the country's rapidly constructed tract housing, they were castles.[64] The outbreak of the Korean War spurred disaster-relief planning in Kingsport by the local chapter of the American Red Cross; city employees, among them Charles K. Marsh, director of public works, were granted military leave as they were inducted into the armed services; and Kingsport units of the Tennessee National Guard—the Second Battalion, 278th Infantry—reported to Fort Devens, Massachusetts, for training.[65] By February 1951, reactivation of Area A of Holston Ordnance Works was well under way. The John J. Harte Construction Company persuaded the mayor and aldermen to allow the use of boilers there, although no fly-ash collectors could be installed on the stacks in fewer than 120 days; town officials wanted confirmation, however, that the devices had been ordered and would be operational as soon as possible. Representatives of Holston Ordnance informed the city during September that they could not have the devices in place before mid-November, and the board did not object to the use of the boilers in the meantime.[66]

The local Cold War mentality received a boost with revelations that a spy ring had touched Kingsport. The Federal Bureau of Investigation arrested Dean Slack on 15 June 1950 in Syracuse, New York, and accused him of having supplied Communist agent Harry Gold with war secrets from Holston Ordnance Works from 1943 to 1944. Slack, who had worked for Eastman Kodak during the 1930s, had also allegedly sold industrial secrets to a friend with Socialist leanings. Later, Slack had become acquainted with Gold, who worked for the spy ring of Klaus Fuchs, billed as a British scientist-traitor. Gold appeared in Kingsport during 1943 and apparently blackmailed Slack, then employed at HOW, into cooperating. After reportedly sneaking a handful of some substance out of the plant, Stack left the model city and worked at Oak Ridge on the Manhattan Project. Indicted on 1 September 1950 in the United States District Court at Greeneville, Tennessee, he pleaded guilty to charges of espionage several days later and received a fifteen-year sentence from the judge, even though the government prosecutors had recommended only ten.[67]

Some citizens constructed fallout shelters, but espionage, war, and the threat of nuclear attack did not weigh heavily on teenagers and young adults in the model city during the fifties. Attending athletic events, "cruising Broad" (the practice of driving up and down Broad Street from Church Circle to the Clinchfield depot), admiring hot cars, or frequenting drive-in movies and restaurants received high priority. Some of their middle-aged parents took their pleasure at lodges maintained by fraternal orders or joined the new Ridgefields Country Club.

Although the sobriety forces managed to convince the Board of Mayor and Aldermen to outlaw beer in 1955, Mr. and Mrs. Kingsport have been known more than once to vote dry and drink wet. The board reversed itself and legalized beer again in 1962.[68]

Dottie Teter became the first Miss Kingsport in 1953. She was persuaded to enter the local contest, the first in a series that could lead to the Miss America competition in Atlantic City, New Jersey, because "it was not going to be a beauty pageant, but 'an all-American-girl-type pageant.' " Also, several of her friends planned to participate, and contestants received free bathing suits. With her prize, a $250 scholarship, she purchased contact lenses so that she would not have to count her steps from one point on stage to another in the Miss Tennessee pageant, the technique she had used in Kingsport to avoid wearing glasses. Although she placed in the top ten at the state contest in Jackson, she decided that beauty pageants were really not for her. Later, as a missionary in the Congo with nuns and priests being killed thirty-five miles away, she recalled thinking how easy it was to be a Christian in Kingsport: "When I was growing up, I thought that if you are good, get a good education, marry a good boy with a good education, and go to church regularly, life will be a success." With maturity and life's calamities, she had discovered that "life is not like 'Ozzie and Harriet,' 'The Waltons,' or 'The Brady Bunch.' "[69]

Dottie Teter's view of life as an eighteen-year-old Miss Kingsport was not unlike that of her peers. This clean-cut, freshly scrubbed, financially comfortable contingent of Kingsport's youth population did not turn out en masse when Elvis Presley, who was just beginning his rise to stardom, played the Civic Auditorium in September 1955. About half of the seats were empty when a country-music crowd stared at an "unusual-looking young boy in his white buck shoes, his bright pink socks, the denim pants, the white shirt unbuttoned down to where his acoustic guitar hung, and his black leather jacket." With his greasy long hair, he looked like a hood, but there was a magic about him. Teenaged girls screamed when he opened his act with "One O'clock, Two O'clock, Three O'clock ROCK!" from the Bill Haley and the Comets hit entitled "Rock around the Clock." A local girl, Billy Mae Smith, went out to the Martinique Restaurant with him for a pepperoni pizza after the show. He took her home, kissed her good night, and left town. Elvis sent her a postcard from New York and a billfold picture, but she never saw him again.[70]

Beginning in 1956, the relative tranquility of the model city was shattered. On 28 January, some 525 members of the Kingsport Local No. 117 of the United Glass and Ceramic Workers of North America struck Blue Ridge Glass Corporation in an attempt to obtain a fifteen-cent hourly raise. The company, then headed by Joseph H. Lewis, president and general manager, and Sam S. Benedict, vice-president and director of public relations, granted a five-cent raise, announced its intentions of remaining in operation, and began to hire replacements for striking employees. Tensions ran high as some returning union members and newly hired workers crossed the picket lines. Incidents of violence occurred at the plant site and even at such downtown locations as Freels Drugstore. Strike-inspired lawlessness spilled over into the communities and countryside of rural Hawkins, Sullivan, and Washington counties. The dynamiting of cars, houses, and the Clinchfield Railroad tracks, as well as gunshots at the strike scene and in residential areas, introduced a level of turbulence that had heretofore been unknown in labor-management relations in Upper East Tennessee. The Kingsport newspapers, though refusing to take a stand against the right to strike, nonetheless denounced the violence and reminded readers that "Kingsport is a decent community where men and women believe in law and order." Newspapers in Bristol, Johnson City, and Knoxville also abhorred the lawless acts.[71]

The murder of Everett Jenkins at his Sulphur Springs home in Washington County on 30 April 1957 at first seemed to be strike-related. Jenkins, a nonunion employee of Blue Ridge Glass Corporation, died when he put his foot on the starter of his dynamite-laden automobile. Rewards in excess of $10,000 were offered for information pertaining to the murder; the company itself posted the first $5,000. His widow blamed the strike for his death, but her alleged lover refused to take a lie-detector test after he was arrested; he was released a short time later. Although she came through the polygraph test "as clear as a crystal," she was subsequently taken into custody and bound over for the crime.[72] That autumn, a jury acquitted her after the testimony of a key witness was discredited, so the murder remained unsolved.

In May 1956, P.J. Miller, president of the local union, in an open letter to the people of the Kingsport area, had charged that the company did not bargain in good faith and had never demonstrated that it could not afford the demand of a fifteen-cent hourly increase. Union representatives, according to Miller, had offered to accept the five-cent raise if indeed Blue Ridge could not afford to meet the higher figure. Worse still, he alleged, the company's president had promised that he would not try to operate the plant during the strike. When the union sent in a skeletal crew to shut down expensive machinery, at the company's request, they learned that Blue Ridge intended to maintain production and to break the strike. Miller admitted that strikers had already lost more money than the requested increase would have produced over several years, but invoking Americana, he observed: "Progress always comes at a high price. Stop and consider just for a moment what the American pioneers lost personally when they left the settled communities of the east and pushed forward with their families over the trackless mountains, into the wild beyond to face savage Indian massacres, the perils of wild nature and unknown dangers of every sort."[73] Donald Berger, district president of the United Glass and Ceramic Workers of North America, with a bid to nativists, blamed the troubles on foreign ownership. Be that as it may, the owners and management of Blue Ridge Glass Corporation were in tune with the sentiments of other industries in the town that were wholly American concerns. Berger lamented that Blue Ridge Glass was "owned by Frenchmen." "About the only way you could get anything out of them," he claimed, "was to practically beat their brains out."[74]

When the National Labor Relations Board held an election to determine bargaining rights for the glass-and-ceramic-workers union on 21 September 1956, the strikers were not permitted to vote. Consequently, by a vote of 597 to 6, the union was decertified. The NLRB validated the results on 24 October. Unemployment compensation then became an issue, and the Tennessee Employment Security Commission finally agreed on 5 August 1957 to make 744 payments for a total of approximately $21,000 to 220 of the 308 claimants who lost their jobs as a result of the strike. Union members who forfeited their jobs subsequently sued the union for breach of contract but lost their suit. Plaintiffs claimed that Berger had told them they could not lose in their dispute with the company and pointed to a $3.5-million strike fund at the union's disposal. When Blue Ridge had offered striking workers the option of returning to their jobs, union officials had reportedly threatened their own members with bodily harm if they exercised that option. The union, which did not deny the threats or that Berger had made such claims, rested its defense on the argument that it accepted no responsibility for unauthorized actions taken and statements made by its representatives.[75]

As labor unrest sent tremors through the staid industrial community, annexation and rezoning that the city government had inaugurated caused further damage to the increasingly fragile cohesion of the Kingsport area. State legislation that was enacted after the Constitutional Convention of 1953 eased annexation proceedings for the cities. By 1955 the process could be accomplished in three ways: (1) a petition from fifty freeholders, followed by an ordinance and a referendum of qualified voters in the area; (2) a petition from a majority of residents and property owners or by municipal initiative, preceded by a notice and public hearing and followed by an ordinance—aggrieved property owners within the proposed area could file a quo warranto suit; and (3) a resolution by the city government to extend corporate limits, followed by a public notice and a referendum of qualified voters in the area—a second election to reflect the will of city residents might also be used. With one election or two, a resolution of annexation required a majority of those voting to become effective. Larger cities might also annex smaller ones at this time. This could be implemented upon petition from 20 percent of the qualified voters in the smaller municipality, followed by an ordinance of the larger city if a majority of voters in the smaller one approved.[76] Kingsport officials found the second option especially to their liking.

During 1956 the Bureau of Public Administration of the University of Tennessee submitted an annexation study that Kingsport officials had requested. The final report explored what impact annexation would have on the future fiscal condition of the city. Researchers suggested that (1) the problems of whether to annex developing areas on the periphery would be continuous and (2) areas adjacent to the city were experiencing population increases at a faster rate than the incorporation. Although Kingsport grew from 11,914 in 1930 to 19,571 in 1950, the percentage of the total population of the metropolitan area that resided inside the city fell from 61 to 44 during the same twenty-year period. The report focused particularly on the centrality of Tennessee Eastman Company and its properties to the annexation question. In addition to the Eastman holdings, other study areas included Fort Robinson, Lynn Garden, Bloomingdale, Preston Woods, Holston Hills, and Ridgefields. TEC's holdings represented approximately 78 percent of the assessed values in all of the study areas combined. Pointing to the advantage of the "very great concentration of taxable property in one study area," the researchers observed that this gave "the city a chance to use this property to help carry the burden of less productive and more expensive areas... a chance to annex comprehensively which it [the city] would otherwise not have." The report suggested that "the city could finance annexation of all of the study areas with little difficulty for eight years following the annexation." Between the ninth and fifteenth years, "substantial additional sums of local money might be needed." After twenty years, resulting costs would "probably begin tapering off and eventually disapppear in about the thirty-fifth year after annexation." Researchers cautioned that the longer annexation was postponed, the more expensive it would be.[77]

Tennessee Eastman was the key to comprehensive annexation during the 1950s. It would be at least twenty-five years, however, before company officials would be favorably disposed—and then only on their own terms. Consequently, the elected officials adopted a piecemeal approach that took in the more desirable areas with significant tax bases and generally ignored the less promising ones. After having added a small tract in the vicinity of Fairmont Avenue and another in the Fairacres area by ordinances during the summer of 1955, they followed up with a large section around Ross N. Robinson Junior High School. In 1958, by ordinance no. 1576, an immense tract to the west of Lynn Garden Drive and north of what would be Stone Drive (Highway 11-W) came under the city's auspices.[78]

Property near this last acquisition became a source of considerable irritation when residents of Sevier Terrace protested the reclassification of property from residential use to tourist accommodations. In the midst of the ensuing struggle, some citizens came to believe that the pursuit of the almighty dollar counted for more at City Hall than the quality of life for the people and the maintenance of neighborhoods. Furthermore, the fate of the downtown commercial area hung in the balance. Signals were curiously mixed. In January 1955, Ralph C. Grant, vice-president and general manager of J. Fred Johnson Company, had informed the Board of Mayor and Aldermen that his firm intended to build a large department store that would occupy two lots at the corner of Broad and Center streets; so he requested the closing of an alley.[79] Such a commitment seemed a testimonial to the vitality of the downtown. A new post office and a new city hall were also in the offing.

In the meantime, however, traffic congestion and parking problems were harbingers of a new era. During the mid-fifties, the construction of a bypass road, named Industry Drive, around the southwest side of town, diverted traffic from the central business district.[80] It also quite inadvertently drained off potential shoppers, because industrial workers who had once passed through the core area bound for home now found it more convenient to avoid downtown and to frequent shopping centers that were beginning to appear. By 1962, for example, Sears Roebuck Company was preparing to locate near a pleasant neighborhood at Green Acres on the east side of town; and Edwin O. Norris, a local attorney representing the Securities Company, which owned the property, spoke to the Board of Mayor and Aldermen about rezoning it.[81] More immediately portentous perhaps for the old established businesses was the construction of the four-lane section of Highway 11-W, which was designated Stone Drive by the town fathers in honor of H.G. Stone.[82] The highly vocal disenchantment of the home owners blurred any omen that this held for the downtown.

The controversy over the rezoning of property in the vicinity of Sevier Terrace from R-2 (residential) to T-A (tourist accommodation) raged for about two years, from 1959 to 1961, and was aired in public hearings, regular meetings of the Board of Mayor and Aldermen, and court proceedings. At stake was the construction of a forty-four-unit motor lodge with swimming pool and restaurant under the Howard Johnson franchise. Attorney Lacy West, representing a group that opposed the change in classification, suggested "that the community might be caught in a scheme for individual profit... rather than community benefit." He pointed out that people in the area had bought property believing that it would remain residential and noted that Kingsport "should be very careful not to sacrifice a good community for the sake of progress." The opposition, including the Sevier Terrace Realty Company, some businessmen, and at least one judge and one physician, expressed surprise at so much hostility, pointed out that the motel would be built with "Kingsport money" and would "employ mostly Kingsport people," and said that this development "would be a valuable asset to Kingsport's growth." At one point, "a delegation, mostly ladies accompanied by their children," besieged the Board of Mayor and Aldermen. This prompted the city fathers to promise to station a policeman at school crossings near Andrew Jackson Elementary School and to request the fencing of the bridge over Lynn Garden Drive to make it safer for children on their way to class.[83]

Confronted with more public protest than had ever before been witnessed in Kingsport, the elected officials unflinchingly changed the zoning to allow tourist accommodations. Irritated home owners soon discovered that this move signaled the opening of a Pandora's box. As one of them observed when the rezoning of Lynn Garden Drive was under consideration a few months later, the rezoning of "one piece of property... seemed to open doors" for subsequent changes.[84] Furthermore, the reclassification of property to permit the construction of the motel marked the first stage of strip commercial development along Stone Drive. During the 1980s, urban sprawl extended for more than ten miles and stood as a remarkable testimonial to limited vision, poor planning, and the unheeded pleas of earlier years "that zoning laws were for the protection of the people."[85]

In fairness to supporters of the Howard Johnson project, it must be noted that Kingsport was without a decent hostelry. The once-gracious Kingsport Inn had deteriorated badly by the 1950s. In December 1957, City Judge Brantley Blue fined the establishment for violation of city ordinances regulating food-handling establishments. Inspectors from the Sullivan County Health Department turned up numerous violations after being forced into action by members of civic clubs who complained of possible food poisoning.[86] The Securities Company, which owned the Kingsport Inn as well as the Homestead Hotel, decided not to renew the lease of the management that operated both establishments. Local buyers acquired the Homestead Hotel, but no one seemed interested in trying to salvage the Kingsport Inn. By 1960 the Dennis heirs had sold the land on which the inn was situated to Millers of Knoxville, whose intent it was to build a large department store. Millers, however, had the chance to buy out its chief competitor in Knoxville and therefore decided against constructing in Kingsport. The old lodging house was demolished, local merchants bought the property for a parking lot, and Millers eventually acquired the J. Fred Johnson Company.[87]

Just before the litigation involving the Howard Johnson Motel was resolved, smoothing the way for its construction, Jack Trayer of Bristol, the president of Kingsport Motor Inn, Incorporated, announced the forthcoming opening of the new 108-room Holiday Inn on Lynn Garden Drive, only a short distance from the proposed motel. Calling Kingsport "a natural as a convention city," he claimed that his company was "trying to bring to Kingsport what we have been told is needed ... more rooms for the traveling public and more meeting rooms for conventions, clubs, and similar gatherings."[88] The Howard Johnson interests and the city reached an agreement on their differences and settled the three suits that had been pending in the Federal District Court at Greeneville, Tennessee; a suit that the developers had brought against the state had been resolved earlier. Instead of making changes in plans that would have put them in compliance with the T-A zoning ordinance, which required that the Kingsport Planning Commission approve construction plans in advance, and certain provisions of the building code, the developers had sought, through a series of lawsuits, to proceed with their original plan.

The settlement, which seemed to favor the city, paved the way for the construction of what had become a sixty-unit structure. Parties to the agreement, in addition to the city and Howard Johnson of Kingsport, Incorporated, were M.J. Morison, Jr., and his wife, Mrs. Annie Laura Morison, as well as Sevier Terrace Realty Company, of which M.J. Morison, Sr., apparently was a principal officer.[89] The resignations of Vice-Mayor J.A. Godwin and Alderman Max Y. Parker in the wake of the settlement appeared to be coincidental. Both were at midpoint in a four-year term, having been elected in 1959. According to a newspaper account, business activities placed demands on their time and spurred their decisions; Parker later recollected that he took advantage of an opportunity to make a trip to Europe. W.W. Cawood, a native of Harlan County, Kentucky, who was engaged in the insurance business, and W.C. Hale, an assistant vice-president of Tennessee Eastman Company who was originally from Jonesboro, Tennessee, were appointed to the unexpired terms.[90] On 13 December 1964 the *Kingsport Times-News* announced that the Howard Johnson Motor Lodge would be sold at auction on 8 January 1965 to satisfy claims by a host of creditors. The City of Kingsport was among those with claims, for unpaid property taxes. The motel subsequently operated as the Tennessee Motor Lodge.

The city fathers also faced considerable opposition when they looked hungrily to the affluent neighborhoods of Ridgefields and Preston Woods during the early 1960s. At a public hearing on the annexation of Ridgefields, Joseph O. Fuller, an attorney speaking as a private citizen, supported the move, claiming that the question was "whether Kingsport is to grow and thrive or whether it is to dry up and become stagnant." Mrs. Paul Scott asked if Tennessee Eastman property, of which there was a large portion in this study area, would be included. Under Tennessee law, a city needed the consent of an industry before its property could be annexed. Tennessee Eastman had consented to the inclusion of some of its property on Long Island in the original Ridgefields annexation area. Businessman W.B. Greene, Sr., opposed the annexation and said the people should have a vote on the issue. The local Chamber of Commerce added its endorsement. The discussions, which began in March 1962, dragged into September. W.W. Cawood, now mayor, stated that the city schools had over nine hundred tuition students, mainly from Ridgefields, Preston Woods, and Colonial Heights, and opined: "If the City is to build schools for these students they should become a part of the City."[91] Indeed, Ridgefields was taken in by ordinance no. 1738, as was the Fort Robinson area; the Preston Woods and Cliffside area, by ordinance no. 1762, in April 1963.[92] In June 1964 the city crossed the north fork of the Holston River and expanded its boundaries into Hawkins County, annexing portions of what was once the old Kingsport Farms, Incorporated. The State Supreme Court upheld this action, which involved 882 acres of eastern Hawkins County, when it was challenged by the suburban town of Mount Carmel.[93]

The city grew dramatically in land area during the 1950s and early 1960s. Coincident with this expansion, serious erosion befell the downtown. Even the once-proud trees that lined city streets succumbed to Dutch Elm disease. In the midst of what some considered progress and others called deterioration, the model city and the immediate area suffered what symbolically as well as literally could be called its most devastating blow. On Tuesday, 4 October 1960, at 4:45 P.M., the time of a shift change, the aniline plant at Tennessee Eastman Company, which had been constructed eighteen months earlier, exploded. A fire, not brought under control until about 8:00 P.M., followed the blast. The deaths, which eventually rose to fifteen, were numbered at eleven by the next morning, with two missing and presumed dead. More than sixty employees were initially listed as injured, although the number may have run as high as two hundred; forty-seven were admitted to Holston Valley Community Hospital and at least eight to other area hospitals and clinics.[94]

Few area residents who heard and felt the explosion that overcast autumn afternoon could ever forget the fear and dread that hung so heavily over Upper East Tennessee and southwestern Virginia. The blast jarred the downtown and was noticeable as far away as Johnson City; smaller explosions followed. Many homes near the plant suffered damage. The ceiling of the Pet Dairy collapsed, the Blue Ridge Glass Corporation suffered some ill effects, and thousands of windows were broken in Kingsport residences and businesses. At the explosion site, one witness later reported, "Everybody in the area was bleeding... it literally rained debris... glass, bricks, and metal... for several minutes. We didn't even try to help anybody who was able to walk." With the fire raging, a volunteer, looking up from a stretcher, prayed aloud, "Please, God, let it rain hard." Within minutes of the blast, local radio stations had passed the word of the disaster. Relatives of Eastman employees—many of whom were just leaving their jobs or were in the locker rooms—could not help but expect the worst.[95]

The switchboards at the plant, the offices of the newspapers, and Kingsport public buildings were swamped with calls; for hours only emergency long-distance communications were accepted. TEC's Public Relations Office went on emergency status, releasing information, including the names of the dead, as quickly as details had been confirmed and families had been notified. Calls came in from all over the United States, as well as from two London newspapers. By late evening, television networks and wire services were transmitting news about the blast all across the country. In Kingsport, people were trying to come to grips with what had happened. Corporal Albert Fletcher of the Police Department reported that when he arrived at the scene, "the first of the injured he saw were two men running from the fire. They were bloody all over, and didn't have on a stitch of clothes. A passing car stopped and took them to the hospital." A reporter, who quickly arrived on the scene, described "a mask of frozen horror" and "contorted faces."[96]

In what were the town's worst moments, Kingsport residents and area citizens were at their best. Holston Valley Community Hospital summoned all of the doctors and nurses in the city. A call for blood also went out, and donors queued up; many of them were used to build up a reserve of blood for the seriously injured. Medical personnel worked diligently through the night. Dr. H. Jim Brown, president of HVCH's medical staff, and William A. Phillips, executive director of the hospital, halted elective medical and surgical admissions until the effects of the disaster could be ascertained. Fifty to sixty members of the Ladies Auxiliary and the Junior Auxiliary provided assistance. Every stretcher and every wheelchair in the building was taken to the ground-floor emergency area; these were followed by roller-mounted beds from the vacant wing. People in Kingsport brought their cars to transport patients who were able to give up their rooms; volunteers handled traffic and served coffee and sandwiches; and clergymen were on hand to offer comfort. The situation at the hospital, according to one reporter, "was reminiscent of pictures of mine explosions—the same anxious faces watching ambulances, cars, and trucks arrive with the injured." The hospital set up a public-address system and gave the names of injured who were being treated, assigned beds, or released. Cries of grief punctuated the sighs of relief. Meanwhile, at the plant, as many as twenty-five ambulances lined up to rush the injured to the hospital. At least five rescue squads were quickly on the site, as several area towns rallied to assist their neighbors. Squads from as far away as Pennington Gap and Abingdon, Virginia, as well as Rogersville and Knoxville, Tennessee, rushed to Kingsport. The Tennessee Highway Patrol stood ready to escort or assist in any way a truck that was carrying a special drug shipment from Atlanta to Kingsport. Fire fighters from Arkansas even offered to fly to Kingsport to help battle the blaze.[97]

On the day after the explosion, with most of the facility back in operation, the local newspapers printed the official statement of the president of Tennessee Eastman Company. James C. White noted that the events of the previous afternoon represented "the worst disaster Tennessee Eastman has suffered in its 40 years of operation." White also expressed his deepest sympathy to the families that had suffered losses and thanked the people of Kingsport and the surrounding area "who so effectively mobilized to aid us at this tragic time."[98] People in the town as well as in the outlying areas felt a deep and abiding loyalty to this company for the jobs it had provided to thousands, for its recreational programs for employees and their children, for its profit-sharing plan, which paid bonuses each March, and for its financial contributions to the commercial, civic, and cultural life of the town and region. It would never have occurred to them not to respond when the industry needed them. Their reaction stemmed from a sense of gratitude and obligation, not from intimidation or fear. In the wake of the tragedy, the local newspapers and the employee newsletter printed the obituary notices of all of the dead, along with their photographs. The town and the region mourned their tragic passing and settled into the grim task of processing insurance claims and repairing damage. At the request of Mayor L.P. Gregory, people all over the city observed a moment of prayer and meditation on Friday, 7 October, at 11:00 A.M.[99]

Details of the explosion remained amazingly sketchy. On 10 November a brief story appeared in the *Kingsport News*, with the company's release stating that the blast may have been caused by "the detonation of a mixture of nitro-benzene, nitric acid and water." Fifteen years later, a *Times-News* staff writer, Mary Kiss, whose husband had been on the job in the Organic Chemical Division when the explosion occurred, called it "The Day Kingsport Wept." She reported that the aniline plant had not been rebuilt (at least not in the same way), and city fire fighters recalled that the tragedy could have been far worse. "If the fire had gotten into the building we were trying desperately to protect, it would have leveled everything out there and would have caused tremendous damage to the city," observed Conner Caldwell, who had been overcome by the effects of aniline poisoning as he and others fought the blaze.[100] The company's image apparently remained untarnished, the public seemingly accepted the explosion as an act of fate, but realistically no one could ever again feel quite as comfortable about this sprawling chemical giant.

Within three years of the explosion at Eastman, the town's second-largest employer, Kingsport Press, fell victim to the longest and most serious strike in the town's history. This company, a fully integrated book-manufacturing operation, originated in the model city; but its reputation was national and international in scope. As early as 1950 the company had claimed that it was the largest complete book-manufacturing establishment in the world. Nine of its fourteen acres downtown were under roof, thirteen hundred workers were on its payroll, and seventy-five thousand books were being produced and shipped each day to all parts of the United States and around the globe.[101] This firm had printed volumes of almost every variety—the miniature classics that measured one inch on a ruler, Bibles, prayer books, encyclopedias, and a random assortment of other types. During the early 1950s the company turned out Dr. Alfred C. Kinsey's famous report *Sexual Behavior in the Human Female.* Area residents considered the Press a good place to work. News that it was hiring drew people from many miles away in Kentucky, Virginia, and the Carolinas. As one source so graphically put it, "Hillbillies brushed up on their reading and writing, put on their shoes, started up their jalopies, and took off for Kingsport whenever they thought there was a chance of getting on."[102]

Much of the good will that the Press's management had cultivated for about four decades collapsed during the peculiar interlude preceding the strike. Edward J. Triebe, the company's president, admitted that he had not believed the allied unions could take the workers out until the deadline approached: "I thought our people had too much sense, that they were too well aware of how deeply their interests were tied in with the Press's, to allow themselves to be dragged out on a strike which they obviously did not want."[103] The highest echelon of national union representation, however, played successfully on local discontent to advance their more comprehensive strategy: namely, undercutting the Kingsport company's competitive price advantage. Claude Smith, president of Pressmen's Local No. 336, described the management, which he claimed wallowed in nepotism, as callously old-fashioned, inattentive to modern trends in labor relations, inept in the selection of supervisors, and unwilling to give the employees a voice in determining working conditions.[104]

Sylvester Petro, a specialist in labor law who had previously had experience as an unpaid organizer for the steelworkers, carefully studied the Kingsport Press strike and concluded that Anthony J. DeAndrade, the international president of the pressmen, "was motivated *primarily*—according to his own statements—by the nationwide or industrywide competitive considerations. This is not to say that the union officials had no interest at all in the men and women employed at Kingsport Press." Petro thought that the real reason for the strike was not "how the Press was being run" but "that the Press's allegedly low labor costs were posing a competitive threat in the industry—that a 'disproportionate amount of work' was going to Kingsport."[105]

In any event, the striking workers at Kingsport suffered the consequences. The town was surrounded by a generally underdeveloped area, and plenty of people—even those who already had jobs elsewhere—were anxious to fill the positions vacated by union members. One of the locals' presidents later commented: "I wish we had given that more thought. The men are going through their life's savings. Many are deeply in debt, though the grocers and tradesmen are going along pretty well. The Hardship Fund helps, but if things continue this way, more and more are going to lose their homes. The strike was a big mistake. I wish we had never called it."[106]

Although the Kingsport Press strike was larger and more far-reaching locally and nationally, its course bears a resemblance to that of the Blue Ridge Glass Corporation's strike seven years earlier. Negotiations broke down, the picket lines went up, and violence plagued the town and surrounding area. The plant remained in operation; the unemployed eagerly rushed to fill the positions created by striking workers; and with the strikers ineligible to vote, the newly hired, who were grateful for their jobs, rejected the striking unions as bargaining agents.

The strike had begun 11 March 1963, when approximately sixteen hundred strikers and sympathizers had gathered outside the Press, marking the onset of a struggle that lasted more than four years. As late as 28 April 1967 a few pickets remained at their posts, although plant employees by this time had soundly rejected the last three unions that had remained active as bargaining agents. When the strike began, Kingsport's safety director, R.L. ("Jim") Eisenbise issued this perfunctory statement: "No violence will be tolerated by either management, labor, or outside individuals."[107] For months, local newspapers reported incidents of lawlessness in the town and in the outlying areas, ranging from the pelting of automobiles with eggs to dynamiting, teargassing, and the exchange of gunshots. Petro wrote: "My talks with people actually victimized during these months has left me with an impression of dread and anxiety that I am afraid is not even remotely conveyed by newspaper headlines and stories."[108] Twenty years after the strike, some of the Press's employees who were terrorized still had unlisted telephone numbers, a practice adopted during those terrible days.

The unions, which must bear most of the responsibility for the local violence, also besought the Press's customers around the country to boycott the stricken company; and they enjoyed some success. Field Enterprises Educational Corporation, a major customer that published *World Book Encyclopedia*, remained loyal; but Encyclopaedia Britannica, Incorporated, reportedly agreed to take its work out of Kingsport and to give it to Plimpton Press in La Porte, Indiana. The unions also demanded that the New York City Board of Education cease using textbooks manufactured at Kingsport Press. The board at first refused, then reversed itself; but finally a court injunction halting the boycott became permanent on 27 October 1966.[109] Contrary to the unions' charges, the Kingsport Press was not guilty of refusing to bargain in good faith; it was only guilty of refusing to yield to union demands in 1963. The company's official position, which never wavered, was set forth in its annual report that year: "The Company has never quarreled with the philosophy of collective bargaining. Unions were voluntarily recognized by Kingsport Press even before the Wagner Act of 1935. Some employees were first represented by a union as far back as 1933. Yet in keeping with the freedoms upon which our country was formed, we believe a man must be free to choose or not to choose union representation, as he, and only he, sees fit."[110] The key to union defeat can be found in the 1964 annual report: "The quality of applicants for employment remains high."[111] National union leadership failed in its objectives with the strike against the Press, and local union members were the pawns. Not many years elapsed before the Press's ownership underwent changes, and this company, like other American printers, found itself hard-pressed to compete with cheap labor elsewhere on the international front.

The prolonged labor unrest, more than any other event in the town's history, seriously undermined the social cohesion of the entire region. It set family members against each other, generated quarrels and fights among schoolchildren, tore neighborhoods asunder, pitted those who had once had jobs but had walked out against those who had not had jobs but had wanted in, and forced some who had once been employed by the Press to leave the area to find work. Petro claimed that the strike hit bottom on 27 March 1965, when a "gloomy, spiritless crew of pickets" outside the plant were braving the raw cold of subfreezing temperatures and wet snow while inside, where the temperature rarely fell below 80° F, executives were working in shirtsleeves and new employees were successfully mastering their tasks.[112]

With the town and its hinterland troubled by labor violence and unrest at the Blue Ridge Glass Corporation and Kingsport Press and disconcerted by the Eastman explosion, other important developments that were affecting Kingsport's industrial base received less attention and made a smaller impression at the time. Chambers of Commerce, however, from Kingsport, Bristol, and Johnson City had begun to explore cooperative approaches to industrial recruitment. In July 1964, directors made a preliminary three-day trip to New York City in an attempt to lure industry to the Tri-Cities. Describing this experiment as "very satisfactory," they planned a similar visit to Chicago.[113] By the late 1950s and early 1960s, land within the incorporation that was suitable for major industrial expansion had almost been exhausted. Meanwhile, surrounding counties had become increasingly interested in industrial development. They had land in abundance; but they did not have utilities, waste-disposal systems, and related services. During Kingsport's early years, the locations of old factories had been determined by the dependence on the railroad as the only reliable method of transportation. This had unfortunate consequences for air quality in the business and commercial core and also for the residential areas rimming the downtown. The glass plant became the first industry to break out of this pattern. With Eastman as its huge and land-acquisitive neighbor, Blue Ridge Glass, if it was to expand, had to look beyond the original site.

In 1959, American Window Glass and Saint Gobain merged and considered relocating their Blue Ridge Glass works, long established at Kingsport, to Louisiana. The Kingsport and Rogersville Chambers of Commerce made a successful concerted effort to persuade company officials to build a new facility on the Hoffman property near Church Hill in Hawkins County. Construction began during the autumn of 1959, and the multimillion-dollar Greenland plant of American–Saint Gobain Corporation opened in 1962.[114] Hawkins County established an industrial commission soon thereafter. County Judge Lyle Ratliff and

County Attorney J.O. Phillips applied to the state for a charter on 25 April 1963, and the document was recorded on 4 May.[115] This represented a conscious decision by county officials to recruit industry and made possible the issuance of industrial-development bonds for site preparation, access roads, and other enticements for prospective manufacturers.

Three other industries soon became neighbors of the glass plant. Officials of Holliston Mills bought land in Hawkins County. That company, which was owned by the McCusker family from the Northeast, had outgrown its downtown location. A processor of book cloth, the firm had been attracted to Kingsport in 1926 because a major supplier of gray goods, Borden Mills (later J.P. Stevens), was already located there, as was Kingsport Press, a principal customer. The Hawkins County plant was built in 1963, and production began in the same year. Another new firm, Alladin Plastics, soon developed near Surgoinsville; it started operations in 1963. A public-relations junket to promote the area, sponsored by the governor, attracted this industry; and the sale of industrial-development bonds for construction provided an additional incentive. Under a lease-purchase plan, Alladin agreed to take possession of the building after twenty years.[116] Kingsport Press bought the vacant buildings of its old neighbor, Holliston Mills, downtown and also built a sister plant in Hawkins County, which opened in 1966.[117]

Keeping the established industrialists satisfied and luring others below the Mason-Dixon line were considered good economics and good politics during the 1960s and 1970s. The governor's involvement with industrial recruitment, as well as the undertakings of local officials from Upper East Tennessee cities and counties, was in keeping with efforts throughout the South, including the Volunteer State, to attract new manufacturing operations. A 1969 study revealed that 66 percent of 308 companies responding considered labor costs and availability crucial to their decisions to locate in Tennessee. The nonunion climate, the inexpensive electrical power supplied by TVA, and an adequate supply of relatively cheap land, buildings, freight, and raw materials also figured prominently.[118]

Meanwhile, the comprehensive vision for a planned city, which antedated World War I and which Kingsport, in many ways, symbolized in 1944, was gone. By the late 1960s, what the model city already represented or was about to become was the product of a more narrowly drawn perspective governed by the progress motif. The territorial growth that had occurred through annexation seemed to suggest that bigger was better; some people felt that the quality of life and the wishes of home owners were being sacrificed in the process. Workers, after the troubles of the 1950s and 1960s, were not as comfortable with their employers as they once had been. The appearance of strip commercial development and shopping centers was posing serious threats to the downtown commercial district. Industry was being forced to decentralize in order to expand. The tight-knit society of the established order was no longer exercising the degree of influence and control it had once maintained. The plan, which had included the residents of all classes within the town, workers from the outlying area, industrialists, and town fathers and which, in varying degrees, they all had once embraced, was well on its way to becoming obsolete.

8

Dismantling the Model City

Around 1966 the City of Kingsport, at an approximate cost of $129,908, engaged Eric Hill Associates of Atlanta to prepare a long-range planning study. Leon S. Eplan, vice-president of the firm, observed two years later that "with or without proper planning, the Kingsport of 1990 will be at least as different as the Kingsport of today is from that of 1946—22 years ago."[1] What in retrospect seems a profound expression of the obvious ran counter to the town's innate conservatism. For some of the residents, the millennium had arrived; they looked on their individual circumstances with personal satisfaction and on those of their community with a smug complacency that hardly prepared them to deal realistically with the cold, hard facts of urban deterioration. This attitude had vexatious consequences when it manifested itself among those who were in a position to exercise influence and provide leadership.

By the late 1960s, the town's direction had passed to citizens who possessed a limited understanding of the past, a perspective confined to the present, in union with a consuming passion for the fast buck and the quick fix, and little ability to anticipate or prepare the city for the future. The inevitability of death and the diminishing public participation of the aged disarmed the town's pioneers. By design and by default, residents sanctioned the dismantling of the physical and social infrastructure of the old model city without finding a satisfactory alternative. For the last two decades, Kingsport has been wandering in the proverbial wilderness. Especially damaging, given its lingering competitiveness, the town has lost its position of being the unchallenged leader of the Tri-Cities. In spite of all of this, Kingsport has rallied on occasion, and its prospects are not completely bleak; the town is down but not out.

A recurring chorus of nostalgia signals Kingsport's obeisance to the past. Resting on previous accomplishments that become all the more glorious as they recede into the past and invoking the names of model-city deities is not an uncommon ritual. Marking the deaths of H.J. Shivell and Morris Sobel in 1984, Tom Yancey III, a staff writer for the *Times-News*, also took the opportunity to summon memories of George Eastman, J. Fred Johnson, and Tom's own grandfather, Dr. T.B. Yancey.[2] In another memorial to Shivell and Sobel, columnist Sally Chiles-Shelburne, too, recalled the contributions of J. Fred Johnson and of John B. Dennis. She reminded her readers that "the patriarchs of early Kingsport are almost gone" and offered up further lamentations: "To honor them properly we need to move forward, change, grow and adapt as quickly and deftly as they did. We need to invest heavily in the future. Then the mantles of succession might fit and be worthy of passing on."[3] A reader of the *Times-News* who obviously found "progress" on the southwestern end of town distasteful demanded to know if the late Harvey Brooks, who had donated a portion of his estate, including the Allandale mansion, to the city after giving almost one hundred acres for the Kingsport University Center, had "really wanted a fast-food joint on his east and west lawn? A bank in his front yard and a drugstore out back?" Although the reader would have been as well advised to ask the Brooks heirs as city officials, he philosophically concluded that "if Mr. Brooks were still alive, he wouldn't have far to go for a Big Mac, would he?"[4]

Recent economic and quality-of-life indicators make it clear that Kingsport and the Tri-Cities should be taken seriously as an industrial, commercial, and residential center. During the 1960s, Eric Hill Associates reported that, by 1959, for every $10 earned by other families in Tennessee, the average Kingsport family had earned $15. And 18 percent of Kingsport families had incomes over $10,000, surpassed only by those of Oak Ridge in a state that averaged only 8 percent. Approximately 29 percent of the town's residents earned more than $10,000 in 1970. Census tract data for 1980 revealed that the Ridgefields neighborhood in the model city was the most prosperous in the Tri-Cities, with an average household income of more than $40,000; but a triangular zone bordered by Main, Sullivan, and Clinchfield streets, with 101 households occupying mostly rental property above businesses, possessed the lowest, $7,635. The First Tennessee-Virginia Economic

Development District reported in 1982 that in retail sales Kingsport outstripped those of the other towns in the district. A survey of purchasing power published in *Sales and Marketing Management* found disposable income in the Tri-Cities to be $20,783 per family in 1984. Even Rand-McNally's controversial 1985 *Places Rated Almanac* placed the Johnson City–Kingsport–Bristol SMSA (Standard Metropolitan Statistical Area) at forty-sixth of the nation's 329 metropolitan areas. Another study whose findings were released in the July 1985 issue of *American Demographics* ranked the Tri-Cities seventh among urban areas as a desirable place in which to live. The Fortune 500 list includes nineteen companies that have divisions in Upper East Tennessee and southwestern Virginia. Eastman Kodak of Rochester, New York, parent to the huge operation at Kingsport, ranked thirtieth in 1984. Piedmont Airlines featured the area in *Pace,* its in-flight magazine, during February 1986, a decision that was determined largely by advertising potential.[5]

Kingsport's current malaise, however, is discernible across two decades during which a cacophony of protest has been rising from the once-harmonious community. From all points on the political spectrum, dissenters who would effect change have taken their texts straight from model-city propaganda and have used it as a battering ram. The Reverend John Price of St. Mark's Methodist Church presented black demands for the immediate and complete integration of the city school system in 1965. Reminding the Board of Education that the "total desegregation of pupils and teachers is taking place all around us," he observed that "it would enhance the image of Kingsport as the Model City if we would do likewise. It's not a sound world when we can outstrip the Russians and travel millions of miles around the world in space while we can't send our children one mile to a white school." A 1965 editorial in the *Kingsport News* stated: "It is nice to know that hard work and planning resulted in building a 'model city.' But unless action is taken soon Kingsport could be known as that 'OLD Model City.' " A 1969 photograph of Broad Street taken by Ken Murray, a cameraman with the local newspaper, bore the caption "On a Clear Day You Can Almost See the Station." If a picture is indeed worth a thousand words, this one made its point. Two years earlier, state officials had conducted an air-quality test and had found Kingsport's pollution problem among the worst in the state.[6]

The "Kingsport spirit" had seemingly hit rock bottom by 1980 when the Downtown Kingsport Association had the temerity to place an artificial Christmas tree on Church Circle. Disconcerted by the hue and cry occasioned by the fake tree, the chairman of the decorations committee admitted that he knew nothing about such matters and said he had relied on the expertise of a Hickory, North Carolina, firm. Three businessmen donated a twenty-five-foot Colorado spruce from their property, and others gave money to buy decorations; citizens rallied to trim the live evergreen. One of the benefactors explained that Church Circle is "kind of holy ground to everyone around here." Such a happy occasion represented the exception. In 1982 the Reverend William Wood, pastor of the First Presbyterian Church, who was surprisingly outspoken for a model-city minister, claimed that Kingsport suffered from "a crisis of the spirit" and declared that "timidity about doing things" had to be eliminated. "You cannot whitewash the fact that there are real problems in this city," he added. In 1985 Tommy Lee Hulse, a mayoral candidate, campaigned unsuccessfully on the slogan "Remodel the Model City"; a distraught dropout denied that Dobyns-Bennett was a model high school; and a religous zealot, fresh from the frenzy of a tent revival near the stockyards, questioned Kingsport's worthiness as "a model city." Likening Kingsport to Sodom and Gomorrah, the native son warned the town of its peril.[7]

The model city was already in serious trouble by the late 1960s, with urban blight downtown and urban sprawl developing on the periphery and around the suburbs. Its establishment had been predicated on both physical and social planning, but planning in Kingsport by the 1960s emphasized the structural, and even this was limited to a piecemeal approach. Joseph Heller, the owner of Joseph's Music Store, headed the Downtown Improvement Committee. The Eric Hill study had observed that the central business district could not maintain its hold on retail sales and would become a service area of law, insurance, and bank offices. In 1985 Heller, still hanging on downtown, confessed that he had not believed these predictions. The business editor for the *Times-News*, Kim R. Kenneson, wrote: "Today, he's giving that study more consideration and believes that if Kingsport's downtown area is to succeed, it's going to have to quit trying to return to what it was years ago, with thriving shops and retail outlets, and search for a new direction—possibly that proposed in the 20-year-old study." The original suggestion for a semimall, a "pedestrian paradise," had received a cool reception.[8]

Complacency rested heavily on the citizenry, and at this critical juncture in the model city's existence, vision was a commodity in dangerously short supply. Heller was not alone in his views. In his first report to the Downtown Improvement Committee in January 1969, he admitted that a few old landmark stores were going out of business, but he argued that they were quickly being replaced by new ones. As "the most spectacular example," he cited the "attractive two-block-long Lowe's building planned for Main Street." A few days earlier, the *Kingsport News* had reported that "the attractive building would screen the sight of the tracks from the streets" and was expected "to help 'revitalize' the sagging Main Street business district." In November 1969 a spokesman for Lowe's revealed that "the new block, brick, and steel one-story building" would stand directly in front of the Clinchfield Railroad Station. The new building's showroom, windows, and sign, he promised, would be directly in line with Broad Street and Church Circle. One angry citizen fired off a letter to the newspapers. Observing that the depot was "one of the few buildings with any character left" and that "most towns and cities" were attempting to renovate and preserve "their older store fronts," she speculated that "the merchants of Kingsport (with a few exceptions) won't be satisfied until all of our older building fronts are replaced with gaudy modern chrome and glass."[9] Strategically placed to block the Clinton Mackenzie-designed depot and to mar the view down Broad Street from Church Circle, the Lowe's building, a crime against urban aesthetics, ranks with the midnight massacre of the trees on the downtown's principal thoroughfare during the 1950s—under cover of darkness—and with its sandbagging a couple of decades later to create parking spaces in the middle of the once-expansive boulevard; brick-and-concrete barriers—euphemistically called planters—followed.

Since the 1960s, Kingsport has carried a heavy burden of residual bitterness, much of which derived from annexation and zoning practices during the 1950s and early 1960s, along with poor judgment, indeed myopia, afterward. Seven years after Highland Park, an area of modest and limited income, had been taken into the city, for instance, the area was still dotted with outdoor toilets; and concerned citizens were waiting impatiently for sewer hookups. The Board of Education, pressed to accommodate children inside the incorporation, announced in May 1966 a moratorium on accepting tuition students. In 1967 the Kingsport Board of Realtors claimed that a severe housing shortage existed in the town. Real-estate brokers also advocated comprehensive zoning. A piecemeal approach, a practice that they had earlier found acceptable to break the resistance of the old commercial establishment, as well as neighborhoods, to strip development, now hampered prospects for shopping centers and hamburger chains.[10]

The underlying bitterness surfaced as recently as 1984, when the *Times-News* published guest commentaries by Keith Stapleton that trumpeted a master plan as a panacea for Kingsport's woes. Stapleton, a native of Kingsport, had grown up in Toledo, Ohio. He returned to his birthplace in 1981, espousing the concept of comprehensive planning.[11] His ideas received some support, but city resident Richard Devaney, in a letter to the editor of the newspaper, vented the long-standing frustration of many. Failing to distinguish between *positive* and *poor* planning, he pointed out that the citizens of Kingsport had become "chary of any plan": "They remember that planning gave us a river port rather than a rail terminal [in the nineteenth century]. They remember that planning prevented us from having convenient access to Interstate-81. They remember that planning delayed the completion of US-23 to the state line for at least 15 years. They remember that planning gave us excess school capacity. And above all, they remember that planning did, in fact, give us Stone Drive."[12]

Physical deterioration in Kingsport is the most obvious manifestation of social fragmentation and loss of community, but the symptoms are less serious than the underlying illness. The social fabric that Johnson wove a half century ago met the exigency of that time and place; but Kingsport has matured, America has changed, and the people of Kingsport and the surrounding area have become more sophisticated. Natives resent such comments of patronizing and often ill-informed newcomers as those made by a woman who claimed that she had come to a better understanding of contemporary Tennesseans after having read Catherine Marshall's novel *Christy*—the story of a young teacher in the Great Smokies during the early years of the twentieth century.[13] In the seventh decade of the twentieth century, mountaineers could no longer be summoned en masse to perform for visiting capitalists or to pander to their overlords—never mind that Appalachia was being discovered again—and the once-obedient blacks no longer accepted the place assigned to them.

The civil-rights crusade, rising ethnic consciousness, the war in Southeast Asia, and Women's Liberation had fractured American society during the 1960s and 1970s. Historian Robert H. Wiebe has written about that period: "The major casualty of the 1960's was a dream of moderation, accommodation, and cohesion, and its passing brought acute feelings of loss and betrayal."[14] Out of this era came the writing of

Harry E. Caudill as a voice crying in the wilderness, railing against the sins of the capitalistic establishment in America's garden; and the polemics of Jack E. Weller who likens Appalachian "folk" to working-class urban ethnics.[15] Political candidates, troops of VISTA workers (Volunteers in Service to America), and waves of photographers and journalists have made their forays into Appalachia to focus national attention on downtrodden mountaineers—a tradition that was established by local colorists of the late nineteenth century and has been nurtured by contemporary photojournalists. The Appalachia that they so painstakingly discovered and continue to discover was and is not Kingsport and its immediate area; yet Kingsport, an America in miniature, has had its own problems. Halfheartedly and reluctantly grappling with civil rights, nearly blind to equal opportunity for women, and untroubled by antiwar protests, the city in 1967 marked its fiftieth anniversary since incorporation as the newspaper mentioned that a young Kingsport soldier had died in South Vietnam on 29 March.[16]

During the 1960s, Kingsport's relatively small black community became restive. For them and their counterparts across the United States, as well as for some whites, equality of opportunity for the black race was an idea whose time had arrived. In the wake of the *Brown* decision, mass demonstrations, and federal civil-rights legislation, racial inequities in the model city became increasingly irksome. Around 1960, when per capita income in Kingsport stood at $5,900, only 55 percent of the city's black families reportedly had incomes that exceeded $3,000; but the median income of nonwhite families was $2,553.[17] As the decade of the sixties commenced, M.C. Stone, chairman of the Board of Education, announced that a desegration plan had been adopted and would go into effect "at such date in the future as may appear to the Board to be consistent with the best interests of the city as a whole."[18] Before a year had elapsed, it was determined that the first grade would be integrated in the autumn of 1961, with a grade being added each year. In this manner, full desegregation could be happily achieved in twelve years. In 1963, municipal officials told the black leaders who were concerned about recreational facilities and safe school crossings that no discrimination existed within the city. School authorities, by August 1964, had decided that all city schools would be fully integrated by 1966. About this time, the black community served notice that it was unwilling to accept delay. Admitting that "times change, and the line of communication between Negro and white communities [is] not very good," an editorial in the *Times-News* noted on 12 September 1964 that "people who tell you confidently that the Negroes are perfectly content with the status quo were proved dead wrong." Black students first registered at Dobyns-Bennett High School in 1965; full integration had been officially accomplished by December 1966.[19]

The atmosphere at the newly constructed Dobyns-Bennett High School, which was futuristic in design and was located just off Memorial Boulevard, remained tense for several years. Name-calling and fights led to near-riot conditions on several occasions. In April and May 1969, for example, white students battled with black students in the hallways; fistfights resulted in suspensions. In 1970, Horace Curry, who had once been president of the local chapter of the National Association for the Advancement of Colored People, filed a $200,000 suit in the United States District Court at Greeneville. Charging that Kingsport officials were subsidizing the other ambulance service and attempting to drive him out of business solely on account of race, he specifically named Mayor Fred Gillette, the four aldermen, and City Manager Charles K. Marsh. The racial turmoil, which climaxed around 1973, led Richard Waterson to seek election to public office. Running a successful race in a town where aldermen are chosen at large, he became the first and, to date, only black alderman and has since risen to vice-mayor. Waterson credited Mayor Richard Bevington for the advancement of blacks in the model city: "I don't believe that had anyone else been mayor that my job would have been as easy. He made a commitment and stuck by it. The mayor has done more to improve race relations than any man in town."[20]

Along with school segregation, hiring practices piqued the black community. When Waterson was elected to City Hall, no blacks were working for the municipality—not even in garbage collection; the reason: "The men kicked about riding with blacks in the cabs." Employment practices have changed; indeed, during the 1980s, Robert Mebane, a black, became personnel director. He was recruited from outside the city to fill the slot which had previously been held by one of the city's highest-ranking female employees, who had been deposed. At least one black usually serves on special commissions. Their small numbers, in 1978 standing at only about fifteen hundred, have been a disadvantage; and future annexation will in all likelihood exacerbate this situation.[21]

Demands for open housing met more with stony silence than with vocal opposition, but a ten-year plan for slum clearance was considered.

In a report to the League of Women Voters on housing conditions in 1967, City Attorney William Weber noted the presence of 404 dilapidated houses and 1,107 deteriorating ones, approximately 85 percent of which were occupied. Black leader Wilbur Hendricks expressed the hope that homes would be found for occupants before they were evicted if the city launched a program of urban renewal. Spokesmen for the black community cited strides made by Johnson City in open housing and slum clearance where the two races lived side by side. In Kingsport, Hendricks observed, his race had simply been "moved from one slum to another." As the issue became more pressing, no real-estate agent could be found in the model city who was willing to pledge that he would never practice discrimination. In 1968 the Human Relations Subcommittee, a biracial group of seven whites and three blacks, of the Citizens Advisory Committee publicly denounced prevailing bigotry: "All are put on note that the city practices racism on a massive scale. How can we honestly avow a Christian faith while tolerating division of our city on racial lines?"[22]

Most blacks could not afford to leave Riverview and the East Sevier–Maple–Dale Street area, but the few who tried ran into solid opposition from property owners. This became increasingly embarrassing as nonwhite professionals at Tennessee Eastman looked for suitable residences. Not until 1974 were blacks able to secure a fair-housing ordinance in Kingsport—a goal they had set for themselves—although state and federal legislation already outlawed discriminatory practices. In the meantime, the local Human Relations Forum, headed by the Reverend Robert Bowman of the Unitarian Church, circulated a petition in support of the Good Neighbor Pledge. Promising to be a good neighbor to any person who moved into the neighborhood and to accept a neighbor's choice to sell or rent his home to whomever he might choose, the pledge seemed innocuous enough; but only about 457 signed it between 1 December 1968 and 19 February 1969. Some townspeople complained that several housewives had affixed their signatures without really understanding the petition.[23]

In spite of the painfully slow process of securing basic human rights for blacks, the conservative white inhabitants of the model city gradually altered their views—outwardly at least—as the small but persistent black community kept them on the defensive. Even the social-studies curriculum at the high school came under scrutiny when a few critics in town demanded that blacks be included in history. Robert Fanslow, a highly regarded white instructor, advised against rushing into Black

Studies; John Bruce, a black citizen, called the matter "an immediate problem"; and Ross Jennings, a former Peace Corps volunteer and a white who was involved with the Good Neighbor Pledge, claimed that the history and social studies being taught in city schools had "great gaps" and were "simply not true." By 1970 the city schools had begun the annual observance of what was then called Negro History Week.[24]

Criticism of the curriculum by minorities seemed relatively insignificant in the face of the racial violence and other turmoil that was confronting the school system during the late sixties. Kingsport had been a town that had taken enormous pride in its schools and had given the educational establishment generous financial support. Most citizens rated the schools highly, although Joseph H. Lewis, a former mayor, observed in 1983, "I don't think they were absolute tops, but I think they [referring to Charles Koffman, principal at Dobyns-Bennett High School, and Ross N. Robinson, superintendent] did a reasonably good job...back then."[25] The 1968/69 academic year passed with continuing racial tension, a mediocre football season, and a defeat in the final moments of the quarterfinals of the state basketball tournament. A few days before the town's fiftieth high-school graduation, a grand jury indicted Dobyns-Bennett's Principal William Neal on three counts stemming from missing funds. The mayor proclaimed the observance of Flag Week, 8-14 June 1969, with the somber message that "during these critical times, it is entirely appropriate that the attention of all citizens be directed toward the ideals of Freedom, Equality, Liberty and Justice on which the country was founded that they may rededicate themselves to these principles."[26] Whether he was referring to civil-rights confrontations, the war in Vietnam, or local conditions, his comment was applicable.

At commencement, Madeline Bush, the valedictorian, in the rhetoric of angry youths of the 1960s, attacked American society "which judges man by his affluence, his job, his home, his material possessions, and discounts his talents as a human being. We have become a nation of bigots. We preach the brotherhood of man but fail to practice it." On this somber note, tears fell, thunderclouds burst, the D-B dome leaked, as it had since its construction, and water accumulated on the floor of the gymnasium. A few months later, Principal Neal was convicted on two counts and was given a three-year probation.[27] Superintendent of Schools Dana Swick moved to a position at George Peabody College for Teachers, and several other administrators and instructors found employment elsewhere.

With the city's school system seemingly in a state of disarray, civic leaders, industrialists, and businessmen continued their efforts to establish a permanent center for higher education in the town. A unified effort, spearheaded by Kingsport resident James Welch and East Tennessee State University professor and administrator Fred McCune, had led to the planning and eventual construction of a permanent home for the Kingsport University Center on property donated by Harvey Brooks at the southwest end of town. Welch, in alliance with McCune, tirelessly hammered away at the conspicuous absence of higher-educational opportunities in the planning of the model city. Their efforts spurred a cooperative venture by East Tennessee State University and the University of Tennessee, which brought day and evening courses and programs at the undergraduate and graduate levels to thousands of area residents for whom higher education heretofore had seemed impossible. The community rallied to raise local contributions, to persuade the governing officials of the two universities of the merits of the idea, and to extract funding from the state. Confronted with bureaucratic obstacles and the attendant delays, the project moved forward at a snail's pace. Opposition to a university center at Kingsport had existed in Johnson City and Washington County, where some people believed that this would undermine the Johnson City campus of East Tennessee State University; by March 1967 the idea was being aired in the press as the state considered a proposed budget that would earmark $1.1 million for the Kingsport effort. The *Bristol Herald-Courier* opined that the whole matter had "been blown all out of proportion by near-hysterical opposition from good people in Johnson City and Washington County." The *Kingsport Times* called the controversy a "frightening trend for the Tri-Cities."[28]

Indeed, this development was foreboding, and the timing could not have been worse. This was a pivotal era for the rapidly growing Upper East Tennessee area, and joint planning and cooperation at this critical juncture was in the best interests of the entire region. Kingsport, which was occasionally accused of "hoarding industry," was not easily moved to cooperative efforts, although the Tri-Cities had undertaken a few ventures aimed at industrial recruitment. Their representatives, along with those from Sullivan and Washington counties, jointly administered and maintained the regional airport. Bristol, Virginia, had also become a partner during the 1960s. In May 1965, a planner from Johnson City told members of the Cosmopolitan Kiwanis Club of Kingsport that their city was the leader of the three in population and economics and that the Tri-Cities needed its guidance. He claimed, however, that Kingsport's vision was limited to its own political boundaries.[29] The *Times-News* soon endorsed the idea of economic cooperation but gave the model city's definition of *cooperation:* "Cooperation should mean 'If we cannot get something we will help one of the other cities in the area to get it.' That is cooperation enough. There is no need to expect one city to sacrifice its own interests for the benefit of another."[30] Johnson City's opposition to the Kingsport University Center made the planned city even less responsive to joint efforts.

Although the press used such phrases as "Golden Triangle" to describe Kingsport, Bristol, and Johnson City and speculated about whether the Tri-Cities would become a metropolis,[31] area leaders made little commitment to comprehensive regional planning. The idea for a Tri-City coliseum, a test case of sorts, soon fell victim to rivalry between Johnson City and Kingsport. As early as 1963, some thought was being given in the model city to expansion of the Civic Auditorium. The Chamber of Commerce, in the same year, filed a report calling for the construction of a new facility, and the newspaper endorsed the idea. In about 1965 the notion of a coliseum to serve the region gained ground; and the Tri-Cities Coliseum Committee, with representation from the various cities and counties, began a study. In a 1968 article, Margy Clark, writing for the *Kingsport Times-News,* attacked the idea, on the basis that Kingsport had not been able to fill the five thousand seats in the Dobyns-Bennett gymnasium for various events. Describing Kingsport as a "No Show" town, she cautioned that word was spreading among booking agents in the big cities. While recognizing a small but steady contingent that supported local performing-arts groups, the symphony, and events sponsored by the Community Concert Association, she correctly asserted that most people were content to stay home and watch television.[32]

Almost five years elapsed before the Coliseum Committee finally presented a 117-page report. Gerald S. Cassell, an Eastman employee who was a resident of Washington County, served as chairman. The report called for a centrally located facility to serve Kingsport, Bristol, Johnson City, and Elizabethton, as well as Sullivan, Carter, and Washington counties in Tennessee and Washington County, Virginia. Other municipalities were also welcome to participate. The committee proposed the purchase of 150 acres near Tri-City Airport and the construction of an $8-million, 164,422-square-foot structure that would include a sports arena, an auditorium–concert hall, and exhibit space.

A private fund drive and a 1 percent sales tax in each participating municipality and county could finance the project. The study group recommended the appointment of a Tri-City Coliseum Authority to continue the planning, oversee the operation, and hire a manager. Projected to seat eight thousand in the sports arena and twenty-seven hundred in the auditorium, the facility could be expected to lose about $40,000 per year; the cost would be divided among the owners by percentages based on retail sales.[33]

The Coliseum Committee invited six hundred area leaders to Sullivan County's Central High School for the unveiling of the plan. Cassell soon expressed his disappointment with the lack of response from governmental representatives. The estimated construction costs and the possibility of new taxes generated little enthusiasm.[34] W.B. Greene, Jr., president of the Carter County Bank in Elizabethton, represented his county on the committee. "Two things happened," according to Greene: "First, Kingsport dropped the cookie; second, about that time Johnson City recognized a Tri-City Coliseum was a marginal possibility, so they went to work on Freedom Hall.... We didn't get cooperation from major industry in Kingsport. The attitude of the city fathers and industry in Kingsport the past 25 years has been, 'We like the way things are, we don't want any change.' " Greene also noted that Johnson City "in the last 15 years has passed the model city of Kingsport in progressive attitude in the public and private sector."[35]

The "hope" expressed by the committee that the Tri-City Coliseum proposal might "forge that missing link" of "regional planning and action" languished. By the mid-sixties, leaders in Johnson City had undertaken comprehensive long-range planning that would transform the town. Johnson City, as planner John Nolen observed during the 1910s, had for many decades been "throttled by a girdle of railroad tracks"[36] and identified as the location of the normal school that evolved into East Tennessee State University. With the Kingsport community less than enthusiastic about a jointly operated civic center, Johnson City moved forward with the Liberty Bell Complex and Freedom Hall on the north side of town; recruited such new industries as Texas Instruments; improved roads and streets; and made a polite if less than triumphant bow to downtown revitalization as development continued beyond the core. Becoming the first of the Tri-Cities to adopt liquor-by-the drink, it preempted the others in attracting new restaurants and hotels. It is also the home of East Tennessee State University's Quillen-Dishner College of Medicine and the Veterans Administration's Mountain Home. Meanwhile, Bristol, Tennessee, has also erected a civic center, Viking Hall. Kingsport has had to make do with the aging and somewhat seedy Civic Auditorium and Fine Arts Center, the school auditoriums, and, at Tennessee Eastman's pleasure, the fine accommodations of its Employee Center.

As environmental concerns garnered increasing attention during the late 1960s and early 1970s, the City of Kingsport, less than cooperative in other areas, willingly shared its pollution problems. In February 1967 the Tennessee Stream Pollution Control Board announced that the sewage-treatment facilities that were being used by several large industrial plants in the model city and between Kingsport and Knoxville were not adequate and therefore were contributing to the pollution of the Holston River. The Tennessee Department of Health in March pointed to serious dust pollution and declared that the "particulate loading" was "possibly the highest in the state." About a year later, Mayor Joseph H. Lewis told the local Jaycees that Kingsport's air-pollution ordinance was a good one, but that "the city's hands" were "tied until the public wakes up and realizes the need for clean air." He added: "The public just doesn't give a damn. The problem is a social one, and each citizen must decide to do his part."[37]

By September 1968, Lewis and the mayors of twenty-one other cities and towns of the First Tennessee-Virginia Economic Development District had proposed a nine-county study of air pollution; the intent, according to Jack Strickland, the district developer, was to determine if an area air-pollution problem did, in fact, exist. If so, uniform ordinances could be put into effect. An editorial in the *Times-News* entitled "Lot of Smoke, Not Much Fire" belittled this gesture and suggested that such talk about pollution surveys seemed a bit futile because Kingsport could not enforce the existing ordinance. "Downtown Kingsport is dirty," the editorial chided, "and it shouldn't be all that difficult to find out where the dust is coming from" without huddling with twenty-one other cities. "The state has had a pollution control board in the 'organization' state for over a year without making any headway....And dumping it on the laps of a 22-city study group will not clean up Kingsport's air." In October the *Times-News* congratulated Lewis for his change in attitude about pollution, citing a recent letter that Lewis had written to legislators in which he stated that "the citizens of Kingsport are vociferous in their demands that this situation be corrected immediately." In January 1970 the newspaper reported that the city's air had failed to meet standards in all three categories of recent testing conducted by the state.[38]

Aggressive reporting by the daily newspapers, which were no longer locally owned, made it more difficult for the local establishment to sweep the town's problems under the rug. Neither industries nor City Hall could completely escape their vigilance, but the threat of lost advertising dollars could temper the attacks and affect the management. The appearance of zealous journalism in the model city coincided with the plethora of urban challenges and the deterioration of the old order, which was nowhere more apparent than in municipal government. Industrialists, throughout most of the city's history, had taken a lively interest in local matters. Joseph H. Lewis, a former chief of the glass plant and one-time mayor, recollected: "In the early days, plant heads used to get together about every two or three months. Not on a fixed schedule—no fixed agenda on the thing. But, we'd have a dinner meeting about every three or four months of that sort, to discuss city affairs and what our position would be." Into the 1960s the slate of candidates remained carefully controlled and the selection of the mayor prearranged, according to Lewis. The "control of city government" had traditionally been in the hands of the industrialists. Lewis recalled: "They wanted a good government, and what they'd try to do was to find people they thought would and could do the job on the thing. And sometimes they'd get somebody from the plants, [and occasionally] somebody from downtown.... They came to me. Jim White and Chamberlin (Hale) got in touch with me and said, 'We'd like to have you run for Board of Mayor and Aldermen.' And I said, 'Gee, I've never given it any thought.' So, I finally went over to talk to Jim White and talk to the people about the thing. I didn't know anything about politics. 'What do I do?' 'Nothing.' " They took care of everything. Lewis admitted that once he had been elected alderman and then mayor, he had depended a great deal on City Manager Charles K. Marsh: "I used to talk to Charlie on the thing [running the city]. He was really the ramrod on it."[39]

Marsh, through an in-house promotion, had become city manager in January 1959, when D.W. Moulton had resigned to become the Tennessee commissioner of highways. Bill Barnett, a staff writer for the *Times-News,* obliquely but incisively challenged Marsh's influence in a 1967 analysis: "There is one potential weakness in the city manager form of government—generally considered the most efficient way to operate a city. There is a danger that the part-time council members may tend to leave everything to the city manager and his staff and merely approve whatever he recommends without giving him sufficient guidelines as to what the citizens want."[40] With the breakdown of the old power structure and the transfer of authority to the city manager, the idea of a truly representative government gained strength. Lewis believed that he was probably the last handpicked mayor of Kingsport and claimed that John Cole had introduced "the idea of a Democratic form of government... a wider representation in Kingsport.... He talked that a lot, and I think it spread, and whether it originated in other people or not... it was about that time that the [behind-the-scenes] selection of the people that would be on the Board of Mayor and Aldermen and later who would be Mayor, stopped."[41]

As alderman, Cole abandoned the unwritten rule of avoiding the open discussion of troublesome issues and regularly introduced subjects at meetings of the board that he believed to be of public interest. It was he who nominated the newly elected alderman Elery Lay, the assistant superintendent of schools, for the town's top political position in opposition to Fred Gillette, the first model-city mayor ever to be challenged by another candidate. Lay's election had already set off a storm of controversy as to whether he could simultaneously receive two salaries from the city, but he had polled the largest popular vote of any alderman in the city's history.[42] The press also discerned a new mood in public relations at City Hall. According to newspaperwoman Joan Roesgen: "It used to be you asked Marsh a simple question like: 'Is today Wednesday?' And he'd answer: 'Let me say this. If yesterday was Tuesday, and tomorrow is Thursday, and Rotary meets at noon, and the Meter Maids are off duty, then it might be safe to make that assumption, unless you're talking about a 40-hour work week, in which case it really would be premature to say.' " Now, he simply replied: "It most certainly is Wednesday—pending approval by the Board of Mayor and Aldermen, of course."[43] In 1971, Roesgen observed that most people were pleased "to see John Cole in the mayor's seat" because he was "probably the only public official who got elected because he did more listening than talking." She added, "Cole writes a lot of 'Dear Charles' memos."[44]

By the 1960s and 1970s the relationship of the industries to the community had undergone a subtle transformation; and a transfer of power had occurred as the upper echelon of Kingsport companies, who had been among the model city's pioneer generation, passed into retirement and succumbed to the vicissitudes of aging. Managers lacked the commitment and zeal of the founders. Under increasing attack from environmentalists, industrialists found themselves on the defensive. A fortress mentality rarely begets creative and positive civic response. Furthermore, Kingsport's commercial-industrial elite has always been basically conservative, a factor that has often been overlooked. Earlier in the town's history, however, the conservatism had been tempered by a sense of mission—a common set of goals. Without that ingredient, the conservatism of the 1960s and 1970s simply supported the status quo. Systems of performance evaluation hardly encouraged fresh innovative approaches, because such ideas, if in fact they existed, generated controversy; harmony ranks above all other criteria in the American managerial model. Consequently, bright and eager male employees in the town's industries and businesses soon learned that in order to succeed they had to be loyal to their companies, attend church regularly, assume an active if innocuous role, join civic organizations, enthusiastically embrace prevailing views, and cultivate the proper image of the family man.

A wife and children, testaments to virility, have been essential to the rising young executive in the model city. Children have been expected to proceed to maturity in the least troublesome manner, with a modicum of dance lessons, music recitals, scouting, and sports, enrollment in respectable colleges, and marriages to suitable individuals. The good wife has known her place and has assumed the role of being a becoming accessory for her husband. In 1967, for example, the *Times-News* ran a feature story entitled "City's First Lady and Council Wives," which emphasized that the family and home were of prime importance to these women. Visible but decorous volunteer work also rated highly. Interestingly, a slightly higher percentage of adult females in Kingsport probably worked outside the home than was true of women elsewhere in Tennessee. In 1960, for example, 38 percent of all women over fourteen were employed; the rest of the state stood at 33 percent, and all urban areas with populations over ten thousand, at 37 percent.[45]

Female social climbers in the model city have always placed a premium on appearance and proper dress. One newcomer observed during a newspaper interview: "The women of Kingsport do dress very fashionably, adding 'I'm a conservative dresser, I like my clothes tailored!'"[46] A feisty denizen of a retirement center, to which some of the Kingsport social order have been transplanted, remarked in 1985, off the record, that her female peers, wives of once-high-ranking executives, dressed rather well and played a good game of bridge, but that was about the extent of their interests. The wives of the industrial-commercial coterie have been expected to scramble, and belonging to the Junior League or to the "right" book club scored points in the game of one-upmanship.

Dynamic leadership has not been forthcoming from this town in which such emphasis has been placed on conforming to middle-class American ideas and values. Indeed, the quality of leadership has plummeted to abysmal levels. An editorial in the *Times-News* in 1980 asked "Why Doesn't Anyone Act?" and four years later, "Can't Anyone Make a Decision Anymore?" "The easiest way to get an issue off your back in government is to create a study group to look at the matter," one writer observed; "it gets it out of the public eye for a while." "Pass it back to committee," opined another; "that seems to be the standard operating procedure for Kingsport's Board of Mayor and Aldermen." When the city's elected officials, in the process of selecting a new city manager, destroyed their individual rating sheets, the newspaper, in November 1984, taunted, "There they go again!... Are our aldermen really so thin-skinned that they're afraid to let the public know how they think?"[47] For three months in 1980, Mayor Gardner Hammond's Long-Range Planning Committee studied the question of why Kingsport had been stagnant in recent years and concluded that it was because of a lack of leadership. While noting "that Kingsport abounds with leadership talent," the committee acknowledged that the challenge was "how to bring the talent into the mainstream of community activity and create an environment that will challenge leaders to function freely and creatively."[48]

The Long-Range Planning Committee called for the establishment of a formal leadership training program and passed the responsibility for implementing it to the Greater Kingsport Area Chamber of Commerce. Before much time had elapsed, *management* and *leadership* had become synonymous. As developed by the chamber in alliance with the Junior League of Kingsport, the Adult Education Department of the city's school system, and the local chapter of the American Society for Training and Development, the initial plan called for these components: Basic Principles of Organization, Time Management, Meeting Leadership and Participation, Face to Face Communications, and Know Your Community. While the town and region awaited what might be "the foundation for a physical and spiritual re-awakening rarely experienced in any community" and while committees cranked out reams of reports, existing problems had not gone away.[49]

Of these, water pollution and air pollution ranked at the top of the list. In this city, citizens had been known to greet each other on the street, sniff the air, rub their hands gleefully, and, in a self-congratulatory fashion, observe, "It smells like money."[50] They had rarely taken kindly to external or internal criticism. If neighbors from surrounding towns ventured to make a derogatory statement, many Kingsport residents assured themselves that the others, obviously jealous of Kingsport industries, would like to have Kingsport's problem. If a resident or a visitor made an unpopular observation, some thought it clever to advise that person of schedules for all modes of transportation out of town. Writer Don Widener, in *Timetable for Disaster,* described the consequences: "When I visited the town in 1953, the town captivated me. Pretty and clean, it seemed to be successfully combining industry and people—retaining its beauty in the bargain." Returning in 1969 was a shocking experience: "A familiar gray smog hid the mountains. The river seemed much dirtier, and smoke was belching from stacks." People reacted nervously and claimed somewhat uncertainly that something was being done about it.[51]

"Beset as she is by most of the evils of population, industrialization and urban sprawl," Widener reasoned, made Kingsport "almost typical." The model city's plight was not as desperate as that of some other areas, he speculated. Kingsport might even be more fortunate than some other towns because it had the industrial base to transform itself—"providing, however, that the people, the officials, and their business leaders recognize the symptoms of decay and move to correct the problems." Sympathetically, he wrote that "it is bad enough when a dusty, ugly little town folds," but "it is downright demoralizing to watch the thousand-cuts process scar a town with the beauty and potential of a Kingsport."[52]

The condition of the Holston River by this time had become desperate. It had once been clean and clear, and as late as 1940 the south fork had reportedly been used for swimming, but sewage and industrial waste had fouled it.[53] The city finally held a referendum to secure approval for a modern sewerage-treatment plant in 1956 and a facility for secondary waste water in 1966. Before the municipality and industries jointly began to give water quality serious attention, a Kingsport nature enthusiast, Thomas Gannaway, claimed that "there was no aquatic life or fish life in the Holston." By the early 1980s he sighted such rough fish as catfish and carp. "I always said," he stated in an interview, "we can have industry and a clean environment."[54]

Reaching such a consensus, if indeed that ever happened, did not come easily; nor is there reason to believe that it should be taken for granted. Efforts to correct environmental abuses in Kingsport owe a great deal to the media and to the national concern for ecology that brought state and federal legislation into existence and encouraged "closet" environmentalists and distressed citizens to become more outspoken. Arthur Smith, a chemical engineer with Tennessee Eastman Company, for example, retired in 1977 after thirty-one years because "he knew his growing interest in environmentalism would rock the company's management." Well-informed, articulate, and fearless, he has been a vigilant defender of Bays Mountain Park and a worthy antagonist of the Kingsport Power Company.[55] Physician J.F. Smiddy, a Kingsport respiratory-disease specialist, has courageously distinguished himself from the model city's medical establishment by drawing connections between air quality and health issues.

On 22 September 1977 an outbreak of pneumonia occurred in Kingsport. Seventy-two cases conformed to the clinical description of Legionnaires' disease; there were twenty-seven confirmed cases and seven presumed ones. Three deaths occurred. In 1978 Dr. Smiddy and J.T. Dondero, head of the investigating team from the Center for Disease Control, presented a paper at the annual meeting of the American Thoracic Society. They noted that Kingsport probably had the "most intense and severe air pollution of any city in Tennessee, related to the presence of a large chemical company and several other polluting industries." At the time of the outbreak, the city had been "under an atmospheric inversion...and a visible cloud with a chemical aroma was present in the town." Eighty-five percent of the victims had connections with a geographic area that included the neighborhoods of Cherokee Village and Gibsontown, as well as Holston Valley Community Hospital. All patients except one lived in Kingsport or its immediate vicinity.[56]

Concern about pollution intensified, but not enough to break the reluctance of most citizens to take a public stance. A 1979 editorial described the situation: "It is one of those topics discussed at cocktail parties and over the dinner table, but rarely in public. Why? Because a lot of folks are plainly worried that an open position could create direct or indirect repercussions against them or the community."[57] Six individuals based in southwestern Virginia, identified as the Kingsport Study Group, had forced the issue in 1978 with an article entitled "Smells Like Money," which was published in *Southern Exposure.* Their thesis was: Chemicals made and used at Tennessee Eastman Company might be damaging the health of plant workers and the public at large. In a full-page spread on 18 June 1978, Mary Kiss of the *Kingsport Times-News* summarized the article and TEC's rebuttal. Eastman's defenders soon made their views known to the newspaper. One of them, the wife of a company chemist, wrote: "I would like to see the authors of the article 'It Smells Like Money' write one on 'Kingsport—The City Without Eastman.' Dr. Smiddy probably wouldn't even have a hospital to examine his patients and make vague allegations about their ailments."[58]

Juliet Merrifield, representing the Kingsport Study Group, responded to Eastman's position, as set forth in Kiss's article:

> Our aim . . . was to air these concerns and stimulate public debate and further research. We are pleased that you were able to persuade the Tennessee Eastman Company to break its long silence on pollution and health issues [TEC had not cooperated with the study group]. . . .
>
> We do not dispute the fact that Tennessee Eastman has been making attempts in recent years to clean up its workplace, water and air pollution, in response to pressure from federal and state regulatory agencies. However, at the same time it has opposed in the courts and the legislature at least two occupational and environmental health measures. Tennessee Eastman opposed the State of Tennessee requirements to control its pollution of the Holston River, took out suit against the state, and forced the Water Quality Control Division to make concessions. And Eastman Kodak lobbied actively and persistently against the passage of even weakened versions of the Toxic Substances Control bill in Congress.[59]

Through the summer of 1978 the *Times-News* reported dangerous levels of ozone in the air over Kingsport. On 23 August the Tennessee Division of Air Pollution Control revealed a recent reading of 135—well above the unhealthful level of 100. Forty-eight hours later, with a reading of 132, the newspaper claimed that "high ozone levels combined with inversion and stagnant air made it difficult for people in Kingsport to breathe"; and it published a photograph with the following explanation: "Stagnant air surrounding the area today made it impossible to see the Clinchfield Depot at the end of Broad Street while standing at Church Circle."[60] About this time, journalist Dan Holman discerned a new odor and a new attitude in the town. Explaining that the town generally had three basic smells emanating respectively from the Mead plant, the Eastman plant, and the sluice on Riverport Road, he found the sluice odor to be dominant that summer. Taking the matter up with a high-ranking Eastman official, he expected the usual spiel—

"how it could not be them because of all the anti-pollution equipment." Instead, his opinion was confirmed. The smell was coming from the solids that were being separated from waste water, and Eastman was in the process of building a 16.5-acre sedimentation basin and dam to alleviate the problem. Holman noted that Eastman had been much more open and far more receptive to questions since "Smells Like Money" had been published.[61]

Nonetheless, pollution had not vanished, and the Kingsport Study Group had not been silenced. Reporter Mary Kiss had written in October 1978: "From any vantage point, it's plain that the Clean Air Amendments of 1970 didn't do the job in Kingsport or in other polluted areas around the country." Although representatives of local business and industry believed that a crackdown might put an end to "progress," a U.S. Chamber of Commerce slide show that had been presented in town had cautioned that "economic growth... could come to a screeching stop" if the law was not enforced.[62] On 29 January 1979, Marcella Fritz, a Barton Street resident who had led her neighbors in a fight against dust and pollution that settled on their homes and automobiles, became the first chairman of the fledgling Kingsport Environmental Health Study Group at its organizational meeting. Helen Matthews Lewis and her cadre from the old Kingsport Study Group, now being identified in the press as the Kingsport Citizens Advisory Group, provided the impetus. Immediate plans called for a public forum on pollution issues. With $75,086 funding from a National Science Foundation grant via the Washington, D.C.–based Public Resource Center, which also subsidized similar projects in Harlan, Kentucky, and Charleston, West Virginia, the Kingsport organization forged links with conservation activists throughout Appalachia. On 21 February, for the first time, city officials and industrial leaders met with the Environmental Health Study Group and made suggestions for a two-day forum, scheduled for 6-7 April.[63]

Soon, however, most industrialists and the business community chose to distance themselves from the Environmental Study Group. By 28 March the Chamber of Commerce had refused to participate, and industrial response proved less than encouraging; but Roger Campbell, administrative assistant to the city manager, had been added to the program. On the eve of the forum, officials of the companies alluded to the backgrounds of the organizers, claimed that they were outsiders attempting to cause trouble for the community, and declined to participate for fear that they would not receive a fair hearing. Lewis, who was affiliated with the controversial Highlander Research and Education Center at New Market, Tennessee, was the target of innuendos. Highlander Folk School, which had originated during the early 1930s at Monteagle, Tennessee, had been deeply involved in labor organizing and the civil-rights movement. The state had revoked the school's charter and confiscated its property around 1960, after repeated assaults from witch-hunters and red-baiters; but the staff had obtained another charter and relocated. Lewis, along with a few other faculty at East Tennessee State University, had also lost her position in 1968 at the height of antiwar protests during the Vietnam era.[64]

For the town's industrial giants, the Kingsport Study Group was a public-relations nuisance, but increasing pressure from regulatory agencies forced them to make serious attempts at compliance with environmental standards; and the *Kingsport Times-News* kept the issue before the public. The Penn-Dixie Cement plant, the favorite local scapegoat, proved to be least cooperative. Although it closed in November 1980, the town still had difficulty meeting air-quality standards. In 1982 Sullivan County was one of more than six hundred counties in forty-nine states in danger of failing to comply with the federal Clean Air Act. A year later, the Environmental Protection Agency ranked the Tri-Cities twelfth among the top twenty urban areas with dirty air. In 1982 a ruptured waste-water line at Tennessee Eastman had dumped chemicals into the south fork of the Holston River. This resulted in a massive fish kill, one of numerous such episodes. An updated listing of hazardous-waste sites, which was compiled by the state's Solid Waste Management Board and released in 1985, included four at Tennessee Eastman Company, one at the AFG (glass plant) dump, and another at the Holston Army Ammunition Plant's Area-A coal-tar trench. Nevertheless, the Tennessee Conservation League named Tennessee Eastman Company, for its considerable efforts, the 1984 Industrial Conservationist; the company has received similar recognition from other groups.[65] In 1982 environmentalist Arthur Smith had noted the difference in the views from Roan Mountain, on the Tennessee–North Carolina line: "Looking toward North Carolina, you see the blue sky meeting the green of the mountains. Turn around toward Tennessee and you see the same blue sky, but at about 3,000 feet there's a dark strip that looks muddy, then the mountains. It's obvious it's there. You don't have to argue about it."[66]

The town's pollution controversy during the 1970s provided much of the impetus for a popularly elected mayor. Discontented citizens conducted a petition drive, calling for a change in the city charter. The first campaign in 1979 pitted incumbent Mayor Gardner Hammond against Alderman Richard Waterson, Edward Steward, Jr., and Gene Shanks. When Waterson, who was also a candidate for reelection as alderman, discovered that the recently passed private act amending the charter prevented him from seeking both positions, he withdrew from the mayoral race. Although this was not much of a contest and although Hammond won the election, the 1981 match between C. Norman Spencer and Ward Huddleston, Jr., was extremely close: Spencer emerged the victor by a three-vote margin. Hardly a solution for all that ails Kingsport, the mayoral election nonetheless has steadily attracted more interest. The 1985 race pitted Thomas W. Todd, a one-term alderman, against Hunter Wright, who had served on the board from 1975 to 1979, and Tommy Lee Hulse, a former Sullivan County purchasing agent. Todd, the establishment candidate, placed third behind Wright, the winner, who was considered most moderate, and the controversial Hulse, whom some believed was the candidate of the underdog, who actually placed second.[67]

In the wake of the troublesome 1970s, the Tennessee Eastman Company has adopted a more visible stance in municipal affairs and civic activities and has reaffirmed its commitment to the community. In October 1980, TEC held a ground-breaking ceremony for its new coal-conversion facility on Long Island and took out a page of advertising in the local newspaper. Toy Reid, general manager of Eastman Chemicals Division, claimed that the Kingsport spirit was "alive and well" but warned of "the dangers of a self-fulfilling prophecy of negativism." He observed that the choice of Kingsport as the site for the new operation represented "Eastman's ultimate vote of confidence in this community—a most tangible expression of the fact that Kingsport's future is also our future. Its health and growth are vital to our company's health and growth."[68] At a subsequent air-quality hearing for the coal-conversion plant, only Arthur Smith, the Eastman retiree, raised a dissenting voice. He said that he wished the plant could have been built somewhere else because the air in Kingsport was already polluted; he dismissed the claims that the facility would have a "benign" effect on the environment by saying that the long-term consequences were simply not known.[69]

On other fronts, TEC has also been active. Reid endorsed the concept of metropolitan government for Sullivan County, although the Greater Kingsport Area Chamber of Commerce rejected the idea, and voters subsequently defeated the proposal during 1982 in all forty-eight precincts.[70] The company, with increasing frequency, has opened its Employee Center to community concerts, ballet performances, and films. Reid, in 1982, endorsed Kingsport's efforts to annex Cook's Valley, but the most significant development came with Eastman's willingness to have its main plant site of approximately 324 acres taken into the incorporation. It should be noted, however, that the company, not the city, set the terms for the three-phase annexation, with the stipulation that the additional tax revenue should be directed toward a much-needed capital-improvements program.[71] TEC, along with other industries and businesses in the Kingsport area, has been a major contributor to the popular and successful week-long summer Fun Fest, inaugurated in the town during the 1980s. On a less pleasant note, the City of Kingsport accused one of the industries, AFG (formerly American–Saint Gobain), of having tapped into the municipal water supply and of having siphoned off millions of gallons without paying for them. The City of Kingsport brought suit for $250,000, but then the Board of Mayor and Aldermen agreed to accept a settlement of about $41,000, to be paid in monthly installments over three years.[72]

The Eric Hill study of the 1960s had focused attention on the model city's need for more parks and recreation areas, and some of the more perceptive citizens shared this view and promoted it. From the 1960s to the 1980s, Kingsport has successfully addressed this matter. Three areas, in particular, stand as evidence: the splendid park on Bays Mountain, at the site of the old reservoir, which was made possible largely through the efforts of such people as Karl Goerdel and Merritt Shobe and through gifts from Tennessee Eastman Company; the small retreat of Glen Bruce Park, between the library and the power-company building; and Riverfront Park, which winds along the south fork of the Holston River and has a pleasant trail, an observation deck, and a bridge to the island. Nonetheless, only careful vigilance has prevented some unfortunate developments. When the fountain in Glen Bruce Park was being constructed, funded by a grant from the Department of Housing and Urban Development, an article in *Reader's Digest* called it a waste of federal money. In response, Mrs. John B. Dennis donated money for it as a tribute to her hubsand.[73] In 1970, as consideration was being given to destroying J. Fred Johnson Park to create an athletic field, the consensus seemed to be that this was too high a price to pay for school sports.[74] The unusual beauty and serenity of Bays Mountain seemed to be in peril in 1983, when Atlantic Richfield Company

(ARCO) proposed to do exploratory drilling for oil and gas and the Board of Mayor and Aldermen seemed to be receptive. The city stood to gain a paltry $17,000 a year for the first five-year lease, with a five-year renewal option at $11,000. In addition, and more importantly, it could expect 12.5 percent royalties from production profits. The newspaper denounced the idea, environmentalists geared up for a major battle, and citizens by the thousands signed petitions. ARCO, in the face of such opposition and of the city's negotiating conditions, withdrew the offer.[75]

The most blatant and visible failure of the model city in recent years has been the blighted and forlorn appearance of the downtown, in tandem with the haphazard and ill-conceived development of Stone Drive. Although declining downtowns and unsightly strip development has been an urban phenomenon in post–World War II America, Kingsport claimed a heritage of reasonably successful planning.[76] Some citizens have been quick to explain away and accept the local situation because of the national pattern.[77] This affords a lame excuse; it did not have to happen, for there had been ample warning. In 1969 a newspaper editorial cautioned that such "strip cities" as Stone Drive created their own set of problems. Pointing to "the ugly profusion of signs, utility poles and unrestricted clutter that defaces the outskirts of so many cities," it asked: "Where are the billboard restraints, the tree and shrubbery planting programs, and the coordination of building designs that might make shopping on Stone Drive pleasant as well as practical?"[78] A 1970 commentary reminded Kingsport of its smugness in the face of problems afflicting its unplanned neighbors and observed, "But out there on Stone Drive we are rapidly creating a motorists' nightmare." In 1983 the same newspaper taunted: "For the last 15 years, Kingsport has enjoyed the music of commercial development on East Stone Drive. But now it's time to pay the piper." Calling it "a nightmare," the newspaper blamed "planning-commission officials, city officials and others who consistently caved in to demands for access from fledgling businesses located along the street." The "only bright spot" would be "if the city would vow not to repeat the mistakes of East Stone Drive on West Stone Drive."[79]

Meanwhile, retail trade in the downtown withered. A veritable explosion of shopping centers and the appearance of Kingsport Mall on East Stone Drive and Eastman Road characterized the 1970s. The Fort Henry Mall, which drained off such major department stores as Penney's, Parks-Belk, and Millers, proved especially damaging for the old commercial district. Significant revitalization of the downtown does not hold a great deal of promise, but if studying a problem—the downtown has been assiduously studied by a wide array of organizations and committees—would guarantee a solution, the core area could anticipate a rosy future. Hopeful indicators include the use of historic zoning, efforts to make the old depot a focal point while ridding the area of the unsightly building that was abandoned when Lowe's left its downtown location, and affiliation with the national "Main Street U.S.A." program. In February 1986 a private corporation, Kingsport Centre, Incorporated, proposed to renovate the existing train station, as well as other buildings that remained in the vicinity from the town's early history, and to produce a new office, shopping, dining, living, and entertainment complex. Although this is an interesting concept, it is still in its early stages, and the outcome remains uncertain.

Ironically, the most vocal opposition to the course of change in the trouble-ridden downtown came when First National Bank of Sullivan County announced plans to build a new home on the Church Circle parking lot, the former site of Kingsport Inn. The bank's commitment both to the central business district and to the new building represented the most promising development of recent years. The local chapter of the American Institute of Architects, however, passed a unanimous resolution opposing the seven-story design, apparently believing that by its scale it would detract from the churches and other buildings in the immediate vicinity. As one local citizen observed, "I wish they had spoken out before the city pruned the trees around Legion Pool so severely or before Lowe's was allowed to build on Main Street and block the train station from view."[80] Bank officials also headed off a 1982 takeover effort by C.H. Butcher, Jr., brother of the convicted felon Jake Butcher, by merging with First American Bank to become First American-Eastern. A lawyer for the financial institution, at this point First Eastern Bank, characterized the Butcher style as "hot money banking," a reference to the technique used by the Butcher banks of transferring funds from one to another and of making unsecured loans to corporate officials.[81]

Kingsport in the mid 1980s, some seventy years after its incorporation, represents a fascinating experiment in American urban planning and development. Born of an era in Appalachian history that was characterized by capitalistic exploitation and the overriding quest for quick profits, it is an enigma. The formula that worked for John B. Dennis and J. Fred Johnson, that special moment and set of circumstances, is not applicable to Kingsport in the 1980s, for each generation must respond to its own set of challenges. While creating the potential for a strong economic base and imbuing their town with the ingredients for a marvelous mythology, they hastened their model city and its population into the future. The founders, especially Johnson, possessed a special panoramic vision, the talent to conceive of and act on behalf of the whole. That nebulous and elusive quality is absent in contemporary Kingsport. The assets of this small city far outnumber its liabilities, but it remains to be seen whether a new and positive vision can be summoned and inculcated, or whether the future will be jeopardized or lost while Kingsport rests on the precarious and quickly decaying remains of the past.

9 Epilogue

The planned industrial city of Kingsport has weathered seven decades as an incorporated municipality. Although it has changed a great deal in appearance and size since 1917 and has lost the vision that launched it, the old model city retains much of its heritage. Several factors have coalesced to spare this city the fate of less successful ventures in Appalachia: an aspiring population that is anxious to take advantage of steady employment and regular cash income; natural resources; the advent of the railroad; northern capital; the concept of interlocking industries; and above all, fortuitous leadership in the person of J. Fred Johnson. Appalachian native laborers still perform the tasks that make the factories work; outside investors retain ownership of most of the industries and many of the businesses; and professionals and managers from the area and elsewhere oversee the operations. Natural resources from the region play a small role; the companies are less dependent on each other; and Interstate-81 and US-23 (designated I-181), as well as greatly improved state roads and air travel, have ended the town's early reliance on the railroad.

The history of modern Kingsport is a twentieth-century experience, and this venture in privately financed modern town planning represents a successful graft of American industrial capitalism in the southern mountains. Economic development in this region has not followed evolutionary patterns of linear descent and continuity. For example, the early ironworks of the eighteenth century did not beget more sophisticated operations, nor did attempts at brick making expand significantly. Instead, the preindustrial efforts of the eighteenth and nineteenth centuries withered and died for lack of capital and access to markets. The appearance of modern industrial capitalism at Kingsport and, with few exceptions, elsewhere in Southern Appalachia marked new beginnings—a distinct separation from the past. Once swept into the mainstream, this region, no less than other American industrial centers, has faced international competition. The cheap labor of the emerging Third World, as well as a plethora of other factors, has undercut conditions that once gave such companies as Kingsport Press (Arcata Graphics/Kingsport as of 1985) and Tennessee Eastman an edge in the national and international markets.

The planning of Kingsport was multidimensional, integrating the physical, the economic, and the social. The conceptualization of Dennis and Johnson had been largely realized by the 1940s. As a consequence, by this point, Kingsport had a sound economic base as a community and as a city, a physical plan with due respect for visual aesthetics, a society that bore the heavy imprint of middle-class values, and a population that, for the most part, shared a common vision. The town functioned—and functioned well—but by no stretch of the imagination did it encourage the flowering of participatory democracy. Property ownership inside the incorporation and among the laborers in the outlying areas, as well as the several industries and the independent Kingsport Improvement Company, distinguished it from such stereotypical company towns as textile-mill villages and coal camps. Furthermore, the civic commitment of the professional-managerial element and the pioneering impulse of early residents cushioned it from the harsher aspects of exploitive capitalism.

At its best, planning is not static; it is subject to altering visions and changing times. Out of the World War II era came new challenges for the model city. External events, the deaths of the original leadership, and new trends in American society intruded upon it, fracturing the old vision. Since that time, Kingsport has witnessed the somewhat limited growth of democratic principles, a considerable geographical expansion, and a more narrowly defined idea of progress. Remnants of the infrastructure remain intact: government by the Board of Mayor and Aldermen and a city manager; basic components of the original physical plan; the churches, clubs, schools, and neighborhoods; and the fundamental conservatism of the population. The community still commits itself to short-term civic projects, but overall direction and long-term goals remain conspicuously absent.

The citizenry bears responsibility on at least two counts. First, probably because of the commercial-industrial nexus of the town's origins, far too much faith has been placed in the Greater Kingsport Area Chamber of Commerce. Although this body has much to commend it, its perspective is basically confined to a one-dimensional view of economic development. Recent staff shake-ups tend to confirm this observation. Corridor annexation by the city to acquire industrial sites suggests the same thing. Second, many residents, particularly the majority of the town's elected officials, seem to misunderstand the traditional role of the city manager. Instead of directing the person in this position, they expect him to guide them. A reform of good-government forces in the United States during the Progressive Era, government by a city manager and a board of mayor and aldermen seemed to be a method for eliminating the worst aspects of machine politics. Nonetheless, it could be easily controlled and manipulated, as indeed it has been for most of Kingsport's history. Johnson and Dennis, at first, exercised careful control, which later passed to an oligarchy of industrialists and businessmen. Currently, with only a pittance for a salary, the mayor and the aldermen generally moonlight as elected officials while holding down full-time jobs or pursuing careers. The community, having moved to a popularly elected mayor, might also consider adequate annual compensation for a demanding position. The election of aldermen by districts or wards, instead of at large, could enhance representation from all segments of the population.

Related to both of the matters just addressed is the tendency of some who are in positions of authority to be unduly impressed by so-called experts, especially those from any place other than Kingsport. City government, to the point of absurdity, in recent years has hired outside consultants, engaged additional legal counsel, and fostered prolonged studies. This method enables the government to avoid making a decision; it also scatters the responsibility. The justice center and proposed civic complex are glaring examples. This tendency may represent a reaction to in-house promotions and to dictatorial decision making in the past, but the consequence is that elected officials forfeit leadership to "experts" who are bound by a mentality born of scientific-management principles of the late nineteenth and early twentieth centuries. Contemporary Kingsport has conclusively demonstrated that awareness of problems and their study do not in and of themselves guarantee satisfactory solutions. Complacency is perhaps a societal disease of present-day Kingsport, just as it is of modern America.

When the Kingsport project was launched, the natives of the area, for the most part, had possessed little or no experience with urbanization; the first-generation labor force therefore had no basis for gauging the model city's development or the performance of its leadership. Increasingly, however, natives of the area have grown to resent the patronizing tone of the experts, as well as those who recruit them. This has been but one of several aspects apparent in the bitter months-long controversy of 1985-86 surrounding City Manager James Zumwalt and Police Chief Arthur LeTourneau, both of whom were recruited from elsewhere in the country for positions that could have been filled by promotions from within the ranks of veteran employees. Furthermore, those on the city's periphery have been less than enthusiastic about annexation in recent years. The relative improvement of county school systems partially accounts for this pattern. Some parents of school-age children, who at one time might have greeted annexation enthusiastically because of the superior Kingsport schools, do not necessarily believe these schools merit the additional tax burden that would come with being taken into the city. The closing of two elementary schools since the 1970s is an obvious indicator of an aging population within the corporate limits. Opposition to annexation, to some degree, can be explained by the desire of local people to distance themselves from the city once the workday is over, to preserve an identity that is fashioned by themselves rather than one that is determined by industrial and commercial forces. It also strongly signals a lack of confidence in Kingsport's leadership.

Kingsport and Upper East Tennessee, as much by default as by design, have become a metropolitan area. The Tri-Cities area has arrived at that special and transient moment when urban amenities and the yet-unspoiled natural beauty of the countryside coalesce. The prosperity of the three cities of Bristol, Johnson City, and Kingsport, along with such peripheral neighbors as Elizabethton, Greeneville, and Rogersville, belies most of the prevailing hillbilly imagery. The Tri-Cities area enjoys the scenic splendor of the Southern Appalachians, but bereft of the poverty that is so often associated with the entire region. Some area people take simple pleasure in their gardens, newly hatched baby chickens, or just an ordinary turnip or potato patch. Multinational corporations, however, recognize that out of these hills come some of the most reliable industrial workers in the world. It is not unusual for employees, cheerfully and voluntarily, to bestow gifts on managers and supervisors at Christmas and, on their own initiative, at one area plant, to organize an annual holiday feast and graciously invite their bosses to dine with them at tables set up on the factory floor. This is a population that is not embarrassed by patriotism, whether getting misty-eyed about Old Glory floating in the breeze, belatedly honoring its Vietnam veterans in the Kingsport Fourth of July parade, or mourning its own dead after the DC-8 crash at Gander, Newfoundland, in December 1985.

The model city's past, though fascinating, is not as glorious as it has, in retrospect, been portrayed by some. Reduced to its lowest common denominator, history can be little more than public relations; and the tendency to trivialize or mythologize the complicated personalities and processes of yesteryear hardly prepares a population to take a serious and sophisticated approach to contemporary problems and issues. Vestiges of the old community and the Kingsport way of doing things still survive among the graying contingent that frequents the symphony performances, those who serve on the board of directors of Holston Valley Community Hospital and Medical Center, and some who take Sunday luncheon at the country club. From absent vision to managerial mentality and to style over substance, the contours of what is wrong—as well as what is right—with America are visible in Kingsport. One can hear a kindly minister on Church Circle intone "Lay not up for yourself treasures upon earth" and in the next breath assure the congregation that Christianity is not opposed to wealth, just to misplaced values. Bays Mountain and Chimney Top really do turn purple at twilight. Wild ducks and other waterfowl grace the south fork of the Holston when it is shallow. Under the azure sky of autumn and the golden haze of October and November, or with the faint greening of a new spring, it is hard not to be a true believer in the "Kingsport spirit."

NOTES

1. INTRODUCTION

1. Stanley Buder, *Pullman: An Experiment in Industrial Order and Community Planning, 1880-1930* (New York: Oxford Univ. Press, 1967); Grace Hooten Gates, *The Model City of the New South: Anniston, Alabama, 1872-1900* (Huntsville, Ala.: Strode Publishers, 1978); James B. Lane, *"City of the Century": A History of Gary, Indiana* (Bloomington: Indiana Univ. Press, 1978); Raymond A. Mohl and Neil Betten, *Steel City: Urban and Ethnic Patterns in Gary, Indiana, 1906-1950* (New York: Holmes & Meier, 1986); and Daniel Schaffer, *Garden Cities for America: The Radburn Experience* (Philadelphia: Temple Univ. Press, 1982); see also Don Harrison Doyle, *The Social Order of a Frontier Community: Jacksonville, Illinois, 1825-1870* (Urbana: Univ. of Illinois Press, 1978); and John S. Garner, *The Model Company Town: Urban Design through Private Enterprise in Nineteenth-Century New England* (Amherst: Univ. of Massachusetts Press, 1984). The successful development of cities owes something to happenstance. Two decades or so ago, such urban historians as A. Theodore Brown and Charles N. Glaab expounded upon this theme: see, for examples, Charles N. Glaab, "Visions of Metropolis: William Gilpin and Theories of City Growth in the American West," *Wisconsin Magazine of History* 45 (Autumn 1961): 21-31; idem, *The American City: A Documentary History* (Homewood, Ill.: Dorsey Press, 1963); Charles N. Glaab and A. Theodore Brown, *A History of Urban America* (New York: Macmillan Co., 1967); and A. Theodore Brown, *Frontier Community: Kansas City to 1870* (Columbia: Univ. of Missouri Press, 1963). Nonetheless, professionally planned cities of the twentieth century merit a more sophisticated analysis than the triad of nature, talent, and luck, although these factors obviously cannot be overlooked.

2. Especially useful are Norman T. Newton, *Design on the Land: The Development of Landscape Architecture* (Cambridge, Mass.: Belknap Press of Harvard University, 1971); Mel Scott, *American City Planning since 1890* (Berkeley: Univ. of California Press, 1969); John W. Reps, *The Making of Urban America: A History of City Planning in the United States* (Princeton, N.J.: Princeton University Press, 1965); and Richard E. Foglesong, *Planning the Capitalist City: The Colonial Era to the 1920s* (Princeton, N.J.: Princeton University Press, 1986).

3. Russell D. Parker, "Alcoa, Tennessee: The Early Years, 1919-1939," East Tennessee Historical Society *Publications,* no. 48 (1976), pp. 84-103; Robert F. Ewald, "Plan for Industrial Community of Alcoa, Tennessee," *Engineering News-Record* 92 (28 Feb. 1929): 364-67; Charles W. Johnson and Charles O. Jackson, *City behind a Fence: Oak Ridge, Tennessee, 1942-1946* (Knoxville: Univ. of Tennessee Press, 1981); and Michael J. McDonald and John Muldowny, *TVA and the Dispossessed: The*

Resettlement of Population in the Norris Dam Area (Knoxville: Univ. of Tennessee Press, 1982).

4. Scott, *American City Planning since 1890,* pp. 110-82; Foglesong, *Planning the Capitalist City,* pp. 3-27.

5. Foglesong, *Planning the Capitalist City,* pp. 124-232.

6. John Loretz Hancock, "John Nolen and the American City Planning Movement: A History of Culture Change and Community Response, 1900-1940" (Ph.D. diss., University of Pennsylvania, 1964), p. 485; and Foglesong, *Planning the Capitalist City*, pp. 167-98.

7. "A Mountain of Debt in Brazil: International Bankers Are Hooked by the Biggest Borrower," *Time,* 25 Aug. 1980, p. 46; "End of a Billion-Dollar Dream: Ludwig Gives Up on His Project to Tame the Amazon Region," *Time,* 25 Jan. 1982, p. 59; Alexander L. Taylor III, "The Master Builders from Bechtel" and "The Jubail Superproject," *Time,* 12 July 1982, pp. 56-58, 60.

8. Eugene A. Conti, Jr., "The Cultural Role of Local Elites in the Kentucky Mountains: A Retrospective Analysis," *Appalachian Journal* 7 (Autumn/Winter 1979/80): 51-68; Margaret Ripley Wolfe, "J. Fred Johnson, His Town, and His People: A Case Study of Class Values, the Work Ethic, and Technology in Southern Appalachia, 1916-1944," ibid., pp. 70-83; and Ronald D Eller, "The Coal Barons of the Appalachian South, 1880-1930," ibid., 4 (1977): 196, 198.

9. John Gaventa, *Power and Powerlessness: Quiescence and Rebellion in an Appalachian Valley* (Urbana: Univ. of Illinois Press, 1980); and E. Bradford Burns, *The Poverty of Progress: Latin America in the Nineteenth Century* (Berkeley: Univ. of California Press, 1980).

10. J.O. Lewis, "The Costliest Railroad in America," *Scientific American Supplement No. 1752* 68 (31 July 1909): 72.

11. Information provided by the Planning Department, City of Kingsport, Tennessee; interview with Nancy Fischman, long-range planner, 4 Sept. 1985; telephone conversation with Fischman, 11 Dec. 1985; *Kingsport Times-News* (hereinafter cited as *Times-News*), 29 July 1980; and Richard Boyer and David Savageau, *Places Rated Almanac: Your Guide to Finding the Best Places to Live in America* (Chicago: Rand McNally, 1985), p. xx and passim. Initial census figures showed a decline in Kingsport's population from 1970 to 1980, 31,938 to 31,697.

12. *Times-News,* 23 July and 1 Nov. 1978, 1 May 1980, 14 June 1985.

13. From *Times-News* clipping files dated 30 March 1975; hereinafter cited as *Times-News* clipping files.

14. *Times-News,* 10 Feb. and 28-29 July 1980; Alfred North Whitehead, *Science and the Modern World* (New York: Macmillan, 1967), p. 197.

15. Interview with Earle Sumner Draper, landscape architect, Vero Beach, Fla., 26-27 June 1978.

16. Lisa Alther, *Kinflicks* (New York: Knopf, 1976), pp. 69-70.

17. Kingsport Study Group, "Smells Like Money," *Southern Exposure* 6 (Summer 1978): 59-67; *Times-News,* 14 Aug. 1980.

18. R.D. Norton, *City Life-Cycles and American Urban Policy* (New York: Academic Press, 1979), p. 5.

19. For an excellent survey of this farm-to-factory phenomenon in the South see Jacquelyn Dowd Hall, Robert Korstad, and James Leloudis, "Cotton Mill People: Work,

Community, and Protest in the Textile South, 1880-1940," *American Historical Review* 91 (April 1986): 245-86.

20. David R. Goldfield, *Cotton Fields and Skyscrapers: Southern City and Region, 1607-1980* (Baton Rouge: Louisiana State Univ. Press, 1982), pp. xi, xiii, 3; see also Blaine A. Brownell and David R. Goldfield, eds., *The City in Southern History: The Growth of Urban Civilization in the South* (Port Washington, N.Y.: Kennikat Press, 1977), pp. 5-22 and passim. In "The End of the Southern City," a paper presented at the Fiftieth Annual Meeting of the Southern Historical Association, on 1 Nov. 1984, in Louisville, Ky., Carl J. Abbott maintains that the urban South actually contains three nontraditional subareas: the Outer South, which includes the major regional cities that have become part of the national urban mainstream; the Middle South, which includes transitional cities that have been rapidly approaching national urban norms; and the Inner South, which contains those older industrial cities and intraregional distribution centers near the region's geographic core. Abbott employs four economic criteria to form his thesis for recent urban divergence in the South: the manufacturing-services ratio; the internationalization of the local economy; the development of a permanent military-defense industry; and the evolution of an information-based economy. Abbott graciously provided me with a copy of this analysis. Kingsport is not included in this study, and the Johnson City–Kingsport–Bristol SMSA receives only passing reference.

21. James C. Cobb, *Industrialization and Southern Society 1877-1984* (Lexington: Univ. Press of Kentucky, 1984), pp. 68-98; and idem, *The Selling of the South: The Southern Crusade for Industrial Development 1936-1980* (Baton Rouge: Louisiana State Univ. Press, 1982), pp. 86-121.

22. Interview with Mrs. H.J. (Genevieve) Shivell, Kingsport pioneer, Kingsport, Tenn., 28 Sept. 1978.

23. *Times-News,* 27 Feb. 1977.

24. Sylvester Petro, *The Kingsport Strike* (New Rochelle, N.Y.: Arlington House, 1967), p. 23.

25. Roy Lubove, "The Urbanization Process: An Approach to Historical Research," in *American Urban History: An Interpretive Reader with Commentaries,* ed. Alexander B. Callow, Jr., 2d ed. (New York: Oxford Univ. Press, 1973), p. 661.

2. FOUNDATIONS OF AN AMERICAN DREAM

1. Lewis Mumford, "Utopia, the City and the Machine," in *Utopias and Utopian Thought,* ed. Frank E. Manual (Boston: Houghton Mifflin; and Cambridge, Mass.: Riverside Press, 1966), p. 3.

2. John A. Piquet, "Low-Cost Methods and High-Class Men," *Industrial Management* 71 (May 1926): 323.

3. Robert H. Wiebe, *The Segmented Society: An Introduction to the Meaning of America* (New York: Oxford Univ. Press, 1975; reprint, London: Oxford Univ. Press, 1979), p. 3.

4. *Kingsport Times,* 22 March 1917. Hereinafter *Times* will refer to *Kingsport Times* unless another city is specified.

5. Gordon S. Wood, *The Creation of the American Republic, 1776-1787* (Chap-

el Hill: Univ. of North Carolina Press, 1969; reprint, New York: Norton, 1972), pp. 418-19.

6. Daniel T. Rodgers, *The Work Ethic in Industrial America, 1850-1920* (Chicago: Univ. of Chicago Press, 1978), pp. xi, 153.

7. Several American historians have elaborated on the theme of nature in the American experience: see, for examples, Henry Nash Smith, *Virgin Land: The American West as Symbol and Myth* (New York: Vintage Books, n.d.; reprint, Cambridge, Mass.: Harvard University Press, 1950); Peter J. Schmitt, *Back to Nature: The Arcadian Myth in Urban America* (New York: Oxford University Press, 1969); John William Ward, *Andrew Jackson: Symbol for an Age* (New York: Oxford Univ. Press, 1955; reprint, Oxford, Eng.: Oxford Univ. Press, 1979), pp. 13-97; and James Oliver Robertson, *American Myth, American Reality* (New York: Hill & Wang, 1981), pp. 113-24.

8. Kingsport Board of Mayor and Aldermen, *Minute Book 3,* 5 Feb. 1929, p. 1179, City Hall; hereinafter cited as Board of Mayor and Aldermen with appropriate minute book, date, and page.

9. Samuel Cole Williams, comp., *Early Travels in the Tennessee Country, 1549-1800* (Johnson City, Tenn.: Watauga Press, 1928; reprint, Nashville, Tenn.: Franklin Book Reprints, 1970), p. 170.

10. Ibid., pp. 169-71.

11. Hancock, "John Nolen and the American City Planning Movement," p. 454.

12. Interview with Mrs. Shivell.

13. Paul A. Counce, "Social and Economic History of Kingsport before 1908" (Master's thesis, Univ. of Tennessee, 1939), p. 66.

14. Ibid.; see also L.R. Ahern, Jr., and R.F. Hunt, Jr., "Notes and Documents: The Boatyard Store, 1814-1825," *Tennessee Historical Quarterly* 14 (Sept. 1955): 257-77; Samuel Cole Williams, "Early Iron Works in the Tennessee Country," ibid., 6 (March 1947): 39-46; and Charles Coffin Ross, ed. and comp., *The Story of Rotherwood: From the Autobiography of Rev. Frederick A. Ross* (Knoxville, Tenn.: Bean, Warters & Co., 1923), pp. 20-21.

15. George L. Fowler, "The Carolina, Clinchfield and Ohio Railway," *Railroad Age Gazette,* 19 March 1909, pp. 539-40.

16. Mark W. Potter, quoted in Frank E. Shaffer, "Here Comes Clinchfield," *Trains,* Aug. 1961, p. 37.

17. Board of Mayor and Aldermen, *Minute Book 4*, 19 Jan. 1937, p. 1625.

18. Charles J. Harkrader, *Witness to an Epoch* (Kingsport, Tenn.: Kingsport Press, 1965), p. 141.

19. "Outline of History of Carolina, Clinchfield & Ohio Railway" (typescript), p. 1, files of the Engineering Department, Clinchfield Railroad, Erwin, Tenn. Since I had access to these materials, most of the Clinchfield Collection has been transferred to the Archives of Appalachia, Sherrod Library, East Tennessee State University, Johnson City, Tenn.

20. Harkrader, *Witness to an Epoch,* pp. 141-42.

21. *Times-News,* 1 July 1956.

22. Ibid.; "Outline of History of Carolina, Clinchfield & Ohio Railway," p. 2.

23. "Historical Events—Carolina, Clinchfield & Ohio Railway" (typescript), p. 1, files of the Engineering Department, Clinchfield Railroad, Erwin, Tenn.

24. Consul G.C. Montagna to Secretary of State Elihu Root, 20 June 1906, and

Montagna to Root, 25 Aug. 1906, Italian Legation in the United States, notes to the Department of State, 1861-1906, National Archives, Washington, D.C., M862.

25. "Historical Events," pp. 2-3.

26. *Times-News,* 1 July 1956.

27. *Johnson City Comet,* 24 Aug. 1905.

28. *Times-News,* 1 July 1956.

29. Harkrader, *Witness to an Epoch,* p. 146.

30. *Bristol Herald-Courier,* 5 Sept. 1908.

31. *Johnson City Comet,* 15 Oct. 1908.

32. Ibid., 28 Jan. 1909.

33. William Way, Jr., *The Clinchfield Railroad: The Story of a Trade Route across the Blue Ridge Mountains* (Chapel Hill: Univ. of North Carolina Press, 1931), p. 112.

34. Albert D. Early, of Milbank, Tweed, Hadley and McCloy, legal counsel for the Securities Company, to the author, 3 Feb. 1978, containing portions of a report prepared by Wiliam B. Franke for the New York Trust Co., 31 Dec. 1938; hereinafter cited as Franke Report.

35. Harkrader, *Witness to an Epoch,* p. 147.

36. Counce, "Social and Economic History of Kingsport," p. 90.

37. Map S-26, May 1906, City of Kingsport, Engineering Department, City Hall.

38. From *Times-News* clipping files dated 13 Feb. 1947.

39. Interview with Albert D. Early, New York, 13 April 1978; and interview with H.J. Shivell, a Kingsport pioneer and the owner of Slip-Not Belting, Kingsport, 28 Sept. 1978.

40. Franke Report, 15 Sept. 1971, containing portions of a 1938 report that he prepared for the New York Trust Co.

41. Ibid.; see also *Deed Book 125,* pp. 79-85, Sullivan County Court House, Blountville, Tenn. In 1926 the Kingsport Improvement Corporation transferred its assets to Kingsport Farms, Incorporated, and these holdings together with assets of other corporations were sold to the newly formed Kingsport Improvement Company; the Kingsport Improvement Corporation was then dissolved. Hereinafter, for simplification, Kingsport Improvement Company will be used as the official designation.

42. Isaac Shuman, "Kingsport, an Unusual City, Built to Make Business for a Railroad," *American City* 22 (May 1920): 471-73; Victor V. Kelsey, "Building a Complete Cycle of Industries," *Scientific American Supplement No. 2181* 84 (20 Oct. 1917): 250.

43. Quotation from *Times-News* clipping files dated 29 Dec. 1957: interviews with Mrs. J. Fred (Elizabeth Doggett) Johnson, Kingsport, Tenn., 6 Feb. and 11 July 1978. Elizabeth Doggett Johnson was the second wife of J. Fred Johnson and the niece of his first wife, Ruth Carter Johnson. The second marriage occurred a few years after Ruth Carter Johnson's death during the 1930s.

44. Interview with Mrs. Johnson, 6 Feb. 1978.

45. Henry F. May, *The End of American Innocence: A Study of the First Years of Our Own Time, 1912-1917* (New York: Knopf, 1959; reprint, Chicago: Quadrangle Paperbacks, n.d. [first Quadrangle paperback ed., 1964]), p. 9.

46. Ibid.

47. Ibid., p. 21.

48. Ibid., p. 30.

49. *Times,* 11 May 1916.

50. Rodgers, *Work Ethic in Industrial America,* pp. 11-13.

51. Interview with Mrs. Johnson, 6 Feb. 1978.

52. For treatment of New South philosophy and its effects on the South, in general, and Tennessee, in particular, see Samuel Boyd Smith, "Joseph Buckner Killebrew and the New South Movement in Tennessee," East Tennessee Historical Society *Publications,* no. 37 (1965), pp. 5-22; C. Vann Woodward, *Origins of the New South, 1877-1913,* vol. 9 in *A History of the South,* ed. Wendell Holmes Stephenson and E. Merton Coulter (Baton Rouge: Louisiana State Univ. Press, 1951); and Paul M. Gaston, *The New South Creed: A Study in Southern Myth-Making* (New York: Knopf, 1970).

53. Copies of correspondence between J. Fred Johnson and George Eastman were provided by Mrs. J. Fred Johnson and are in my possession.

54. Interview with Mrs. Johnson, 6 Feb. 1978.

55. Charles J. Harkrader to a mutual friend, 27 Dec. 1971, courtesy of Mrs. J. Fred Johnson; copy in my possession.

56. Speech delivered by Perley S. Wilcox, "Tennessee Eastman Corporation: The First Twenty-Five Years," 15 March 1947 (copy provided by Mrs. J. Fred Johnson).

57. Interview with Shivell.

58. Telephone conversation with Mrs. Johnson, 6 Dec. 1978.

59. Thomas R. Ford, "The Passing of Provincialism," in *The Southern Appalachian Region: A Survey,* ed. Thomas R. Ford (Lexington: Univ. of Kentucky Press, 1962), pp. 25-26.

60. Wood, *Creation of the American Republic,* p. 70.

61. David M. Potter, "The Quest for National Character," in *The National Temper: Readings in American Culture and Society,* ed. Lawrence W. Levine and Robert Middlekauff, 2d ed. (New York: Harcourt Brace Jovanovich, 1972), pp. 14-15.

62. E.W. Palmer, "An Appreciation," in *John Frederick Johnson* (n.p., n.d.), a bound volume of clippings, telegrams, and sympathy notes, in the possession of Mrs. J. Fred Johnson, when I had access to it.

63. Interview with Draper.

64. Bernard Bailyn et al., *The Great Republic: A History of the American People* (Lexington, Mass.: D.C. Heath, 1977), p. 295.

65. J. Fred Johnson to H.A. Morgan, 13 July 1933, papers of Allen Dryden, Sr. (copy courtesy of Nellie M. McNeil), Kingsport, Tenn.

66. *Times,* 22 March 1917 and 4 July 1919.

67. Interview with J.T. Roller, realtor, Kingsport, Tenn., 25 Sept. 1978.

68. "Kingsport City Plan," p. 3, John Nolen Papers, John M. Olin Library, Cornell University, Ithaca, N.Y., box 26, file 1.

69. H. Ray Dennis to John Nolen, 22 March 1916, ibid.

70. Ibid.

71. John Nolen to H. Ray Dennis, 24 April 1916, ibid.

72. Fred Johnson to John Nolen, 29 April 1922, ibid., file 5.

73. Last will and testament of J. Fred Johnson, probated 7 Oct. 1944, *Will Book No. 5,* pp. 443-47, Sullivan County Court House, Blountville, Tenn.

74. *Times-News* clipping files dated 16 Sept. 1973; Estelle Penn to Mrs. J. Fred Johnson, 6 Oct. 1944, in the possession of Mrs. Johnson, when I had access to it; and interview with Shivell.

75. This photograph was submitted by Mrs. Kathleen Groseclose for a contest

sponsored by the *Times-News.* It was printed in the *Times,* 2 July 1953; a clipping is in the photograph collection (P. C. 147-49), Tennessee Room, J. Fred Johnson Memorial Library [Kingsport Public Library], Kingsport, Tenn.; hereinafter cited as Kingsport Public Library.

76. Letters from several servicemen are contained in *John Frederick Johnson.*

77. Wood, *Creation of the American Republic,* pp. 68-69.

78. *Kingsport: Its Growth, Housing and Industries* (Kingsport, Tenn.: n.p. [Kingsport Improvement Company], 1920), p. 14. Thomas B. Yancey III of Kingsport, Tennessee, provided me with a copy.

79. F.M. Kelly to J. Fred Johnson, 22 May 1939 (courtesy of Mrs. Johnson). For the contrast between Kingsport and Elizabethton, Tenn., see John Fred Holly, "The Social and Economic Effects Produced upon Small Towns by Rapid Urbanization" (Master's thesis, Univ. of Tennessee, 1938).

80. *Times,* 5 April 1917.

81. Piquet, "Low-Cost Methods and High-Class Men," pp. 322-23.

82. Charles Stevenson, "A Contrast in 'Perfect' Towns," *Nation's Business,* Dec. 1937, p. 20.

83. Interview with Mrs. Johnson, 11 July 1978.

84. For studies of the Red Scare see Robert K. Murray, *Red Scare: A Study of National Hysteria, 1919-1920* (Minneapolis–St. Paul: Univ. of Minnesota Press, 1955; 1st McGraw-Hill paperback ed., New York: McGraw-Hill, 1964); and William Preston, Jr., *Aliens and Dissenters: Federal Suppression of Radicals, 1903-1933* (Cambridge, Mass.: Harvard Univ. Press, 1963; 1st Harper Torchbook ed., New York: Harper & Row, 1966). See also Stanley Coben, "A Study in Nativism: The American Red Scare of 1919-20," *Political Science Quarterly* 79 (March 1964): 52-75.

85. Wilcox, "Tennessee Eastman Corporation."

86. *Kingsport: Its Growth, Housing and Industries,* pp. 24 and 26.

87. Howard Long, *Kingsport: A Romance of Industry* (Kingsport, Tenn.: Sevier Press, 1928), p. 84.

88. John Nolen, *New Towns for Old: Achievements in Civic Improvement in Some American Small Towns and Neighborhoods,* introduction by Albert Shaw (Boston: Marshall Jones Co., 1927), p. 62.

89. Interview with Mrs. S.P. (Penelope) Platt, Kingsport pioneer, Kingsport, Tenn., 21 July 1978.

90. Orlando Patterson, *Ethnic Chauvinism: The Reactionary Impulse* (New York: Stein & Day, 1977).

91. Piquet, "Low-Cost Methods and High-Class Men," p. 323.

3. ARTIFACTS OF THE PLANNED CITY

1. *Kingsport: Past, Present, and Future* (Kingsport: Rotary Club of Kingsport, c. 1980), p. 4. The efforts of the industrial agents of the CC & O to secure the location of industries along the entire route are well documented in the Carolina, Clinchfield and Ohio Railway Collection, Archives of Appalachia, Sherrod Library, East Tennessee State University, Johnson City.

2. Walter F. Smith, *Kingsport Press, Inc.: Bookmakers to America* (New York: Newcomen Society in North America, 1959), p. 9.

3. *Times-News,* 19 June 1958.

4. Interview with Shivell.

5. Interview with Draper.

6. Ibid.

7. *Times,* 4 and 25 Jan. 1921; see also Joseph Hyde Pratt, "Good Roads Movement in the South," *Annals of the American Academy of Political and Social Science* 35 (Jan. 1910): 105-13; and Howard L. Preston, *Automobile Age Atlanta: The Making of a Southern Metropolis, 1905-1935* (Athens: Univ. of Georgia Press, 1979), pp. 31-34, 145-47.

8. Interview with Nora and Lidia Harrison, American History Project in Local History, information collected and written by Jim Brockman, Bill King, and Jane Shivell, Tennessee Room, Kingsport Public Library; *Kingsport Sentinel,* 14 Oct. 1910.

9. Stuart Seely Sprague, "Alabama and the Appalachian Iron and Coal Town Boom, 1889-1893," *Alabama Historical Quarterly* 45 (Summer 1975): 85-91; idem, "Investing in Appalachia: The Virginia Valley Boom of 1889-1893," *Virginia Cavalcade,* Winter 1975, pp. 131-43; and idem, "The Great Appalachian Iron and Coal Town Boom of 1889-1893," *Appalachian Journal* 4 (Spring/Summer 1977): 216-23.

10. Marshall W. Fishwick, "Boom Days in Virginia," *Iron Worker,* Spring 1959, p. 7.

11. Charles Blanton Roberts, "The Building of Middlesborough: A Notable Epoch in Eastern Kentucky History," *Filson Club Quarterly* 7 (Jan. 1933): 18-33; see also Gaventa, *Power and Powerlessness,* passim.

12. Long, *Kingsport,* pp. 157, 165; John A. Piquet, *Kingsport: The Planned Industrial City* (Kingsport: Rotary Club, 1946), pp. 21-22. An earlier version of this book appeared in 1937. Unless otherwise indicated, the 1946 edition is the one being cited.

13. Long, *Kingsport,* p. 157; Franke Report.

14. Ibid., pp. 241-42.

15. *Philadelphia Public-Ledger,* 16 Nov. 1916.

16. Long, *Kingsport,* p. 258; *Times,* 29 June 1916.

17. *Times,* 11 May 1916 and 8 March 1917; papers of W.C. Hattan, courtesy of Mary Hattan Bogart, Erwin, Tenn.

18. *Times-News,* 11 April 1976.

19. Interview with Draper.

20. Photograph [c. 1915], Tennessee Room, Kingsport Public Library.

21. *Public-Ledger,* 16 Nov. 1916; *Times,* 11 Jan. 1917.

22. Charles C. May, "Some Aspects of Industrial Housing: The Need for Maintenance Measures, a Housing Enterprise at Kingsport, Tennessee, Clinton Mackenzie, Architect," unidentified article, Nolen Papers, box 26, file 7.

23. Dr. T.B. Yancey to F.W. Lovejoy, 6 Feb. 1922, quoted in *Times-News,* 27 Feb. 1983.

24. Interview with Mrs. Johnson, 6 Feb. 1978.

25. W.C. Hattan diary, Sept. 1915.

26. Ibid., 25 Nov. 1915.

27. Ibid., 29 Nov. 1915.

28. Joseph H. Sears to H. Ray Dennis, 28 Dec. 1915, and Sears to John Nolen, 28 Dec. 1915, Nolen Papers, box 26, file 1. John L. Hancock writes in his dissertation, p. 454, that T.H. Sears of the American Society of Landscape Architects recommended

Nolen to the Dennis brothers. A careful scrutiny of Nolen's papers, corroborated by an interview with Mrs. S. Phelps (Penelope Sears) Platt, daughter of Joseph H. Sears, indicates that Nolen was recommended by publisher Joseph H. Sears of D. Appleton and Co., a friend of John B. Dennis's; interview with Mrs. Platt. My notes, being at variance with some of Hancock's citations, were rechecked by Kathleen Jacklin, archivist at Cornell's John M. Olin Library. Jacklin concluded that there were "miscitations" in Hancock's dissertation; Kathleen Jacklin to the author, 9 Dec. 1981. Some incongruities, however, might be explained by the possibility that while writing his dissertation, Hancock had access to material that was not included in the papers eventually acquired by Cornell University.

29. John Hancock, "John Nolen: The Background of a Pioneer Planner," *Journal of the American Institute of Planners* 26 (Nov. 1960): 302-12; Albert Nelson Marquis, ed., *Who's Who in America, 1916-1917* (Chicago: Marquis Co., c. 1917), p. 1815; and a biographical sketch contained in John Nolen, ed., *City Planning: A Series of Papers Presenting the Essential Elements of a City Plan,* 2d ed. (New York: D. Appleton and Co., 1929), pp. xxiii, xxiv.

30. Hancock, "John Nolen: The Background of a Pioneer Planner," p. 303.

31. Ibid., p. 307.

32. Ibid., p. 306.

33. Newton, *Design on the Land,* pp. 479, 487; and Scott, *American City Planning since 1890,* p. 314.

34. Hancock, "John Nolen and the American City Planning Movement," p. 462.

35. *Times,* 10 June 1919.

36. Nolen, *New Towns for Old,* p. 52.

37. John L. Hancock, "Planners in the Changing American City, 1900-1940," in *American Urban History: An Interpretive Reader with Commentaries,* ed. Alexander B. Callow, Jr., 2d ed. (New York: Oxford Univ. Press, 1973), p. 604.

38. Interview with Draper.

39. Correspondence contained in Nolen Papers, box 26, file 1.

40. Interview with Draper.

41. Hancock, "John Nolen and the American City Planning Movement," pp. 460-61.

42. Hattan diary.

43. John Nolen to H. Ray Dennis, 6 Jan. 1916, Nolen Papers, box 26, file 1.

44. List of payments to Clinton Mackenzie and John Nolen by the Kingsport Improvement Co., 21 Sept. 1920, provided by Mrs. Johnson. The billings are randomly dispersed in the Nolen Papers, box 26, files 1-5.

45. J. Fred Johnson to John Nolen, 3 April 1916, Nolen Papers, box 26, file 1.

46. *Bristol Herald-Courier,* 9 April 1916; and *Times,* 3 Aug. 1916 and 1 March 1917.

47. Muriel Millar Clark Spoden, *The Early Years on Bays Mountain in Sullivan County* (Kingsport, Tenn.: Franklin Printing Co., 1975), pp. 24, 31-32.

48. Interviews with Draper and Mrs. Johnson.

49. *Times,* 5 Sept. 1919.

50. Report of E.A. Douglas, 16-26 Jan. 1919; Harlan P. Kelsey to John Nolen, 29 March 1919; and H. Ray Dennis to Nolen, 3 Sept. 1919—all in Nolen Papers, box 26, file 2.

51. H. Ray Dennis to John Nolen, 19 Aug. 1919, ibid.

52. J. Fred Johnson to John Nolen, 28 May 1919, ibid.

53. *Times,* 8 Aug. 1919; minutes of Board of Mayor and Aldermen, *Minute Book 1,* 3 July and 5 Aug. 1919, pp. 332, 354.

54. J. Fred Johnson to E.A. Douglas, 2 June 1919, Nolen Papers, box 26, file 2. The word *Negro* almost always appeared with a lower case *n*, and it was not unusual for it to be misspelled in correspondence between principals in Kingsport's development.

55. E.A. Douglas to John Nolen, 13 June 1919, ibid.

56. Hancock, "John Nolen and the American City Planning Movement," p. 453.

57. *Times,* 5 April 1917; and H. Ray Dennis to John Nolen, 30 Jan. 1920, Nolen Papers, box 26, file 3; see also Harkrader, *Witness to an Epoch,* pp. 148-49.

58. Herbert R. Sands to H. Ray Dennis, 1 Feb. 1917, and Bureau of Municipal Research, *Memorandum Report of the Proposed Charter for the City of Kingsport, Tennessee,* Jan. 1917, both in Bureau of Municipal Research Archives, Institute for Public Administration, New York City; Charter of 1917 for the City of Kingsport, copy from Kingsport Public Library; and Long, *Kingsport,* pp. 96-97.

59. Harold A. Stone, Don K. Price, and Kathryn H. Stone, *City Manager Government in Nine Cities* (Chicago: Public Administration Service, 1940), pp. 521-22; *Times,* 24 Feb. 1920.

60. John Nolen to H. Ray Dennis, 6 Jan. 1916, Nolen Papers, box 26, file 1.

61. Ibid., 28 April 1916.

62. Map S-26.

63. H. Ray Dennis to John Nolen, 6 Aug. 1917, Nolen Papers, box 26, file 1.

64. John Nolen to H. Ray Dennis, 8 Aug. 1917, ibid.

65. Arthur C. Comey and Max S. Wehrly, *Planned Communities,* pt. 1 of *Urban Planning and Land Policies,* vol. 2 of the Supplementary Report of the Urbanism Committee to the National Resources Committee (Washington, D.C.: Government Printing Office, 1939), pp. 35, 37.

66. John Nolen to H. Ray Dennis, 10 Feb. 1916, Nolen Papers, box 26, file 1.

67. "Suggestions for Tentative Program for Kingsport, Tenn.," ibid.

68. Hancock, "John Nolen and the American City Planning Movement," p. 455.

69. *Times,* 10 June 1919.

70. John Nolen to Grosvenor Atterbury, 4 Nov. 1919, Nolen Papers, box 26, file 3.

71. Interview with Early.

72. H. Ray Dennis to John Nolen, 5 Feb. 1917, and Nolen to Dennis, 6 Feb. 1917, Nolen Papers, box 26, file 1.

73. Earle S. Draper to John Nolen, 15 Feb. 1917, ibid.

74. Earle S. Draper to John Nolen, 17 Feb. 1917, ibid.

75. John Nolen to J. Fred Johnson, 5 March 1917, ibid.

76. Plans for Kingsport, contained in Nolen Papers.

77. Nolen, *New Towns for Old,* p. 63.

78. Ibid.; Frances Mary Hughes, "Where Planned Beauty Blossoms in an Industrial Community," *American City* 43 (Dec. 1930): 141.

79. H. Ray Dennis to John Nolen, 3 April 1919, Nolen Papers, box 26, file 2.

80. *Times,* 20 June 1919.

81. H. Ray Dennis to John Nolen, 23 Oct. 1918, Nolen Papers, box 26, file 2.

82. *Times,* 3 and 6 Feb. 1920.
83. John Nolen to H. Ray Dennis, 8 Aug. 1917, Nolen Papers, box 26, file 1.
84. "Kingsport City Plan," ibid.
85. Interview with Draper.
86. H. Ray Dennis to John Nolen, 1 Feb. 1917, Nolen Papers, box 26, file 1.
87. Nolen, *New Towns for Old,* p. 53.
88. H. Ray Dennis to John Nolen, 7 June 1918, Nolen Papers, box 26, file 2.
89. Interview with Draper.
90. H. Ray Dennis to John Nolen, 7 June 1918, and Nolen to Dennis, 11 June 1918, Nolen Papers, box 26, file 2; interview with Draper.
91. Clinton Mackenzie, *Industrial Housing* (New York: Knickerbocker Press, 1920), pp. 3-42.
92. Ibid., p. 4.
93. Nolen, *New Towns for Old,* pp. 62, 64.
94. H. Ray Dennis to John Nolen, 23 Sept. 1916, Nolen Papers, box 26, file 1.
95. H. Ray Dennis to John Nolen, 7 March 1917 and 15 Oct. 1918, ibid., files 1 and 2 respectively.
96. H. Ray Dennis to John Nolen, 13 Feb. 1919, ibid., box 26, file 2.
97. J. Fred Johnson to John Nolen, 15 May 1919, ibid.
98. W.M. Bennett to Board of Mayor and Aldermen, n.d., contained in minutes of the Board of Mayor and Aldermen, *Minute Book 1,* 3 July 1919, p. 332.
99. H. Ray Dennis to John Nolen, 3 March 1920, Nolen Papers, box 26, file 3.
100. Mackenzie, *Industrial Housing,* pp. 36, 37.
101. Paul R. Frost to John Nolen, 28 July 1920, Nolen Papers, box 26, file 4.
102. Report on visit of Raymond W. Blanchard, 24-27 Aug. 1920, ibid.
103. U.S., Department of Commerce, Bureau of the Census, *Fourteenth Census of the United States, 1920: Population* (Washington, D.C.: Government Printing Office, 1922), 3:971; *Fifteenth Census of the United States, 1930: Population* (Washington, D.C.: Government Printing Office, 1932), 3:903.
104. Reps, *Making of Urban America,* p. 524.
105. John Nolen, *New Ideals in the Planning of Cities, Towns and Villages* (New York: American City Bureau, 1919), p. 7.
106. Ibid., pp. 10-11.
107. John Nolen, "The Planning of Industrial Cities," *American City* 21 (Dec. 1919): 514.
108. *Times,* 6 and 20 June and 23 Dec. 1919, 23 Jan., 20 April, 23 July, 26 Nov., and 14 Dec. 1920, and 27 Feb. 1927.
109. Interview with Draper, who indicated that the Georgian style was used in Kingsport because New York architects seemed to think that it was appropriate for the South.
110. *Times,* 27 Feb. 1927; H.C. Brooks built Spanish-style bungalows on one block of Myrtle Street in 1923; see Long, *Kingsport,* photograph between pp. 82 and 83; see also Board of Mayor and Aldermen, *Minute Book 2,* 29 May 1928, pp. 1113-14.
111. *Times,* 16 Jan. 1920.
112. Gwendolyn Wright, *Moralism and the Model Home: Domestic Architecture and Cultural Conflict in Chicago, 1873-1913* (Chicago, Ill.: University of Chicago Press, 1980), pp. 231-53.

113. Interviews with Mrs. Platt and Mrs. Shivell.

114. Clinton Mackenzie to John Nolen, 29 April 1920, Nolen Papers, box 26, file 3; Mackenzie to Nolen, 1 Nov. 1920 and 19 March 1923, and Nolen to H. Ray Dennis, 5 and 11 Nov. 1920, ibid., file 5.

115. *Times,* 2 and 23 Jan. 1920 and 11 Jan. 1921.

116. Interview with Draper.

117. S. Herbert Hare, "The Planning of the Industrial City of Longview, Washington," *Proceedings of the American Society of Civil Engineers* 53 (Aug. 1927): 1177-83, particularly 1177. See also the following articles by Hare: "The Planning of a New Industrial City," *American City Magazine* 29 (Nov. 1923): 501-3; and "The Planning of Jefferson Square at Longview, Washington," *Parks and Recreation* 15 (Nov. 1931): 116-20. See also B.L. Lambuth, "The Planning of Longview, Washington," *Journal of the Town Planning Institute of Canada* 6 (Aug. 1927): 131-35; idem, "A Small City Whose Growth Is Aided and Controlled by a Plan," *American City Magazine* 35 (Aug. 1926): 186-91; and "Longview: A City-Planned Community," *Architect and Engineer* 81 (April 1925): 99-104.

4. BUILDING AN INDUSTRIAL COMMUNITY

1. *Times,* 27 Feb. 1927.

2. *Times-News* clipping files dated 29 Dec. 1957.

3. Franke Report; *Times,* 25 July 1919.

4. *Baltimore Sun,* 8 Dec. 1916.

5. Billy M. Jones, *Magic with Sand: A History of AFG Industries, Inc.* (Wichita, Kans.: Wichita State Univ. Center for Entrepreneurship, College of Business Administration, 1984), p. 88. Interview with Karl Goerdel, Jasper Ketron, and Howard Wilson, Fall Branch, Tenn., 12 Dec. 1979; all of these men were familiar with early Kingsport and had connections with Tennessee Eastman Co. from its infancy. Goerdel and Ketron retired from that company, and Howard Wilson worked there as a summer employee in his youth and later acted as legal counsel for Eastman on occasion. *Kingsport: Its Growth, Housing and Industries,* p. 6; *Times,* 2 July 1920; and *Times-News* clipping files dated 1, 8, and 15 Dec. 1974.

6. Copy of payroll of American Wood Reduction Co., provided by Jasper Ketron, in my possession; Wilcox, "Tennessee Eastman Corporation"; Earle L. Rauber, "Kingsport: An Industry Pattern," *Monthly Review* (Federal Reserve Bank of Atlanta) 30 (31 Aug. 1945): 83; and *Times,* 18 July 1919.

7. *Times,* 4 July 1919; Stone, Price, and Stone, *City Manager Government in Nine Cities,* p. 522.

8. *Public-Ledger,* 16 Nov. 1916.

9. *Times,* 11 May 1916.

10. *Public-Ledger,* 16 Nov. 1916.

11. *Times,* 9 Jan. 1920.

12. *Herald and Tribune,* quoted in *Times,* 11 May 1916; the *Times* was designated the official paper by the city government; see Board of Mayor and Aldermen, *Minute Book 1,* 28 March 1917, p. 6.

13. *Times*, 17 May 1917 and 18 July 1919; *Kingsport: Its Growth, Housing and Industries,* p. 9.

14. *Times*, 10 May 1917, 10 June and 31 Oct. 1919, 27 Feb., 16 March, and 16 April 1920, and 18 Feb. 1921; Rauber, "Kingsport," p. 82.

15. *Times,* 29 June 1916.

16. Ibid., 15 July 1919; interview with Shivell.

17. *Times,* 10 June and 12 Aug. 1919, 13 and 20 Jan., 11 June, and 23 July 1920; Board of Mayor and Aldermen, *Minute Book 1,* 15 March 1917, p. 1.

18. *Times,* 4 Jan. 1921; H. Ray Dennis to John Nolen, 13 Feb. 1919, Nolen Papers, box 26, file 2; Raymond W. Blanchard to Nolen, 16 Jan. 1920, ibid., file 3.

19. Rauber, "Kingsport," p. 82; interview with Shivell.

20. Rauber, "Kingsport," p. 82; interview with Shivell; Long, *Kingsport*, p. 242.

21. Long, *Kingsport,* p. 173.

22. *Times,* 18 Jan. 1917.

23. Russell Baker, *Growing Up* (New York: St. Martin's Press, 1982; 1st Signet ed., New York: New American Library, 1984), pp. 64-65.

24. Jones, *Magic with Sand,* pp. 87-88; *Times*, 4 July and 7 Nov. 1919, 16 July and 10 Dec. 1920.

25. R.F. Brewer to J.J. Campion, 26 May 1910; W.M. Ritter to George H. Mead, 17 Oct. 1912; Mead to Ritter, 21 Oct. 1912; Ritter to Mark W. Potter, 28 Oct. 1912—all in the Clinchfield Collection, box 38.

26. Herrymon Mauer, *In Quiet Ways: George H. Mead, the Man and the Company* (Dayton, Ohio: Mead Corp., 1970), p. 90; see also *Times,* 29 June 1916 and 20 Jan. 1920.

27. Mauer, *In Quiet Ways,* pp. 120-22, 221, 262-63; see also clipping labeled *Bristol Courier,* 1922, Clinchfield Collection, box 38.

28. *Times,* 18 July, 11 Nov., 5, 9, and 12 Dec. 1919.

29. *World Book Encyclopedia,* 1982, s.v. "Influenza," by Robert E. Marquis.

30. Board of Mayor and Aldermen, *Minute Book 1,* 11 Oct. 1918, pp. 215-16; interview with Mrs. Johnson, 6 Feb. 1978.

31. *Times,* 8 July 1919; Board of Mayor and Aldermen, *Minute Book 1*, 17 Oct. 1919, p. 368; *Kingsport: Its Growth, Housing and Industries,* p. 26; Piquet, "Low-Cost Methods and High-Class Men," p. 319.

32. *Times,* 31 July and 14 Nov. 1919.

33. Ibid., 16 Jan., 3, 6, and 17 Feb. 1920, and 18 Jan. 1921.

34. Dr. George G. Keener to Board of Mayor and Aldermen, 24 Sept. 1921, read into *Minute Book 1*, 27 Sept. 1921, pp. 483-84.

35. Piquet, *Kingsport,* p. 129.

36. Ross, *Story of Rotherwood,* pp. 20-21.

37. Frank Netherland, "The Old Elm and Dam" (guest editorial), *Times-News,* 19 March 1982; Clara Smith Reber, *Church Hill, Tennessee: Area History, 1754-1976* (Rogersville: East Tennessee Printing Co., 1977), p. 52.

38. *Times-News,* 7 Oct. 1984.

39. *Times,* 1 and 8 Feb. 1917.

40. Frank Gould, "Kingsport, Tennessee: Where the Mountain People of the Cumberlands Are Being Taught the Advantage of Industry," *Manufacturer's Record* 88 (10 Dec. 1925): n.p.

41. *Times,* 6 June 1919; Long, *Kingsport,* pp. 185-87.

42. *Times,* 4 Nov. 1919; Long, *Kingsport,* pp. 185, 194, 220; Piquet, *Kingsport,* pp. xiii, 193.

43. *Times,* 11 July 1919.

44. For discussions of perceptions of Appalachia see Henry D. Shapiro, *Appalachia on Our Mind: The Southern Mountains and Mountaineers in the American Consciousness, 1870-1920* (Chapel Hill: Univ. of North Carolina Press, 1978), passim; James C. Klotter, "The Black South and White Appalachia," *Journal of American History* 66 (March 1980): 832-49; and Margaret Ripley Wolfe, "The Appalachian Reality: Ethnic and Class Diversity," East Tennessee Historical Society *Publications* nos. 52 and 53 (1981-82), pp. 40-60.

45. Roderick Nash, "The American Cult of the Primitive," *American Quarterly* 18 (Fall 1966): 521.

46. Interview with Mr. and Mrs. Shivell.

47. Interview with Draper.

48. Wilcox, "Tennessee Eastman Corporation."

49. Ibid.; and Long, pp. 89-90.

50. Wilcox, "Tennessee Eastman Corporation"; Long, *Kingsport,* pp. 89-90.

51. Wilcox, "Tennessee Eastman Corporation"; Long, *Kingsport,* pp. 89-90; and *Times,* 8 June 1920.

52. Interview with Shivell.

53. Wilcox, "Tennessee Eastman Corporation."

54. Report on visit of Raymond W. Blanchard; H. Ray Dennis to John Nolen, 1 Nov. 1920, Nolen Papers, box 26, file 5; *Times,* 28 Dec. 1920; and Long, *Kingsport,* pp. 238-39.

55. Wilcox, "Tennessee Eastman Corporation."

56. J. Fred Johnson to F.W. Lovejoy, 18 March 1932, in my possession.

57. J. Fred Johnson to George Eastman, 6 March 1926, in my possession.

58. Information drawn from correspondence in my possession; Wilcox, "Tennessee Eastman Corporation."

59. F.M. Lovejoy to J. Fred Johnson, 15 March 1932, in my possession; Carl Sandburg, *Complete Poems* (New York: Harcourt, Brace & World, 1950), pp. 446-47. Sandburg wrote: "My work is finished. Why wait?" For discussion of George Eastman's civic and cultural contributions to Rochester, N.Y., see Blake McKelvey, *Rochester: The Quest for Quality, 1890-1925* (Cambridge, Mass.: Harvard University Press, 1956), pp. v-vii, 1, 9, 45-50, 62, 70, 76, 109, 142, 166, 184, 205-6, 210, 212, 214, 222, 233, 236-37, 240-41, 251, 256-59, 260-62, 267, 269, 290, 293, 295, 297-98, 303, 305-6, 315-19, 323, 326, 330, 336-37, 340-41, 344-47; and idem, *Rochester: An Emerging Metropolis, 1925-1961* (Rochester, N.Y.: Christopher Press, 1961), pp. v-vi, 1-3, 9-12, 13, 17-18, 20-24, 29, 35, 39, 42-45, 47, 59-60, 66-67, 72, 79-80, 87, 90, 105, 109-11, 113, 125, 127, 132, 137, 141, 152-53, 162, 165-66, 196, 209, 213-16, 226, 265-67, 269-75, 288, 311, 317-19, 340, 344, 346-47.

60. Telegram, J. Fred Johnson to P.S. Wilcox, 17 March 1932; Johnson to W.G. Stuber, 17 March 1932; Johnson to F.M. Lovejoy, 18 March 1932—all in my possession; Board of Mayor and Aldermen, *Minute Book 3,* 24 March 1932, p. 1353.

61. Rauber, "Kingsport," p. 83.

62. Wilcox, "Tennessee Eastman Corporation."

63. Rauber, "Kingsport," p. 83.

64. Sidney D. Kirkpatrick, "Building an Integrated Industry in Times of Depression," *Chemical and Metallurgical Engineering* 40 (May 1933): 236.

65. J. Fred Johnson to George Eastman, 11 May 1931, in my possession.

66. Rauber, "Kingsport," p. 84.

67. Ibid., p. 82; Long, *Kingsport,* pp. 276-77. See also William H. Stone, "Book Production on Enormous Scale by Huge Printing Plant at Kingsport, Tenn.," *Manufacturer's Record* 83 (8 March 1923): 67-72; and *Bookmakers to America* (Kingsport: Kingsport Press, 1948).

68. Rauber, "Kingsport," p. 84; Long, *Kingsport,* pp. 276-77; Stone, "Book Production on Enormous Scale," pp. 67-72; *Bookmakers to America.*

69. Rauber, "Kingsport," p. 83.

70. Long, *Kingsport,* pp. 277-78.

71. J. Fred Johnson, as told to Arthur van Vlissingen, Jr., "Neighbors I: Paper, Book-Cloth, and Books—a Unit," *Factory and Industrial Management,* April 1928, p. 749.

72. Rauber, "Kingsport," p. 85; Long, *Kingsport,* pp. 271-72; and *Times-News,* 27 Feb. 1983.

73. Rauber, "Kingsport," p. 85.

74. Johnson, "Neighbors I," pp. 749-51; and "Neighbors II: How a Dozen Plants Work Together," *Factory and Industrial Management,* May 1928, p. 971.

75. Interview with Mrs. Johnson, 6 Feb. 1978.

76. Interview with Draper.

77. Piquet, "Low-Cost Methods and High-Class Men," p. 318, a photograph of the whole town turning out to welcome the Bordens.

78. Interview with Wilson.

79. Long, *Kingsport,* pp. 203-4; *Times,* 27 Feb. 1927.

80. Long, *Kingsport,* p. 121.

81. Johnson, "Neighbors II," pp. 972-73.

82. Long, *Kingsport,* p. 181; Piquet, *Kingsport,* pp. 191-92; and Rauber, "Kingsport," p. 85.

83. *Times,* 27 Feb. 1927.

84. Johnson, "Neighbors II," pp. 973-74.

85. *Times,* 27 Feb. 1927.

86. Ibid., 18 and 25 Jan. 1917; 27 Jan., 27 Feb., and 3 Sept. 1920; 7 Jan., 4 and 25 Feb. 1921; Board of Mayor and Aldermen, *Minute Book 1,* 13 June 1917, p. 23.

87. *Times,* 19 April and 4 May 1921; *Times-News,* 27 Feb. 1983.

88. Interview with Shivell.

89. Interviews with Mrs. Johnson.

90. Board of Mayor and Aldermen, *Minute Book 1,* 26 July-16 Aug. 1917, pp. 33-55.

91. Piquet, "Low-Cost Methods and High-Class Men," pp. 320-21.

92. Board of Mayor and Aldermen, *Minute Book 2,* 15 Jan. and 19 Feb. 1924, pp. 709-10, 716.

93. Lawrence W. Levine, "Progress and Nostalgia: The Self-Image of the Nineteen Twenties," in *The American Novel and the 1920's,* ed. Malcolm Bradbury and David Palmer, Stratford-upon-Avon Studies 13, under the general editorship of John Russell Brown and Bernard Harris (London: Edward Arnold, 1971), pp. 36-56.

94. Blaine A. Brownell, *The Urban Ethos in the South, 1920-1930* (Baton Rouge: Louisiana State Univ. Press, 1975), pp. 125-55 and passim.

95. *Times,* 6 June 1919, 20 Jan. 1920, 29 March and 12 April 1921.

96. *Times-News* clipping files dated 11 June 1946.

97. Ibid., 1 June 1952; *Times-News,* 28 Feb. 1982 and 27 Feb. 1983.

98. C.E. Allred, assisted by J.C. Fitch, *Effects of Industrial Development on Rural Life in Sullivan County, Tennessee* (Knoxville: University of Tennessee *Record* Extension series, May 1928), passim.

99. Johnson, "Neighbors I," p. 747.

100. George Tindall used the phrase "business progressivism" to describe the reforms of the 1920s in the South; see Tindall, *The Emergence of the New South, 1913-1945* (Baton Rouge: Louisiana State Univ. Press, 1967). One of two recent attempts at scholarly analysis of Kingsport embraces Tindall's "business progressivism"; see Edward L. Ayers, "Northern Business and the Shape of Southern Progress: The Case of Tennessee's 'Model City,' " *Tennessee Historical Quarterly* 39 (Summer 1980): 208-22. This article relies heavily on secondary sources and promotional pieces. The other is Wolfe, "J. Fred Johnson," pp. 70-83; see also Margaret Ripley Wolfe, "Changing the Face of Southern Appalachia: Urban Planning in Southwest Virginia and East Tennessee, 1890-1929," *Journal of the American Planning Association* 47 (July 1981): 252-65.

101. Floyd W. Parsons, "Everybody's Business: A New Kind of Town," *Saturday Evening Post*, 25 Oct. 1919, p. 44.

102. Piquet, *Kingsport,* p. viii.

5. THE HUMAN FACTOR

1. *Times,* 27 Feb. 1927.

2. From interviews of senior citizens in Hawkins County, Tenn., conducted by Lou Ann Lawson, a student in my Tennessee history course, summer 1978, under my direction.

3. Gaventa, *Power and Powerlessness;* Harry M. Caudill, *Night Comes to the Cumberlands: A Biography of a Depressed Area* (Boston: Little, Brown, 1963); Jack E. Weller, *Yesterday's People: Life in Contemporary Appalachia* (Lexington: Univ. of Kentucky Press, 1965); John Alexander Williams, *West Virginia and the Captains of Industry* (Morgantown: West Virginia Univ. Library, 1976); Mack H. Gillenwater, "Cultural and Historical Geography of Mining Settlements in the Pocahontas Coal Field of Southern West Virginia, 1880-1930" (Ph.D. diss., Univ. of Tennessee, 1972); Allen Batteau, ed., *Appalachia and America: Autonomy and Regional Dependence* (Lexington: Univ. Press of Kentucky, 1983); David E. Whisnant, *Modernizing the Mountaineer: People, Power, and Planning in Appalachia* (Boone, N.C.: Appalachian Consortium Press, 1980); Appalachian Land Ownership Task Force, with an introduction by Charles C. Geisler, *Who Owns Appalachia? Land Ownership and Its Impact* (Lexington: Univ. Press of Kentucky, 1983); Helen Matthews Lewis, Linda Johnson, and Donald Askins, eds., *Colonialism in Modern America: The Appalachian Case* (Boone, N.C.: Appalachian Consortium Press, 1978); Lewis acknowledges "Middle Class Islands" in "Subcultures of the Southern Appalachians," *Virginia Geographer* 3 (Spring 1968): 2-8.

4. Interviews with Mrs. Johnson.

5. *Times-News,* 3 April 1983.

6. Ronald D Eller, *Miners, Millhands and Mountaineers: Industrialization of the Appalachian South, 1880-1930* (paperback ed., Knoxville: University of Tennessee Press, 1982), pp. xxiii-xxiv, 242.

7. See Shapiro, *Appalachia on Our Mind;* Klotter, "Black South and White Appalachia," pp. 832-49; Wolfe, "Appalachian Reality," pp. 40-60; and David E. Whisnant, *All That Is Native and Fine: The Politics of Culture in an American Region* (Chapel Hill: Univ. of North Carolina Press, 1983).

8. *Times,* 25 May 1916; interview with Mrs. Platt.

9. Interview of Frank L. Cloud, American History Project in Local History.

10. *Times-News* clipping files dated 11 June 1946 and 1 June 1952.

11. Interview with Mrs. Johnson, 6 Feb. 1978.

12. Interview with Draper.

13. U.S., Department of Commerce, Bureau of the Census, *Thirteenth Census of the United States, 1910: Population* (Washington, D.C.: Government Printing Office, 1913), 3: 750-51, 758-59; Southern Education Board, "Educational Conditions in the Southern Appalachians," *Bulletin of the Southern Education Board* 1 (May 1902): 17-19; and idem, "Educational Conditions in Tennessee," ibid. (Dec. 1902): 3-29. U.S. Department of Commerce, Bureau of the Census, *Historical Statistics of the United States: Colonial Times to 1970* (Washington, D.C.: Government Printing Office, 1975), 1:382.

14. Lester R. Wheeler, "The Intelligence of East Tennessee Mountain Children," *Journal of Educational Psychology* 23 (May 1932): 354, 359, 370.

15. Idem, "A Comparative Study of the Intelligence of East Tennessee Mountain Children," *Journal of Educational Psychology* 33 (May 1942): 323-24, 333.

16. Interview with Ketron, Goerdel, and Wilson; A.M. Jungmann, "How a City Insured Itself," *Business,* Aug. 1920, p. 24, included in Nolen Papers, box 26, file 7.

17. Assistant Industrial Agent to S. & F. Manufacturing Co., 7 March 1913, Assistant Industrial Agent to Ehrman Overall Co., 20 Feb. 1913, and Assistant Industrial Agent to Freedland Overall Co., 16 April 1913, Clinchfield Collection, box 32.

18. D.C. Boy to R.F. Brewer, 29 Sept. 1916, and Assistant Industrial Agent to Villa and Brothers, 25 May 1916, ibid., box 56. The CC&O industrial agents' emphasis on cheap labor is in line with industrial recruitment elsewhere in the South; see Cobb, *Industrialization and Southern Society,* pp. 68-98; and idem, *Selling of the South,* pp. 86-121.

19. Interview with Mrs. Johnson, 6 Feb. 1978.

20. Interview with Ketron and Goerdel.

21. Ibid.

22. *Times,* 22 March 1917.

23. Board of Mayor and Aldermen, *Minute Book 1,* 18 and 20 June 1918 and 4 June 1919, pp. 175-78, 316; and *Times,* 4 May 1920.

24. *Times,* 27 June and 21 Oct. 1919; Board of Mayor and Aldermen, *Minute Book 1,* 24 June 1919, pp. 327-28; *Minute Book 3,* 21 Jan. and 19 Aug. 1930, pp. 1239, 1263.

25. *Times,* 21 Oct. 1919; Board of Mayor and Aldermen, *Minute Book 1*, 20 Oct. 1919, p. 369.

26. *Times,* 27 June, 1 and 4 July 1919.

27. Smith, *Kingsport Press,* p. 12; *Times,* 18 March 1921.

28. Interview with Goerdel.

29. Interview with Mrs. Johnson, 6 Feb. 1978.

30. Interview with Ketron and Goerdel.

31. From the *Echo* (Kingsport High School) 1 (Jan. 1918): 12.

32. Sidney G. Gilbreath to J. Fred Johnson, 25 Feb. 1913, Papers of President Sidney G. Gilbreath, Archives of Appalachia, Sherrod Library, East Tennessee State University, Johnson City, box 9.

33. Fred W. Alexander, *The Kingsport Public School, Kingsport, Tenn.: A Report Prepared by the Department of Rural Education, East Tennessee State Normal School* (Johnson City, Tenn.: Muse-Whitlock Co., 1915), pp. 8, 15.

34. Anna Lee Mitchell to Sidney G. Gilbreath, 2 Feb. 1916; Gilbreath to J. Fred Johnson, 12 Sept. 1916, and Johnson to Gilbreath, 14 Sept. 1916, Gilbreath Papers, boxes 14 and 16 respectively.

35. *Fourteenth Census,* 3:964, 968, 971.

36. Dr. T.B. Yancey to F.W. Lovejoy, 6 Feb. 1922.

37. *Times,* 18 and 21 Jan. 1921.

38. Ibid., 11 May, 29 June, 3 and 31 Aug., and 9 Nov. 1916.

39. Ibid., 23 April, 15 June, 20 July 1920; T.B. Yancey to F.W. Lovejoy, 6 Feb. 1922.

40. *Times,* 25 May 1916, 10 May 1917, 6 June, 4 and 25 Nov. 1919, and 16 March 1920.

41. Ibid., 22 March 1917, 4 July 1919, and 4 Jan. 1921.

42. *Bristol Herald-Courier*, 10 Feb. 1970 (photograph included).

43. *Times,* 23 Jan. and 23 March 1920, and 7, 8, 9, and 11 June 1921; Board of Mayor and Aldermen, *Minute Book 3,* 3 April 1928, p. 1075.

44. From *Times-News* clipping files, 11 June 1946.

45. Nellie McNeil, *Allen Dryden: Sullivan County Architect, Residences, 1922-1940* (prepared for the Sullivan County Historical Society Essay Contest and printed by the Sullivan County Historical Society, c. 1981), n.p. [1-8].

46. *Times-News,* 1 May 1980.

47. Interview with Goerdel; data about White, Smith, Palmer, Triebe, and Edwards are drawn from Ben Haden, *Kingsport, Tennessee: A Modern American City—Developed through Industry* (Kingsport, Tenn.: Kingsport Press, 1963), n.p.

48. *Times-News,* 19 Feb. 1980 and 27 Feb. 1983.

49. Ibid., 27 Feb. 1983.

50. Ibid., 6 March 1983.

51. Margy Clark, "Kingsport's First Ladies," *Kingsport Times-News Weekender,* 8 Nov. 1975, from *Times-News* clipping files.

52. From interviews of senior citizens in Hawkins and Sullivan counties in Tennessee and Scott County, Virginia, conducted by Lou Ann Lawson, Michael Cox, and Mickey Hamm, students in Tennessee history courses, summer 1978 and winter 1979, under my direction.

53. J. Fred Johnson to Dr. A.E. Morgan, 8 Sept. 1936, on file under Kingsport Biography (J. Fred Johnson), Kingsport Public Library.

54. Transcript of funeral service of Mr. J. Fred Johnson, 5 Oct. 1944, included in *John Frederick Johnson.*

55. Vertical file material, Kingsport Public Library.

56. Interview with Draper.

57. Clark, "Kingsport's First Ladies."

58. Interview with Draper.

59. Interview with Ketron.

60. From interviews of senior citizens.

61. Nolen, *New Towns for Old,* p. 55; interview with Mrs. Johnson, 6 Feb. 1978; and *Encyclopedia of Education,* 1971 ed., s.v. "Gary Plan," by Marvin Lazerson.

62. *Times,* 17 June and 1 July 1919; *Fourteenth Census,* 3:971.

63. Board of Mayor and Aldermen, *Minute Book 1,* 18 May and 17-19 and 24 July 1917, pp. 17, 30-32; 14 Sept. 1920, p. 423; and *Minute Book 2,* 18 April 1925, pp. 814-15; *Times,* 27 Feb. 1927.

64. Board of Mayor and Aldermen, *Minute Book 1,* 7 Feb. and 4 March 1919, pp. 247, 252; *Times,* 20 June 1919.

65. Board of Mayor and Aldermen, *Minute Book 1,* 23 Nov. 1920, 24 July and 7 Aug. 1923, pp. 435, 552, 555; *Minute Book 2,* 19 Feb. 1924, 17 Feb. and 18 Dec. 1925, pp. 717, 786, 852; *Minute Book 3,* 30 Oct. 1928, p. 1171; *Times,* 27 Feb. 1927 (photograph included).

66. *Times-News,* 6 May 1983.

67. *Fourteenth Census,* 3:971.

68. Mary Kiss, "Cement Hill: Where Kingsport Was Born," *Times-News,* 11 April 1976.

69. *Fourteenth Census,* 3:971; Clark, "Kingsport's First Ladies."

70. David Allen Hoover, "Community Development and the History of High School Football in Kingsport, Tennessee, 1920-1934" (Master's thesis, East Tennessee State University, 1981), passim.

71. Details from Johnson's photographs and pass to Holston Ordnance Works, Tennessee Eastman Corporation, construction areas A and B and Civic Auditorium; he had the pass to the defense plant as a courtesy. A copy of the pass was made available by Mrs. Johnson.

72. Interview with Draper.

73. Interview with Shirley Smith, city employee, Kingsport, Tenn., 7 Nov. 1978.

74. Board of Mayor and Aldermen, *Minute Book 2,* 6 May 1927, p. 976; *Minute Book 3,* 24 Jan. and 8 May 1928, pp. 1055, 1110.

75. Garry Wills points out that the art of resignation employed by George Washington only enhanced his grandeur and popularity; self-deprecation apparently served the same purpose for Johnson. See Garry Wills, *Cincinnatus: George Washington and the Enlightenment* (Garden City, N.Y.: Doubleday, 1984), passim.

76. *Times-News* clipping files, 9 Sept. 1973.

77. J. Fred Johnson to J.W. West, 19 Jan. 1944, Kingsport Biography (J. Fred Johnson), Kingsport Public Library.

78. J. Fred Johnson to Sidney G. Gilbreath, 10 May 1916, and to Anna Lee Mitchell, 8 May 1916, Gilbreath Papers, box 15.

79. Interview with Roller.

80. Sam Anderson to Mrs. J. Fred Johnson, 14 Oct. 1944, with comments to Masonic group included, in *John Frederick Johnson.*

81. Ibid.

82. City directories can be found in the Tennessee Room of the Kingsport Public Library.

83. Last will and testament of J. Fred Johnson; *Times-News* clipping files, 29 Sept. 1974.

84. Last will and testament of Johnson.

85. *Johnson City Press-Chronicle*, 8 March 1936; interview with Mrs. Johnson, 6 Feb. 1978.

86. Interview with Mrs. Platt; Clark, "Kingsport's First Ladies."

87. *Times,* 1 and 31 July, 5 Sept. 1919, and 8 March 1921; *Times-News,* 12 Feb. 1982 and 27 Feb. 1983; *Times-News* clipping files, 15 April 1975; and Board of Mayor and Aldermen, *Minute Book 1,* 17 July 1917, p. 30.

88. Interview with Mrs. Platt; see also Wendy Kaimer, *Women Volunteering: The Pleasure, Pain, and Politics of Unpaid Work from 1830 to the Present* (Garden City, N.Y.: Anchor Press, Doubleday, 1984).

89. Lynn Y. Weiner, *From Working Girl to Working Mother: The Female Labor Force in the United States, 1820-1980* (Chapel Hill: Univ. of North Carolina Press, 1985), passim.

90. Alexander, *Kingsport Public School,* p. 12; Board of Mayor and Aldermen, *Minute Book 1,* 18 May 1917, p. 17; and *Times,* 6 June 1919.

91. *Times,* 3 Sept. 1920 and 27 Feb. 1927; Clark, "Kingsport's First Ladies"; and *Times-News,* 8 Feb. 1982.

92. *Times-News* clipping files, 5 Oct. 1975.

93. *Times,* 8 July 1919 and 27 Feb. 1927.

94. James A. Hodges, "Challenge to the New South: The Great Textile Strike in Elizabethton, Tennessee, 1929," *Tennessee Historical Quarterly* 23 (Dec. 1964): 343-57; see also Jacquelyn Dowd Hall, "Disorderly Women: Gender and Labor Militancy in the Appalachian South," *Journal of American History* 73 (Sept. 1986): 354-82.

95. "Tennessee Industrial Experiment: Tennessee 1929," records of the National Board of the Young Women's Christian Association, Sophia Smith Collection, Smith College, Northampton, Mass., box 27.

96. Clark, "Kingsport's First Ladies."

97. McNeil, *Allen Dryden,* pp. [8-9].

98. *Times-News* clipping files, 16 Sept. 1973.

99. Kiss, "Cement Hill."

100. Interview with Goerdel and Ketron.

101. Interview with Mrs. Rhea E. (Gladys Smeltzer) Wolfe, a former employee of Borden Mills and area resident, Church Hill, Tenn., 1 June 1985.

102. Hazel Jones to Louise Leonard, 27 May 1930, Southern Summer School Papers, American Labor Education Service Records, Labor-Management Documentation Center, Martin P. Catherwood Library, Cornell University, Ithaca, N.Y., box 12.

103. Interview with Goerdel, Ketron, and Wilson.

104. Ibid.

105. Interview with Ketron.

106. Ford, "Passing of Provincialism," pp. 32-33.

107. Interviews of senior citizens.

108. *Times,* 8 July and 23 Dec. 1919; Jungmann, "How a City Insured Itself," pp. 21-24, esp. p. 22.

109. *Fourteenth Census,* 3:971.

110. Allred, with Fitch, *Effects of Industrial Development on Rural Life in Sullivan County, Tennessee,* pp. 33, 39.

111. *Times,* 26 April and 20 Sept. 1917, 1 July 1919, 30 January, 19 and 23 March, 9 April 1920, and 27 Feb. 1927; *Times-News,* 20 April and 31 Oct. 1982; *Times-News* clipping files, 1 April 1973 [?].

112. *Times,* 19 April 1917; *Times-News* clipping files, 12 Aug. 1973; and Clark, "Kingsport's First Ladies."

113. Conal Furay, *The Grass-Roots Mind in America: The American Sense of Absolutes* (New York: New Viewpoints, 1977), pp. 44, 55.

114. Interview with Mr. and Mrs. Shivell.

115. Furay, *Grass-Roots Mind in America,* p. 43.

116. Levine, "Progress and Nostalgia," pp. 36-56; and Roderick Nash, *The Nervous Generation: American Thought, 1917-1930* (Chicago: Rand McNally, 1970), pp. 4, 126.

117. Long, *Kingsport,* p. 98.

6. THE MODEL CITY IN DEPRESSION AND WAR

1. Howard Long, "Kingsport Moves Forward," *Manufacturer's Record* 102 (19 July 1933): 20.

2. *Times,* 2 and 13 Oct., 3 Nov. 1929, and 3 Jan. 1930; *Times-News* clipping files, 15 July and 25 Nov. 1973; *Kingsport City Directory,* 1926, pp. 58-59; Heritage Federal Savings and Loan Association, *1978: The Heritage Years,* published report of Heritage Federal Savings and Loan Association; and Piquet, *Kingsport* (1937), pp. 187, 188.

3. H. Ray Dennis to John Nolen, 15 March 1933, and Clinton Mackenzie to Nolen, 26 May 1933, Nolen Papers, box 26, file 6.

4. Franke Report.

5. Ibid.

6. Interview with Draper; Piquet, *Kingsport* (1946), pp. 294-96.

7. Interview with Draper; Haden, *Kingsport,* n.p.

8. Earle Sumner Draper to John Nolen, 22 Dec. 1920 and 11 April 1921, and Nolen to Draper, 14 April 1921, Nolen Papers, box 73.

9. Clinton Mackenzie to John Nolen, 9 June 1933, ibid., box 26, file 6.

10. Interview with Draper.

11. Nolen, *New Towns for Old,* p. 63; H. Ray Dennis to John Nolen, 15 March 1933, Nolen Papers, box 26, file 6; *Times-News* clipping files, 15 July and 25 Nov. 1973.

12. J. Fred Johnson to George Eastman, 18 Feb. 1932, in my possession; *Times-News* clipping files, 7 Oct. 1973.

13. J. Fred Johnson to George Eastman, 18 Feb. 1932.

14. Ibid.

15. Program of the Opening Exercise, the Holston Valley Community Hospital, Kingsport, Tenn., 9 Aug. 1935, from Johnson Papers.

16. Ibid.; *Times-News* clipping files, 29 Dec. 1957.

17. *Times-News* clipping files, 15 July 1973; Board of Mayor and Aldermen, *Minute Book 3,* 7 Jan., 4 Feb., 3 June, and 7 Oct. 1930 and 17 Feb. 1931, pp. 1238, 1241, 1254-55, 1270, 1272, 1286; and *Minute Book 4,* 5 Feb. 1935, p. 1477.

18. *Times-News* clipping files, 2 Dec. 1973; Board of Mayor and Aldermen, *Minute Book 3*, 17 Feb., 10 March, 21 April, 16 June, 14 July, 6 Oct., and 3 Nov. 1931, pp. 1286, 1289, 1302, 1316-17, 1320, 1336, 1340-41; 5 Jan., 19 April, and 6 Sept. 1932, pp. 1346, 1355, 1372; *Minute Book 4,* 17 July and 18 Dec. 1934, pp. 1447, 1470; 20 Aug. 1935, p. 1497; 18 Feb. and 3 March 1936, pp. 1526, 1535; 7 Dec. 1937, p. 1722; and 17 May 1938, p. 1761; and *Times-News*, 4 Jan. 1976.

19. *Times-News* clipping files, 17 Feb. 1974.

20. Ibid., 27 May and 11 Nov. 1973.

21. Ibid., 26 and 30 June, 7 July, and 22 Dec. 1974, 12 Oct. and 14 Dec. 1975.

22. Board of Mayor and Aldermen, *Minute Book 4*, 18 Sept. and 2 Oct. 1934, pp. 1457, 1458.

23. *Times-News* clipping files, 19 Oct. 1975; *Times-News*, 15 Nov. 1981.

24. John Nolen to J. Fred Johnson, 8 Feb. 1933, and Johnson to Nolen, 15 Feb. 1933, Nolen Papers, box 26, file 6.

25. *Knoxville Journal,* 19-21 April 1933.

26. H. Ray Dennis to John Nolen, 19 April 1933, and Clinton Mackenzie to Nolen, 26 May and 28 July 1933, Nolen Papers, box 26, file 6.

27. *Times-News* clipping files, 6 Jan. 1974.

28. Board of Mayor and Aldermen, *Minute Book 3,* 14 April 1931, p. 1296; 17 Jan. and 5 Dec. 1933, pp. 1398, 1423; *Minute Book 4,* 7 May 1935, p. 1485; *Times-News* clipping files, 20 Jan. 1974 and 29 July 1975.

29. J.E. Moreland to Daniel C. Roper, 2 May 1935, Works Progress Administration Records, National Archives, Washington, D.C., RG 69, reel A 1509.

30. *Times-News* clipping files, 20 July 1975.

31. Works Progress Administration Proposal, 5 Sept. 1935, and G.W. Vance, W.S. Holyoke, and Marion Sell to Harry Berry, 6 Sept. 1935, in WPA Records; see also *Times-News* clipping files, 23 Nov. 1975; and Dedication Program, McKellar Tri-City Airport, Tenn., 5 Nov. 1937, n.p. [7], from the Johnson Papers.

32. Project Proposal; Dedication, n.p. [8]; notes on substance of long-distance telephone call between Col. Sumpter Smith and Col. Harry S. Berry, 15 Jan. 1937, and between Digby and Ruddy, 17 April 1935; and R.M. Jones to J.H. Digby, 27 April 1937, WPA Records.

33. How many times Appalachia has been discovered depends to a great extent on who is counting. Robert Munn identifies four distinct stages: a literary discovery beginning in the 1850s, a missionary discovery of the 1890s, a renewed interest during the 1930s, and that of the 1960s. Such careful delineations assume chronological boundaries that are virtually impossible to ascertain. See Robert H. Munn, "The Latest Rediscovery of Appalachia," *Mountain Life and Work* 40 (1963): 25-30.

34. Board of Mayor and Aldermen, *Minute Book 3,* 17 Oct. 1933, p. 1421; *Times-News* clipping files, 26 May 1974.

35. Stevenson, "Contrast in 'Perfect' Towns," pp. 18-20 and passim.

36. Garet Garrett, "Roads Going South: The Story of a Town," *Saturday Evening Post,* 3 Sept. 1938, p. 60.

37. Willson Whitman, "Three Southern Towns III: Kingsport: They Planned It," *Nation,* 21 Jan. 1939, pp. 88-90; idem, *God's Valley: People and Power along the Tennessee River* (New York: Viking Press, 1939), pp. 176-84.

38. Stevenson, "Contast in 'Perfect' Towns," passim.

39. U.S., Department of Labor, Women's Bureau, Correspondence Related to Surveys, National Archives, Washington, D.C., RG 86, box 329; idem, *Employment of Women in Tennessee Industies,* bulletin no. 149 (Washington, D.C.: U.S. Government Printing Office, 1939), p. 57 and passim.

40. Stevenson, "Contrast in 'Perfect' Towns," passim.

41. National Recovery Administration, Industrial and Social Branch, Kingsport Hosiery Mills File, National Archives, Washington, D.C., RG 402, tray 4238; Piquet, *Kingsport* (1937), p. 174.

42. NRA, Industrial and Social Branch, Kingsport Hosiery Mills File.

43. Piquet, *Kingsport* (1937), pp. 176-77.

44. Telephone conversation with Jerry Beck, son of Ray Beck, 22 July 1985; Piquet, *Kingsport* (1937), p. 176.

45. O.W. Huddle, "Kingsport's 'Cheap Labor,' " in "Letters to the Editors," *Nation*, 1 April 1939, p. 387.

46. Telephone conversation with Beck.

47. Stone, Price, and Stone, *City Manager Government in Nine Cities,* p. 507.

48. Ibid., p. 520.

49. Ibid.

50. Petro, *Kingsport Strike,* pp. 62-63; see also Elizabeth Faulkner Baker, *Printers and Technology: A History of the International Printing Pressmen and Assistants' Union* (Westport, Conn.: Greenwood Press, 1957), p. 316 and passim; and International Printing Pressmen and Assistants' Union of North America, *Illustrated Story of a Remarkable Humanitarian and Educational Institution of Nationwide Importance* (Cincinnati, Ohio: S. Rosenthal, 1910), passim.

51. Federal Conciliation and Mediation Service, Subject and Dispute Files, National Archives Annex, Suitland, Md., RG 280, and Guide to RG 280, National Archives, Washington, D.C.

52. *Times-News* clipping files, 25 Feb. 1973; Whitman, "Three Southern Towns III," p. 90.

53. Stone, Price, and Stone, *City Manager Government in Nine Cities,* pp. 512-21.

54. Board of Mayor and Aldermen, *Minute Book 2,* 5 July 1927, p. 995; *Minute Book 3*, 9 June and 7 July 1931, pp. 1314-15, 1318; and telephone conversation with Shelburne Ferguson, Jr., 25 July 1985.

55. *City Directories,* 1926, 1934-35, and 1939.

56. Telephone conversation with Ferguson; Board of Mayor and Aldermen, *Minute Book 4*, 21 Aug. 1934, p. 1453.

57. *Times-News* clipping files, 25 Feb. 1973.

58. Whitman, "Three Southern Towns III," p. 90; interview with Goerdel.

59. Comey and Wehrly, *Planned Communities,* pp. 35-36.

60. Interview with Goerdel; Board of Mayor and Aldermen, *Minute Book 5,* 4 July 1939, pp. 1882-83.

61. Comey and Wehrly, *Planned Communities,* p. 39; Stone, Price, and Stone, *City Manager Government in Nine Cities,* pp. 519-20.

62. Board of Mayor and Aldermen, *Minute Book 5,* 2 July 1945, pp. 2281-82.

63. *Dedication, Kingsport Civic Auditorium and Armory,* 9 March 1940, n.p. Johnson Papers; Board of Mayor and Aldermen, *Minute Book 4,* 7 Dec. 1938, p. 1823; *Minute Book 5,* 3 Jan. 1939 and 20 Feb. 1940, pp. 1835, 1950.

64. Board of Mayor and Aldermen, *Minute Book 5,* 21 Feb. and 21 March 1939, pp. 1849, 1857; 15 Oct., 5 and 12 Nov., and 19 Dec. 1940, pp. 2002-3, 2012-13, 2026; 23 April and 20 May 1941, pp. 2060-61, 2064.

65. Ibid., 22 July 1941, p. 2078; Paul Oppermann, "The Tri-Cities Planning Project: A Pilot Case in Cooperative Planning," *American Institute of Planners' Journal* 8 (July 1942): 11-17.

66. "A Virgin Residential Market," *Architectural Forum* 66 (June 1937): 546-47.

67. Piquet, *Kingsport* (1946), p. 307.

68. Comey and Wehrly, *Planned Communities,* p. 39.

69. Willson Whitman, "Slum Clearance in Kingsport," in "Letters to the Editors," *Nation,* 3 June 1939, p. 656.

70. Piquet, *Kingsport* (1946), pp. 299-303; Board of Mayor and Aldermen, *Minute Book 5,* 7 and 21 Feb., 2 May, 6 June, and 1 Aug. 1939, pp. 1840, 1845, 1868, 1874, 1887; 7 Jan. 1941, p. 2028.

71. Board of Mayor and Aldermen, *Minute Book 5,* 16 Dec. 1941, p. 2112; 3 and 17 Feb. 1942, pp. 2116-19.

72. Interview with Mrs. Ruth Badger Anderson, a former employee of Fraser-Brace Construction Co. and Holston Ordnance Works, Kingsport, Tenn., 23 July 1985.

73. James Phinney Baxter III, *Scientists against Time* (Cambridge, Mass.: MIT Press, 1968), pp. 253-59; historical files and clippings, Holston Army Ammunition Plant, Kingsport, Tenn. (hereinafter cited as HAAP).

74. Ibid.

75. Kirkpatrick, "Building an Integrated Industry in Times of Depression," pp. 236-40; "Test-Tube Love Seat," *Time,* 26 Feb. 1940, pp. 74-75.

76. Historical files and clippings, HAAP.

77. Ibid.; National Defense Research Committee of the Office of Scientific Research and Development, "Supplementary Invention Report on RDX," prepared by Benton A. Bull, 20 Oct. 1942, Office of Scientific Research and Development Records (hereinafter cited as OSRD Records), National Archives, Washington, D.C., RG 227, box 28.

78. National Defense Research Committee, "Supplementary Invention Report on RDX," pp. 18-19; historical files and clippings, HAAP.

79. Dr. Ralph Connor to Dr. Roger Adams and Dean Frank C. Whitmore, 25 March 1942, OSRD Records.

80. National Defense Research Committee, "Supplementary Invention Report on RDX," p. 19; historical files and clippings, HAAP.

81. Historical files and clippings, HAAP; Ralph Connor to James B. Conant, 4 May 1942, OSRD Records.

82. Historical files and clippings; Advance Payment Bond, Contract of Eastman Kodak Company with United States of America, 6 June 1942, from a series of loose-leaf notebooks containing contracts, HAAP, Kingsport, Tenn.

83. War Department Contract with Tennessee Eastman Corporation, 6 July 1942, from loose-leaf notebooks, HAAP.

84. Board of Mayor and Aldermen, *Minute Book 5*, 17 Feb. 1942, p. 2119. For discussion of the impact of defense contracts and military installations on American cities see Roger W. Lotchin, ed., *The Martial Metropolis: U.S. Cities in War and Peace* (New York: Praeger, 1984).

85. Historical files and clippings (*Times-News,* 9 Dec. 1945), HAAP; unidentified clipping from scrapbooks of Mrs. Ralph (Eileen) Williams, Kingsport, Tenn.

86. Historical files and clippings, HAAP; Board of Mayor and Aldermen, *Minute Book 5,* 25 June, 22 July, 1 and 15 Sept. 1942, pp. 2142, 2145, 2150, 2152; *Times-News* clipping files, 8 July 1973.

87. Historical files and clippings, HAAP.

88. Program, Army-Navy Production Award, 6 Dec. 1943, Kingsport, Tenn., from Johnson Papers; flyer on USNS *Kingsport,* in Williams scrapbooks.

89. Piquet, *Kingsport* (1946), pp. 309, 313.

90. Historical files and clippings, HAAP.

91. Ibid.; Supplement to Contract, 6 July 1942, loose-leaf notebooks, HAAP; and Baxter, *Scientists against Time,* p. 258.

92. Clinton Engineer Works–Tennessee Eastman Corporation, Oak Ridge, Tenn., C.E.W.–T.E.C. History, Jan. 1943 to May 1947 (mimeographed), prepared for the United States Atomic Energy Commission and submitted 10 June 1947 by Dr. F.R. Conklin, works manager, pp. 1-10, copy in my possession, courtesy of Mrs. M. Lacy (Julia) West.

93. C.E.W.–T.E.C. History, passim; *TEC News,* 1 Aug. 1985.

94. C.E.W.–T.E.C. History, pp. 26-27 and passim; *TEC News,* 1 Aug. 1985.

95. C.E.W.–T.E.C. History, passim. For a history of Oak Ridge during the war years see Johnson and Jackson, *City behind a Fence*; and for a treatment of the contributions of American women on the home front see Susan M. Hartmann, *The Home Front and Beyond: American Women in the 1940s* (Boston, Mass.: Twayne, 1982); see also D'Ann Campbell, *Women at War with America: Private Lives in a Patriotic Era* (Cambridge, Mass.: Harvard Univ. Press, 1984).

96. Piquet, *Kingsport* (1946), p. 201.

97. Transcript of Robert St. John, "The Story of a City," NBC Programs, 31 Oct. and 1 Nov. 1944, compliments of WKPT Radio Station, "The Nation's Model Station," from Johnson Papers.

7. KINGSPORT IN TRANSITION

1. Unidentified clipping, Williams scrapbooks.

2. Last will and testament of J. Fred Johnson; and material from *John Frederick Johnson.*

3. Clippings from the Johnson scrapbooks; *Times-News* clipping files, 13 Feb. 1947; and Board of Mayor and Aldermen, *Minute Book 5,* 15 Jan. 1946, p. 2323.

4. Interview with Shivell; and interview with Wilson and Goerdel.

5. Haden, *Kingsport,* n.p.

6. *Times-News* clipping files, 28 March 1962.

7. Haden, *Kingsport,* n.p.

8. *Times-News,* 18 March 1973.

9. Ibid., 6 May 1983.

10. *Kingsport, Tennessee: An American City* (prepared in response to requests for information occasioned by Robert St. John's broadcasts), n.p., from Johnson Papers.

11. Ibid.

12. Charles Stevenson, "Where They Planned for Peace," *National Municipal Review*, Feb. 1946, p. 63.

13. *Kingsport, Tennessee: Founded for a Purpose, Built According to Plan—and Patterned in the American Tradition* (1948), n.p., from the Johnson Papers.

14. *Kingsport, Tennessee: An American City*, n.p.

15. Henry S. Churchill and Roslyn Ittleson, *Neighborhood Design and Control: An Analysis of the Problems of Planned Subdivisions* (New York: National Committee on Housing, 1944), p. 22.

16. Rauber, "Kingsport: An Industry Pattern," p. 87.

17. Stevenson, "Where They Planned for Peace," pp. 62-66, 76.

18. Charles Stevenson, "A Town That Planned for Peace," *Reader's Digest*, March 1946, pp. 39-42.

19. *Times-News*, 17 June 1979.

20. Board of Mayor and Aldermen, *Minute Book 8*, 19 April 1955, p. 93.

21. *Times-News*, 27 April 1983.

22. Ibid., 5 Jan. 1984.

23. Interview with Bill Towers, retired executive vice-president of the Holston Electric Cooperative and a former chairman of the Hawkins County Industrial Commission, Rogersville, Tenn., 10 July 1981; interview conducted by Larry Cravens, graduate student in history at East Tennessee State University and a teacher at Cherokee High School, Rogersville, Tenn.

24. *Times-News*, 5 Jan. 1984.

25. Facts concerning transportation are drawn from *Kingsport, Tennessee: An American City*, passim; and Piquet, *Kingsport* (1946), pp. 227-60.

26. *Times-News*, 8 May 1983.

27. Ibid., 3 Feb. 1985. See Kenneth T. Jackson, *Crabgrass Frontier: The Suburbanization of the United States* (New York: Oxford Univ. Press, 1985), pp. 231-45 and passim; see also John S. Lang, with Dan Collins and Patricia A. Avery, "The Legacies of WWII," *U.S. News and World Report*, 5 Aug. 1985, pp. 38-52.

28. Conversations with Kenneth and Madelyn Thomas, Kingsport, Tenn., over several years.

29. Board of Mayor and Aldermen, *Minute Book 5*, 2 July 1946, p. 2363; and *Minute Book 6*, 5 Nov. 1946, p. 1535.

30. Telephone conversation with Lee Garner, Kingsport Development Co., Kingsport, Tenn., 2 Aug. 1985.

31. *Kingsport, Tennessee: An American City*, n.p.

32. *Times-News*, 8 May 1983.

33. Ibid., 5 Feb. 1981.

34. Ibid.

35. Ibid., 31 Oct. 1982.

36. Clipping from Williams scrapbooks.

37. *Times-News*, 8 May 1983.

38. Board of Mayor and Aldermen, *Minute Book 5*, 17 Oct. 1944 and 7 Aug. 1945, pp. 2253, 2287.

39. Ibid., 7 May 1946, p. 2350.

40. Ibid., 16 July 1946, p. 2367.

41. Ibid., 6 and 20 Aug., 3 Sept. 1946, pp. 2370-77, 2399.

42. Ibid., *Minute Book 8*, 8 April 1955, p. 89; and *Times-News*, 10 April 1955.

43. Board of Mayor and Aldermen, *Minute Book 6,* 3 June 1947, p. 1597.

44. Piquet, *Kingsport* (1946), pp. 217-18.

45. Franke Report.

46. Job file 9707, Kingsport, Tenn., Olmsted Associates Papers, Library of Congress, Washington, D.C., container B518.

47. Board of Mayor and Aldermen, *Minute Book 9,* 30 Dec. 1958, p. 36.

48. Interview with Early.

49. Upper East Tennessee Office, Tennessee State Planning Commission, *Housing in the Kingsport Area: A Preliminary Report to the Kingsport Planning Commission, June 1956,* passim.

50. Ibid., pp. 14-15, 19.

51. Kingsport City Government, *Your City: Kingsport, a Report on its Government, 1948 and 1949,* April 1950, passim.

52. Board of Mayor and Aldermen, *Minute Book 6,* 16 Sept. 1947, p. 1629.

53. Kingsport City Government, *Your City* (1948 and 1949), passim; see also Kingsport City Scrapbooks, 1946-56, Kingsport Public Library, which include clippings pertaining to the opposition of Pennsylvania-Dixie Cement Corp. to the pollution ordinance.

54. Planimetric Map, Planning Department, Kingsport, Tenn.

55. Roy S. Nicks, "City-County Separation in Tennessee: Case Study of Kingsport and Sullivan County" (Master's thesis, University of Tennessee, 1957), p. 105.

56. See, e.g., Jackson, *Crabgrass Frontier,* pp. 231-45 and passim.

57. Board of Mayor and Aldermen, *Minute Book 6,* 6 Dec. 1949, p. 1892; see also Kingsport City Government, *Your City* (1948 and 1949), p. 7; and Planimetric Map.

58. City of Kingsport, *Kingsport Reports to the People, 1950 and 1951,* n.p.; Planimetric Map.

59. Board of Mayor and Aldermen, *Minute Book 7,* 16 Jan. 1951, p. 42.

60. Ibid., *Minute Book 7,* 5 May 1953 and 6 July 1954, pp. 357, 486; and *Minute Book 8,* 7 Sept. 1954, p. 6.

61. *Times-News* clipping files, 1 July 1973.

62. City of Kingsport, *Kingsport Reports to the People*, n.p.

63. Board of Mayor and Aldermen, *Minute Book 8,* 8 Oct. 1954, p. 15.

64. Jackson, *Crabgrass Frontier;* Reynolds is quoted in James T. Patterson, *America in the Twentieth Century: A History* (New York: Harcourt Brace Jovanovich, 1976), p. 373; see also pp. 371-408.

65. Board of Mayor and Aldermen, *Minute Book 7,* 5 Sept. 1950, p. 11; and Rotary Club, *Kingsport: The Planned Industrial City* (Kingsport: Rotary Club, 1951), pp. x-xi.

66. Board of Mayor and Aldermen, *Minute Book 7,* 6 Feb. and 18 Sept. 1951, pp. 44, 144.

67. Clipping, Williams scrapbooks.

68. Board of Mayor and Aldermen, *Minute Book 8,* 17 May and 7 June 1955, pp. 101, 105-6; and *Minute Book 9,* 6 March 1962, pp. 370-71.

69. *Times-News*, 2 July 1978.

70. Clipping, Williams scrapbooks.

71. The section pertaining to the Blue Ridge Glass Corp. strike is based on clipping files and other documents provided by Eugene Harris, Human Resources, AFG Industries, Corporate Office, Kingsport, Tenn.

72. Ibid.

73. Ibid.

74. Ibid.

75. Ibid.

76. Nicks, "City-County Separation in Tennessee," pp. 105-8.

77. Roy S. Nicks, Edward S. Overman, and Simon Perry, *Kingsport and Annexation* (Knoxville: Bureau of Public Administration, Univ. of Tennessee, Nov. 1956), pp. ii, 3, 7, 10, 114, 144-45, and passim.

78. Board of Mayor and Aldermen, *Minute Book 8,* 5 July 1955, pp. 117-19, and 23 March 1956, pp. 219-20; Planimetric Map.

79. Board of Mayor and Aldermen, *Minute Book 8,* 4 Jan. 1955, p. 29.

80. Ibid., 20 Dec. 1955, p. 156.

81. Ibid., *Minute Book 9,* 24 April 1962, p. 412.

82. Ibid., *Minute Book 8,* 3 July 1956, p. 248.

83. Ibid., *Minute Book 9,* 17 March 1959 to 4 April 1961, passim.

84. Ibid.

85. Ibid., 24 April 1962, p. 412.

86. *Times-News,* 12 Dec. 1957.

87. *Times-News* clipping files, 13 Jan. 1974.

88. *Times,* 4 April 1961; in the meantime, plans had proceeded for the Downtowner Hotel at the corner of Center and Shelby streets; see *Times,* 29 July 1959, and *Kingsport News,* 31 July 1959.

89. *Times,* 5 April 1961; *Kingsport City Directories,* 1957 and 1959, pp. 346 and 392 respectively.

90. *Times,* 17 April 1961; Board of Mayor and Aldermen, *Minute Book 9,* 18 April 1961, p. 291; telephone conversation with Max Y. Parker, Kingsport, Tenn., 30 Sept. 1985.

91. Board of Mayor and Aldermen, *Minute Book 9,* 20 March 1962, pp. 387-98, 7 Aug. 1962, p. 437, 21 Aug. 1962, pp. 438-41, and 18 Sept. 1962, p. 449; *Times-News* clipping files, 4 Jan. 1968.

92. Planimetric Map.

93. *Times-News* clipping files, 1 Jan. 1966.

94. Details for the section pertaining to the explosion at Tennessee Eastman Co. are drawn from the TEC clipping files in the Tennessee Room, Kingsport Public Library, and from the Williams scrapbooks. The death toll was confirmed by a telephone conversation with June Crofts, TEC Public Relations, 30 Sept. 1985; see also *Times-News,* 5 Oct. 1975.

95. Ibid.

96. Ibid.

97. Ibid.

98. Ibid.

99. Ibid; Board of Mayor and Aldermen, *Minute Book 9,* 18 Oct. 1960, p. 246.

100. *Times-News,* 5 Oct. 1975.

101. Kingsport Press, *Bookmakers to America* (Kingsport, Tenn.: Kingsport Press, 1948); Stone, "Book Production on Enormous Scale," pp. 67-72; details for this section are drawn from clippings and other materials in the Kingsport Press files, Tennessee Room, Kingsport Public Library; see also City of Kingsport, *Kingsport Reports to the People,* n.p.

102. Clipping from Kingsport Press files, dated 16 Sept. 1953; Petro, *Kingsport Strike,* p. 23.

103. *Times,* 18 May 1967.

104. Kingsport Press files.

105. Petro, *Kingsport Strike,* p. 74.

106. *Times,* 21 May 1967.

107. Ibid., 11 March 1963.

108. Petro, *Kingsport Strike,* p. 114.

109. Ibid., pp. 110-131.

110. Kingsport Press, Inc., *Annual Report, 1963,* n.p.

111. Ibid., *Annual Report, 1964,* n.p.

112. *Times-News,* 23 May 1967.

113. *Times-News* clipping files, 23 July and 5 Aug. 1964.

114. Interview with Towers; information provided by Personnel Department, AFG Industries, Inc., Greenland Plant, Church Hill, Tenn.; and *News,* 23 Oct. 1962.

115. Files of the Hawkins County Industrial Commission, Rogersville, Tenn.

116. Interview with Towers; information provided by Alladin Plastics, Surgoinsville, Tenn.

117. Kingsport Press files, including clippings dated 24 July and 4 Sept. 1964.

118. Cobb, *Selling of the South,* pp. 213-14.

8. DISMANTLING THE MODEL CITY

1. *News,* 17 June 1966 and 13 Dec. 1968; many newspaper citations in this chapter are drawn from Kingsport City Scrapbooks, 1946 to the present, Tennessee Room, Kingsport Public Library.

2. *Times-News,* 13 May 1984.

3. Ibid., 14 May 1984.

4. Ibid., 26 Jan. 1981.

5. Clipping, 5 April 1963, Kingsport City Scrapbooks; and *Times-News,* 18 Aug. 1968, 27 Nov. 1982, 15 April 1984, 11 April, 23 June, 24 July, 27 Aug., and 29 Oct. 1985.

6. *News,* 3 Sept. and 6 Oct. 1965, 31 March 1967; *Times-News,* 16 March 1969.

7. *Times-News,* 11 and 21 Dec. 1980, 14 July 1982, 12 May, 31 July, and 29 Oct. 1985.

8. Ibid., 17 May and 7 June 1970, 16 June 1985. A copy of the Central Business District Concept Plan, prepared by Eric Hill Associates for the City of Kingsport, Sept. 1969, is on file in the Planning Department, City Hall, Kingsport, Tenn.

9. *Times,* 24 Jan., 14 Nov., and 28 Dec. 1969; *News,* 14 April 1966 and 17 Jan. 1969.

10. *Times,* 20 March 1963; *News,* 26 May 1967; *Times-News,* 28 May 1967; and clipping, 4 May 1966, from Kingsport City Scrapbooks.

11. *Times-News,* 15, 17, 18, and 20 July 1984.

12. Ibid., 10 Aug. 1984.

13. Ibid., 1 Dec. 1968.

14. Wiebe, *Segmented Society,* p. 9.

15. Caudill, *Night Comes to the Cumberlands;* and Weller, *Yesterday's People.*
16. *Times-News,* 2 April 1967.
17. Ibid., 18 Aug. 1968.
18. *News,* 8 April 1960.
19. Ibid., 20 Jan. 1961, 5 Sept. 1963, 7 Aug. 1964, and 2 Dec. 1966.
20. Ibid., 23 April and 25 May 1969; *Times,* 17 March 1970; and *Times-News,* 9 July 1978.
21. *Times-News,* 9 July 1978.
22. *News,* 12 and 13 Sept. 1967; and *Times-News,* 29 Sept. 1968 and 9 July 1978.
23. *Times-News,* 29 Sept. 1968 and 9 July 1978; *Times,* 15 Oct. 1968; and *News,* 19 Feb. 1969.
24. *Times,* 14 March 1969 and 12 Feb. 1970.
25. Interview with Joseph H. Lewis, an early Kingsport resident, employee of Blue Ridge Glass Corp., and alderman and mayor, Kingsport, Tenn., 14 Dec. 1983, Oral History Collection, Tennessee Room, Kingsport Public Library.
26. *Times,* 4 June and 27 Oct. 1969; and *News,* 10 June 1969.
27. *News,* 10 June 1969; *Times-News,* 14 Sept. 1969; *Times,* 27 Oct. 1969.
28. *News,* 10 and 15 March 1967; *Bristol Herald-Courier,* quoted in *News,* 23 March 1967; *Times,* 19 March 1967.
29. *Times,* 19 May 1965 and 19 March 1967.
30. *News,* 20 July 1965.
31. *Times-News,* 7 April 1968.
32. *News,* 15 Feb. and 21 Nov. 1963; *Times-News,* 27 Oct. 1968.
33. *Times-News,* 15 March 1970 and 5 July 1981.
34. Ibid., 29 March 1970; *Times,* 11 March 1970.
35. *Times-News,* 5 July 1981.
36. Ibid.; John Nolen to H. Ray Dennis, 7 Feb. 1916, Nolen Papers, box 26, file 1.
37. *News,* 7 Feb. and 31 March 1967; *Times,* 23 Feb. 1968.
38. *Times-News,* 8 Sept. and 27 Oct. 1968, 11 Jan. 1970.
39. Interview with Lewis.
40. *Times-News,* 10 Dec. 1967.
41. Interview with Lewis.
42. *Times-News,* 13 July 1969; and *Times-News* clipping files, 22 Feb. 1970.
43. *Times-News* clipping files, 22 Feb. 1970.
44. Ibid., 29 Aug. 1971.
45. *Times-News,* 9 July 1967 and 18 Aug. 1968.
46. Ibid., 1 Dec. 1968.
47. Ibid., 24 Sept. 1980, 4 Oct. and 29 Nov. 1984.
48. Ibid., 19 Aug. 1980; *Times,* 18 Aug. 1980.
49. *Times-News,* 26 April, 27 Sept., and 23 Oct. 1981.
50. Interview with Wilson.
51. Don Widener, *Timetable for Disaster* (Los Angeles: Nash Publishing, 1970), p. 221.
52. Ibid., p. 222.
53. Ibid., p. 221.
54. *Times-News,* 28 Feb. 1982.

55. Ibid., 28 Feb. 1982, 18 Oct. 1984, and 3 March 1985.

56. Ibid., 21 May 1978.

57. Ibid., 5 April 1979.

58. Kingsport Study Group, "Smells Like Money," pp. 59-67; *Times,* 27 June 1978.

59. *Times,* 13 July 1978.

60. Ibid., 23 and 25 Aug. 1978.

61. Ibid., 8 Aug. 1978.

62. *Times-News,* 22 Oct. 1978.

63. *Times,* 30-31 Jan. and 22 Feb. 1979.

64. Ibid., 28 March and 5 April 1979; for information on Highlander see Aimee I. Horton, "The Highlander Folk School: A History of the Development of Its Major Programs Related to Social Movements in the South, 1932-1961" (Ph.D. diss., Univ. of Chicago, 1971); and Hulan Glyn Thomas, "The Highlander Folk School: The Depression Years," *Tennessee Historical Quarterly* 23 (1964): 358-71; and Bill Moyers, "The Adventures of a Radical Hillbilly: An Interview with Myles Horton," *Appalachian Journal* 9 (Summer 1982): 248-85.

65. *Times-News,* 14 Aug. 1980, 6 Feb. 1981, 22-24 April and 15-16 July 1982, 18 Sept. 1983, 5 Jan., 7 Feb., 7 April, and 18 Aug. 1985.

66. Ibid., 28 Feb. 1982.

67. *Times,* 5 April 1979; and *Times-News,* 8 May 1985 and passim.

68. *Times-News,* 12 Oct. 1980.

69. Ibid., 25 Nov. 1980.

70. Ibid., 16 and 27 Dec. 1981 and 13 Jan. 1982.

71. Ibid., 3 Oct. 1984 and passim.

72. Ibid., 21 July 1982.

73. Charles Stevenson, "The Great Society's Wondrous 'War' Budget," *Reader's Digest,* April 1967, p. 51; and *News,* 4 April 1967.

74. *Times-News,* 1 Nov. 1970.

75. Ibid., 24 Feb. to 16 June 1983 and passim.

76. Jane Jacobs, *The Death and Life of Great American Cities* (New York: Vintage Books, 1961), passim; see also such sources as David R. Goldfield and Blaine A. Brownell, *Urban America: From Downtown to No Town* (Boston, Mass.: Houghton Mifflin, 1979), pp. 355-405; Zane L. Miller, *The Urbanization of Modern America: A Brief History* (New York: Harcourt Brace Jovanovich, 1973), pp. 199-229; Claude S. Fischer, *The Urban Experience,* 2d ed. (San Diego: Harcourt Brace Jovanovich, 1984), pp. 271-93; Howard P. Chudacoff, *The Revolution of American Urban Society,* 2d ed. (Englewood Cliffs, N.J.: Prentice-Hall, 1981), pp. 263-303; Herbert J. Gans, "The Failure of Urban Renewal," in *American Urban History: An Interpretive Reader with Commentaries,* ed. Alexander B. Callow, Jr., 3d ed. (New York: Oxford Univ. Press, 1982), pp. 455-69; and Philip Langdon, "Burgers! Shakes!" *Atlantic,* Dec. 1985, pp. 74-89.

77. Interview with Wilson and Goerdel.

78. *Times-News,* 7 Sept. 1969.

79. Ibid., 12 Aug. 1970 and 27 Nov. 1983.

80. Ibid., 13 and 24 April 1980.

81. Ibid., 8 April 1982; see also *The Tennessean and the Knoxville Journal, Borrowed Money, Borrowed Time: The Fall of the House of Butcher,* 18 Nov. 1983.

INDEX

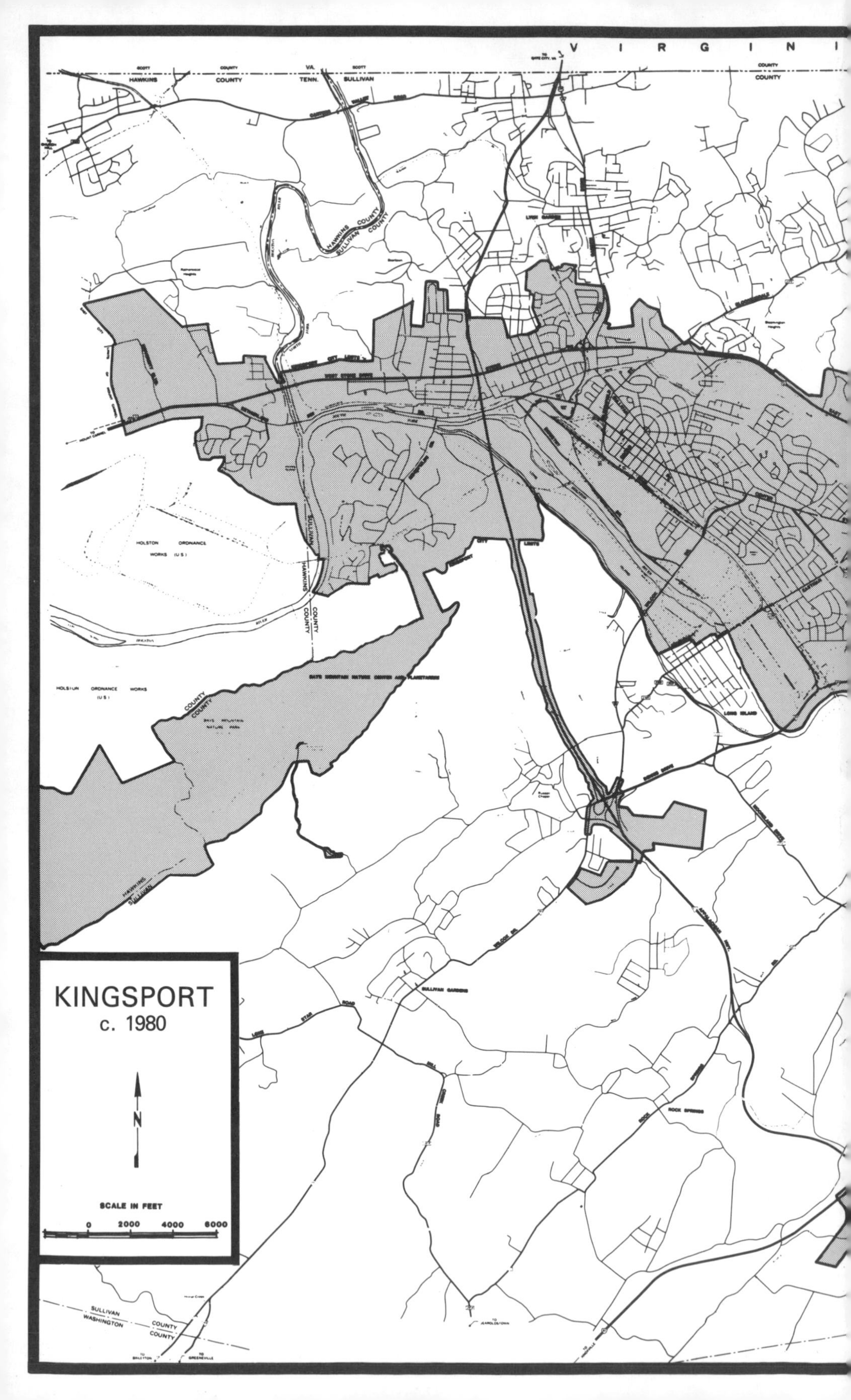
KINGSPORT
c. 1980
N
SCALE IN FEET
0
2000
4000
6000
V I R G I N I
SCOTT
HAWKINS
COUNTY
VA.
TENN.
SULLIVAN
COUNTY
HAWKINS COUNTY
SULLIVAN COUNTY
HOLSTON ORDNANCE
WORKS (U.S.)
HOLSTON ORDNANCE WORKS
(U.S.)
SULLIVAN
HAWKINS
COUNTY
COUNTY
COUNTY
SULLIVAN
WASHINGTON
COUNTY
COUNTY